# The Philosophy and Art of Wang Guangyi

Aesthetics and Contemporary Art

Series Editors: Tiziana Andina and David Carrier

Philosophers and cultural historians typically discuss works of art in abstract terms. But the true significance of art for philosophy, and philosophy for art, can only be established through close analysis of specific examples. Art is increasingly being used to introduce and discuss problems in philosophy. And many works of art raise important philosophical issues of their own. But the resources available have been limited. *Aesthetics and Contemporary Art*, the first series of its kind, will provide a productive context for that indispensable enterprise.

The series promotes philosophy as a framework for understanding the study of contemporary arts and artists, showcasing research that exemplifies cutting-edge and socially engaged scholarship, bridging theory and practice, academic rigour and insight of the contemporary world.

Editorial Board

Alessandro Arbo (University of Strasbourg), Carla Bagnoli (University of Modena and Reggio), Leeza Chebotarev (Private Art Advisor), Paolo D'Angelo (University of Roma Tre), Noël Carroll (CUNY), Diarmuid Costello (University of Warwick), Maurizio Ferraris (University of Turin), Cynthia Freeland (University of Houston), Peter Lamarque (University of York), Jonathan Gilmore (CUNY), Luca Illetterati (University of Padova), Gao Jianping (Chinese Academy of Social Sciences), Birte Kleemann (Michael Werner Gallery), Joachim Pissarro (CUNY), Sara Protasi (University of Puget Sound), Shen-yi Liao (University of Puget Sound), Ken-Ichi Sasaki (Nihon University), Elisabeth Schellekens (University of Uppsala), Vincenzo Trione (IULM, International University of Language and Communication, Milan).

Forthcoming in the Series

*Aesthetics, Philosophy, and Martin Creed*, edited by Elisabeth Schellekens and Davide Dal Sasso

*Art, Fashion, Popular Culture, and the Up-Ending of Tradition* by Adam Geczy and Vicki Karaminas

*Contemporary Chinese Art, Aesthetic Modernity and Zhang Peili* by Paul Gladston

*Visual Metaphor in Contemporary Art and Analytic Philosophy* by Mark Stall Brandl

# The Philosophy and Art of Wang Guangyi

Edited by
Tiziana Andina and Erica Onnis

BLOOMSBURY ACADEMIC
LONDON • NEW YORK • OXFORD • NEW DELHI • SYDNEY

BLOOMSBURY ACADEMIC
Bloomsbury Publishing Plc
50 Bedford Square, London, WC1B 3DP, UK
1385 Broadway, New York, NY 10018, USA

BLOOMSBURY, BLOOMSBURY ACADEMIC and the Diana logo are trademarks of
Bloomsbury Publishing Plc

First published in Great Britain 2019
This paperback edition published in 2021

Copyright © Tiziana Andina, Erica Onnis and Contributors, 2019

Tiziana Andina and Erica Onnis have asserted their right under the Copyright, Designs and
Patents Act, 1988, to be identified as Editors of this work.

Series Design: Irene Martinez Costa
Cover image: Wang Guangyi, Famous Paintings Covered with Quick-Drying
Industrial Paint – Delacroix (1989), oil on canvas, 120x100cm

All rights reserved. No part of this publication may be reproduced or
transmitted in any form or by any means, electronic or mechanical,
including photocopying, recording, or any information storage or retrieval
system, without prior permission in writing from the publishers.

Bloomsbury Publishing Plc does not have any control over, or responsibility for, any
third-party websites referred to or in this book. All internet addresses given in this
book were correct at the time of going to press. The author and publisher regret any
inconvenience caused if addresses have changed or sites have ceased to exist, but can
accept no responsibility for any such changes.

A catalogue record for this book is available from the British Library.

A catalog record for this book is available from the Library of Congress.

ISBN: HB: 978-1-3500-1937-9
PB: 978-1-3502-3114-6
ePDF: 978-1-3500-1938-6
eBook: 978-1-3500-1940-9

Series: Aesthetics and Contemporary Art

Typeset by Newgen KnowledgeWorks Pvt. Ltd., Chennai, India

To find out more about our authors and books visit www.bloomsbury.com
and sign up for our newsletters.

# Contents

List of Figures . . . vii
Notes on Contributors . . . x

Introduction  Chinese Contemporary Art: Between Deconstruction and Construction  *Tiziana Andina* 安提强 *and Erica Onnis* 欧雯 . . . 1

Part I  Defining the Human and Humanizing the Divine

1  Gratings, Barriers, and Boundaries: Wang Guangyi's Transcendental Painting  *Luca Illetterati* 意泑 . . . 17
2  Wang Guangyi: Popular Study on Anthropology  *Demetrio Paparoni* 德沐 . . . 31

Part II  Duplicating the Scene

3  Wang Guangyi's "Material Spirit": A Religion Embodied in Art  *Tiziana Andina* 安提强 . . . 41
4  The Tears of Pictures: Duplication and Inflection in Wang Guangyi's Oeuvre  *Enrico Terrone* 容恒 . . . 51

Part III  Bridging the Cultural Divide through Pop

5  On the Meanings of Propaganda  *Erica Onnis* 欧雯 . . . 71
6  A Critique of Wang Guangyi's *Great Criticism: Coca-Cola*  *Xian Zhou* 周宪 . . . 87

Part IV  Words and Images: Two Instruments to Describe the World

7  Wang Guangyi: On Contemporary Pop Art, "Covers," Remix, and Political Theology  *Babette Babich* 巴比特．芭比希 . . . 111
8  The Globalist Dimension of Art: Wang Guangyi and Transculturalism  *Davide Dal Sasso* 沙毅奇 . . . 147

## Part V  Erasing the Emotions

9   Grief and the Power of the Mind  *Carola Barbero* 宝凯乐    171
10  Reasoning with Idols: A Conversation with Wang Guangyi
    *Andrew Cohen*    181

## Part VI  The Circle of Life: Presenting and Representing Food

11  Food Art, a Hymn to Nature  *Mary Bittner Wiseman* 明玛丽    191
12  Food in Wang Guangyi's Art  *Nicola Perullo* 裴倪轲    205

## Part VII  In Dialogue with Wang Guangyi

13  Nothingness, God, the Soul, and the World: A Conversation with
    Wang Guangyi  *Demetrio Paparoni* 德沐    223
14  Dark Learning, Mysticism, and Art: A Conversation with Wang
    Guangyi  *Yan Shanchun* 严善錞    243

Index    281

# Figures

Permission for use of these images has been granted by the respective artists listed below.

Cover: Wang Guangyi, Famous Paintings Covered with Quick-Drying Industrial Paint—Delacroix (1989), oil on canvas, 120 × 100 cm

| | | |
|---|---|---|
| 0.1 | Tiziana Andina and Erica Onnis in the studio of Wang Guangyi. Beijing, August 2018 | 12 |
| 1.1 | Wang Guangyi, *Red Rationality—Revisions of Idols* (1987), oil on canvas, 160 × 200 cm | 18 |
| 1.2 | Wang Guangyi, *Frozen North Pole No. 24* (1984–85), oil on canvas, 68 × 86 cm | 20 |
| 2.1 | Wang Guangyi, *Passport n. 2* (1995), oil on canvas, 150 × 120 cm | 32 |
| 2.2 | Wang Guangyi, *VISA Project* (1994), installation with artificial fur, pictures, wooden boxes, screen printing, etc. 120 × 80 × 60 cm (33 pieces) | 33 |
| 2.3 | Wang Guangyi, *Popular Study on Anthropology: Race and Aesthetics* (2017) | 33 |
| 3.1 | Wang Guangyi, *New Religion—The Last Supper* (2011), oil on canvas, 400 × 1600 cm | 45 |
| 3.2 | Wang Guangyi, *Great Criticism—Marlboro* (1992), oil on canvas, 175 × 175 cm | 46 |
| 4.1 | Wang Guangyi, *Post-Classical—Death of Marat A* (1987), oil on canvas, 116 × 166 cm | 55 |
| 4.2 | Wang Guangyi, *Mao Zedong AO* (1988), oil on canvas, 150 × 360 cm | 57 |
| 4.3 | Wang Guangyi, *Chinese Tourist Map: Beijing* (1989), oil on canvas, 120 × 150 cm | 58 |
| 4.4 | Wang Guangyi, *Death of the Guide* (2011), oil on canvas, 400 × 600 cm | 62 |
| 4.5 | Wang Guangyi, *Holy Sindone* (2013), oil on canvas, 100 × 70 cm | 64 |
| 5.1 | Maoist Era Posters. Above: 破四旧 *Pò sì jiù* (Destroying the "four olds," 1966). Below: 无产阶级文化大革命万岁; | |

|  |  |  |
|---|---|---|
|  | *Wúchǎnjiējí wénhuà dà gémìng wànsuì* (Long Live the Great Proletarian Cultural Revolution) | 74 |
| 6.1 | Wang Guangyi, *Great Criticism—Coca-Cola* (a. 1990, oil on canvas, 200 × 200 cm; b. 1999, oil on canvas, 200 × 180 cm; c. 2002, oil on canvas, 200 × 200 cm; d. 2003, oil on canvas, 120 × 150 cm; e. 2006, oil on canvas, 200 × 300 cm) | 97 |
| 6.2 | Wang Guangyi, *Great Criticism—Coca-Cola* (a. 2005, oil on canvas, 150 × 120 cm; b. 2005, oil on canvas, 60 × 70 cm) | 98 |
| 7.1 | Andy Warhol, *Mao* (1974) | 116 |
| 7.2 | Andy Warhol, *Marilyn Diptych* (1962) | 117 |
| 7.3 | Wang Guangyi, on the right, *Mao Zedong: Red Grid No. 2* (1988), oil on canvas, 150 × 130 cm; on the left, *Mao Zedong: Red Grid No. 1* (1988), oil on canvas, 150 × 130 cm | 120 |
| 7.4 | Babette Babich, *People Wash*. February 22, 2000 | 122 |
| 7.5 | Wang Guangyi, *Great Criticism: Andy Warhol* (2002), oil on canvas, 300 × 200 cm | 124 |
| 7.6 | Babette Babich, *Denkerei*. Berlin, Kreuzberg, May 14, 2012 | 126 |
| 7.7 | Shi Xinning, *Duchamp Retrospective Exhibition in China* (2000–1) | 132 |
| 7.8 | Jeff Koons, *Made in Heaven* (1989) | 134 |
| 8.1 | Wang Guangyi, *Inflammable and Explosive* (1989), installation with cotton, plastic bags, etc. 50 × 60 × 35 cm/piece (3 pieces) | 157 |
| 8.2 | Wang Guangyi, *Things-in-Themselves* (2012), installation with sacks of rice and rice bran, etc. Variable dimensions | 163 |
| 10.1 | Wang Guangyi, *Water, East Wind, Golden Dragon* (2007–8), installation (cast iron/fiberglass, pictures, etc.), size of the car model: Size: 500 × 190 × 165 cm | 186 |
| 11.1 | Wang Guangyi, *Small Criticisms—Banana* (1992) oil on canvas, 150 × 120 cm; *Danone* (1993) oil on canvas, 100 × 100 cm; *Mango* (1992) oil on canvas, 100 × 100 cm; *Tooth* (1992) oil on canvas, 100 × 100 cm; *Une Pomme* (1993) oil on canvas, 100 × 100 cm | 194 |
| 11.2 | Wang Guangyi, *24-Hour Food Degeneration Process* (1997), installation with Plexiglas, water, fruits, food, and photographs, etc. Variable dimensions | 198 |
| 12.1 | Wang Guangyi, *Quarantine—All Food Is Potentially Poisonous* (1996), installation with official Chinese health quarantine |  |

|  | propaganda images, metal racks, wooden shelves, food, etc. Variable dimensions | 208 |
|---|---|---|
| 12.2 | Wang Guangyi, *Gentle Black* (1985), oil on canvas, 85 × 70 cm | 211 |
| 12.3 | Wang Guangyi, *The Era of Materialism* (2000), installation with printed matter, wooden boxes and food, etc. Dimensions variable | 214 |
| 13.1 | Wang Guangyi, *Daily Life* (2014), oil on canvas, 150 × 120 cm | 224 |
| 13.2 | Wang Guangyi, *Pietà* (2011), oil on canvas, 400 × 600 cm | 229 |
| 13.3 | Wang Guangyi, *Cold War Aesthetics—People Living in Fear* (2007–8), installation with colored fiberglass and video, 215 × 60 × 30 cm/each sculpture | 236 |
| 14.1 | Wang Guangyi, *The Materialist* (2001), sculpture with fiberglass and millet, about 180 × 120 × 60 cm | 261 |

# Notes on Contributors

**Tiziana Andina** 安提强 is associate professor of philosophy and director of the research center Labont - Center for Ontology at the University of Turin. Her publications include: *Arthur Danto: Philosopher of Pop* (2011), *The Philosophy of Art: The Question of Definition. From Hegel to Post-Dantian Theories* (2013), *Bridging the Analytical Continental Divide. A Companion to Contemporary Western Philosophy* (2014) and *What Is Art? The Question of Definition Reloaded* (2017). She is co-editor of the international series *Brill Research Perspectives in Art and Law* and of the international series *Analytic Aesthetics and Contemporary Art* (Bloomsbury Academic).

**Babette Babich** 巴比特．芭比希 is professor of philosophy at Fordham University in New York City and Visiting Professor of Theology, Religion, and Philosophy at the University of Winchester. She has published 8 books including: *The Hallelujah Effect: Music, Performance Practice and Technology* (2016 [2013]), *Un politique brisé. Le souci d'autrui, l'humanisme, et les juifs chez Heidegger* (2016). Author of over 250 journal articles and book chapters, she has edited 14 collected volumes, including, most recently: *Reading David Hume's "Of the Standard of Taste"* (2019), *Hermeneutic Philosophies of Social Science* (2017). She has been executive editor of the journal *New Nietzsche Studies* since 1996.

**Carola Barbero** 宝凯乐 is associate professor of philosophy of language at the University of Turin. Her research areas range between philosophy of language and philosophy of literature; in particular, she has worked and written a lot on empty names, on the metaphysics and ontology of fictional entities, on aesthetics and emotions, and on the paradox of fiction. She is the author of many papers; among her books are *Madame Bovary: Something Like a Melody* (2005), *Who Fears Mr. Hyde?* (2010), *Philosophy of Literature* (2013).

**Andrew Cohen** is an independent filmmaker and journalist whose work is devoted to effecting social change and protecting human rights. He produced, directed or wrote several award-winning documentaries such as *Dealers among Dealers* (1996), *Killing Kasztner* (2008), *Ai Weiwei: Never Sorry* (2012), *The World Before Her* (2012), *Hooligan Sparrow* (2016), *Human Flow* (2017), *Ximei* (2019). Cohen directed and wrote a nine-part series of short films on China's leading contemporary artists in collaboration with Art Asia Pacific. His latest feature-length documentary, *Beijing Spring* (2019) chronicles China's first democracy movement and battle for artistic freedom from 1978–82.

**Davide Dal Sasso** 沙毅奇 holds master's degrees in philosophy and art history. He received his PhD in philosophy from the University of Turin in 2017. His research is focused on the relationship between philosophy, aesthetics, and contemporary art, with a particular interest in questions concerning conceptualism and the role of praxes in arts. He is the editor of the new edition of Ermanno Migliorini's *Conceptual Art* (2014).

**Luca Illetterati** 意泐 is professor of theoretical philosophy at the University of Padua. His main scientific interests are in the area of German philosophy, philosophy and artworks, philosophy of translation, and metaphilosophy. He is president of the Italian Society for Theoretical Philosophy, scientific coordinator of Padova University Press, and a member of the board of directors of the International Hegel Society (Internationale Hegel-Vereinigung). Among his publications: *Purposiveness: Teleology between Nature and Mind* (2008); *Hegel* (2010); *Filosofia Classica Tedesca: Parole Chiave* (2016).

**Erica Onnis** 欧雯 is a PhD student in theoretical philosophy at the University of Turin (FINO Consortium), where, since 2015, she is a member of the Labont – Center for Ontology. Since 2017, she is also seminar lecturer and teaching assistant in Theoretical Philosophy. Her research interests lie in metaphysics, philosophy of science, and Chinese language and philosophy.

**Demetrio Paparoni** 德沐 is art critic, curator, and essayist. He has been professor of the history of modern and contemporary art at the University of Vienna and at the University of Catania. He contributed to monographs for recent anthological exhibitions in Italy on the works of Andy Warhol, Keith Haring, Jean-Michel Basquiat, David LaChapelle, Edward Hopper, and Roy Lichtenstein and has created multiple television documentaries for the Rai Educational channel. Among others, he has written on Wang Guangyi (2013), Rafael Megall (2014 and 2017), Morten Viskum (2016), Ljubodrag Andric (2016), Vibeke Slyngstad (2017), Natee Utarit (2018), and Ronald Ventura (2018).

**Nicola Perullo** 裴倪轲 is professor of aesthetics at the University of Gastronomic Sciences in Pollenzo. His current main areas of research concern the relations between taste, perception, creativity, and education. He is one of the main international experts of the relations between food and philosophy. Some of his more recent works in this field: *Taste as Experience* (2016); *Can Cuisine Be Art? A Philosophical (and Heterodox) Proposal* (2017), *Wineworld. New Essays on Wine, Taste, Philosophy, and Aesthetics*, Rivista di Estetica, n. 51/2013.

**Enrico Terrone** 容恒 received a degree in electronic engineering from the Politecnico di Torino and then a PhD in philosophy from the Università di Torino. He taught "History of Film and Film Criticism" at the Università del Piemonte Orientale. He currently is associate researcher at Collège d'études mondiales,

Paris. He has published papers in international journals such as *British Journal of Aesthetics, The Monist, Film and Philosophy,* and *Philosophy of the Social Sciences.* He works on philosophical issues concerning aesthetics, technology, and social ontology. His primary area of research is philosophy of film.

**Mary Bittner Wiseman** 明玛丽 is professor emerita of philosophy at Brooklyn College and at the Graduate Center of the City University of New York. Author of *The Ecstases of Roland Barthes* (1989 and 2017) and editor of *Subversive Strategies in Contemporary Chinese Art* (Brill, 2011), she has published on aesthetics, Chinese contemporary art, ethics, and the philosophies of art and literature. *Picturing Women: From Titian to Kiki Smith* is in manuscript form.

**Xian Zhou** 周宪 is professor of aesthetics and director of the Institute for Advanced Studies at Nanjing University, China. His research fields include aesthetics, art theory, and visual culture. He is the author of over a hundred articles and a dozen books in Chinese, including *Traveling Theory between Cultures* (2017), *What Is Aesthetics?* (2015), *The Turn of Visual Culture* (2008), and *Critique of Aesthetic Modernity* (2005).

**Yan Shanchun** 严善錞 is a Chinese visual artist born in Hang Zhou in 1957. He graduated from Zhejiang Academy of Fine Arts in 1983 and then began teaching at Hubei Fine Art Institute. He is currently deputy director and a first-class artist of Shenzhen Fine Art Institute, and the curator of Shenzhen International Ink Painting Biennale. Among his solo exhibitions are *Yan Shanchun: A Decade of Paintings and Prints* (Beijing, 2017) and *Yan Shanchun: West Lake* (Beijing, 2016 and New York, 2015).

# Introduction Chinese Contemporary Art: Between Deconstruction and Construction

Tiziana Andina 安提强 and Erica Onnis 欧雯

Sometimes different worlds meet, and when this happens it is usually a good thing. An example of this can be found in contemporary art where, in unexpected ways, the Western and Eastern (especially Chinese) artistic traditions have recently shown similar interests despite their diametrically opposite background cultures. For this reason, among the many interpretations used to decipher contemporary art—no matter the latitude where it was made—the most popular one is to consider it a deconstructive and typically postmodern practice.[1]

This idea is surprising for several reasons. In particular, it is surprising to make a direct and scarcely problematized association between postmodernism and contemporary art, and it is even more surprising to think that there should be some relation between the typically Western philosophical concept that goes by the name of postmodernism and Chinese culture, including contemporary Chinese art. We will therefore try to provide reasons for these perplexities, considering them in relation to Wang Guangyi's art, which is both a particular and a paradigmatic case. So, let's start from the question of postmodernism, that is (perhaps a little counterintuitively), from philosophy.

## Postmodernism as a Worldview

First of all, we believe it may be useful to offer some insights about philosophical postmodernism. Clarifying what it is will allow us to understand its various applications: that is, postmodernism in art and in criticism. To offer first a historical contextualization and a definition, we can say that postmodernism is a movement that developed in Western philosophy toward the end of the twentieth century. Postmodern theory is characterized by a notably skeptical orientation, determined by radical and extreme subjectivism, oriented toward a strongly relativistic worldview. This core of ideas is based on an intrinsically suspicious theoretical attitude toward reason.

Perspectivism, of course, has its champions: first of all the French philosopher Jean-François Lyotard who, in 1979, coined the term "postmodern" in *La condition postmoderne*.[2] In this book, Lyotard argues that the contemporary age has seen the end of the great narratives that characterized modernity. In other words, until the twentieth century, the great philosophical systems have produced meaning, offering values and conditioning the way of thinking of thousands of people. All this, according to Lyotard, ended with the acknowledgment of the failure of humanity's attempted emancipation (at least in the West). What was left—as a sort of ideological residue—was fragmentation: of theories, of ideas and—in a sense that we are going to define—of artistic production. In other words, philosophy had assumed the task of deconstructing the metaphysics on which the great systems of the past were founded; what survived was a variety of practices and worldviews that were all equally legitimate and sustainable.

Lyotard's book would probably not have been so popular if, at the end of the nineteenth century, a giant of philosophy—Friedrich Nietzsche—had not made this prospect possible by starting the greatest and most effective project of criticism of Western philosophy and culture. In fact, Nietzsche is the philosopher who developed the most extensive and systematic deconstruction of the cornerstones of traditional metaphysics: subject, external world, and truth.[3] For each of these concepts, various metaphysicians have written thousands of pages: traditionally, the subject was understood as a thinking and unitary substance on which the knowledge of the external world is based; the external world was seen as a reality in which we can intervene, and which we can manipulate through knowledge and science; truth was a form of knowledge based on the adaptation of the subject to the world. First Nietzsche and then postmodernism—one of the minor legacies of Nietzsche's philosophy—have powerfully and systematically dismantled each of the great narratives linked to these concepts.

Nietzsche was convinced that Western metaphysics was based on a lie: the idea that man is able to know the truth. For him, this belief was marked by a clear anthropological bias and was entirely false. Man cannot know the truth because the truth simply does not exist; what does exist is what has determined the human aspiration to the truth—that is, man's need to feel protected by a perspective that he believes to be true and therefore stable. However, human beings should know that the truth is entirely the result of their own construction, something that does not exist outside human needs and that, indeed, depends on them. The constructions of Western metaphysics, according to Nietzsche, would therefore be the product of the uncertain and fragile human nature, which would have led man to build a solid and ordered theoretical universe, one that is far more such than reality itself.

The result was the construction of a maze of concepts—a maze that ended up reifying life by claiming that those concepts adequately described it.[4] In reality, in Nietzsche's view it makes no sense to speak of truth because the epistemological dimension in which we exist is—and can only be—typically human, and therefore circumscribed to the sphere of the human. *Ergo*, it literally does not make sense to speak of truth, in the strong meaning of the term. If this is the case, it is clear that the only consequence that can follow from these premises is that the main task of philosophy amounts to the genealogical critique of metaphysical systems. Nietzsche, in fact, engaged precisely in such a task, which was later undertaken, as we said, by postmodernism.

However, it does not seem possible to have deconstruction without reconstruction. Nietzsche himself expressed the temptation to provide his own metaphysics, alternative to the many theories of metaphysics he was deconstructing. Such a metaphysics presents very clear and definite traits. In essence, the German philosopher offered two theoretical indications: the first was that deconstruction had to be absolute—that is, devoid of ideological residues. The second was that the main outcome of deconstruction would involve recognizing an essential trait of the natural world on the one hand, and of human nature in particular on the other—that is, the will to power. On the one hand, metaphysics is nothing but the product of our being all too human, since it is humans who have elaborated it to meet their needs; however, on the other hand, the will to power—namely the central element of Nietzschean metaphysics—is something that exists and can be grasped in nature.

Ultimately, therefore, Nietzsche proposes a metaphysics that is aware of human limitations—a metaphysics relative to those limits. This is what postmodernists, fundamentally more radical than Nietzsche, miss: the idea that essentially there is no escaping metaphysics; not for lack of trying but simply because it is impossible. The idea that permanent deconstruction is a sustainable prospect is fallacious for many reasons. Above all, Nietzsche's skeptical hypothesis—that is, the idea that knowledge is a measure of the human being, and that there is no escaping this measure because the world is a sort of opaque and dumb entity—is a possibility, but has no true foundation. It could be so, of course; we cannot exclude it. But, on the other hand, it is not clear why we should claim in our theories that it is undoubtedly the case.[5] The hypothesis that Nietzsche asks us to support is, in the final analysis, theoretically burdensome without presenting any real advantage in terms of knowledge—so much so that when he presented his vision of the world Nietzsche himself ended up outlining a metaphysics, however weakened in its foundations.

## Contemporary Art and Deconstruction

Since the early twentieth century, deconstruction has been a major component of art, as evidenced by the progressive rejection of mimetic representation, the decomposition of forms, the dematerialization of the medium, up to the extreme position of conceptualism, according to which art can be reduced to an idea, that is, the conceptual content of the work.[6] A similar conclusion had already been drawn by Hegel in his philosophy of art.[7] However, Hegel also indicated that, once art reached its peak it would turn to philosophy because, in fact, the latter would be the only option left. Instead, it is not clear what conceptual artists thought about the dematerialization of art. Once art had lost its body, because of the artists' choices, one had to continue to make art even if it was not at all clear how to do so.[8] And, in fact, especially since the second half of the twentieth century this has been the case: we have continued to make art even if it is still unclear how we should do so.

Since then, however, two important things have happened: philosophy has overcome the postmodernist disarray and with all due precautions has started again to take an interest in metaphysics;[9] meanwhile, art seems to have found a different destiny: it has not recomposed, still largely bearing the signs of the fracture that started with the twentieth century—in the name of such as Picasso, Duchamp, and the avant-garde—and continued with the idea that the fate of art is dematerialization (which is a little bizarre, especially coming from artists). In the twentieth century, artists claimed that they should make art in the freedom to express themselves as they considered most appropriate, without setting any limits to their practices, deconstructing the traditional canons. Often, they pushed the aesthetic property *par excellence*—beauty—to the edge of artistic production, using common objects to create artworks, as in the case of ready-mades, or replacing the concrete art object with an action or performance.

The work of art became an object of rather marginal interest in the art world, while the latter—namely the socioeconomic circuit in which the actors of the sector operate—was increasingly seen as akin to the financial market.[10] Two covers of *The New Yorker*, though realized at different times, show well how the attention of the public and experts has progressively shifted from the artwork itself to the world around it, probably also because the reading and understanding of the artwork had become increasingly complicated the more it moved away from traditional production.

Both covers express the same idea: works of art are there, but the audience is distracted and mainly interested in conversation (*The New Yorker*, January 22, 1944); alternatively, the art is even physically separated from the majority of the audience, who are busy chatting in a room adjacent to that of the exhibition (*The New Yorker*, March 6, 2017). Which is to say: art or, better, artworks have ended up at the edge of the art world and people are rather interested in talking, perhaps also because of the excessive self-celebratory posture of much contemporary art.

It is in this context that contemporary Chinese art has entered the relatively foreign Western cultural horizon, only partially comprehending its profound meanings and dynamics. This phenomenon can be seen as a full commingling of the two cultures—Western and Eastern—which have little in common, but which have found in art the least unfit place for dialogue. This dialogue was possible because Western contemporary art has proved to be particularly hospitable, that is, ready to recognize both different practices and artistic forms, and the value of commingling, in view of the exploration of different languages. And it did this not so much to underline the fluidity of reality or the inconsistency of the idea that there is one truth to discover, as claimed by philosophical postmodernism, but rather because in this historical phase art has also experienced its potentialities from an ontological point of view. Artists have tried to push the arts to the extremes of expression, not only bending them to the representation of emotions, but also inducing them to question their expressive limits. A sort of meta-art, as philosophers would say.

The main tool used in this phase was the deconstruction of ancient models so as to experiment with radically new ones. In this way, contemporary art has been able to take on a number of forms, styles, and practices, for which it is difficult to find comparisons in the past, and thanks to which contemporary Chinese art could integrate into the Western context without losing its own identity and deep nature. As we will show in this book, Wang Guangyi's work is an excellent example of this mediation-creation. This cultural exchange went from East to West, so to speak: Chinese artists were to first to look westward. And they did so in two rather traditional ways: by appropriating Western-style themes and practices, and by adding further deconstruction to the deconstruction of contemporary Western art of the early 1900s. Since the 1990s, in fact, Western deconstruction artists themselves have begun to be deconstructed by Chinese artists. It was a sort of second-level deconstruction, whose spirit, in truth, had not been foreign to the twentieth-century avant-gardes.

The deconstruction of Western art by Chinese artistic movements had multiple objectives, but the main one consisted in replacing the Western cultural model with the Chinese one, using—this is a most interesting paradox—the same expressive tools as did Western art. In addition to all this, it is important to make a further consideration. Unlike the West, Chinese contemporary art is being faced with significant political ostracism. This is not too surprising given that, in a political regime that exalts the paternalistic role of the state, art is conceived as a useful tool for achieving common goals. In this sense, art becomes an ideological tool that political power aims to control for its own purposes.

In the case of traditional arts, a cultural policy of this kind may have some logic, but things become evidently more complicated if this logic is to be applied to the avant-garde arts which, programmatically, are reluctant to convey the ideas of political power. Often, they are even completely reluctant to deal with social and political issues. Thus, for a long time, Chinese political power has been rather dismissive toward contemporary art, preferring other forms. The situation changed when political leaders perceived that this form of art could penetrate foreign cultural contexts and, consequently, contribute to the consolidation of Chinese politics in nonstandard ways.[11] In other words, those in power sensed that this type of art could bring China outside of its borders.

Toward the end of the seventeenth century, Chinese art came into contact with the most important Western painting techniques—such as perspective, oil painting on canvas, and chiaroscuro—thanks to the Jesuit, Giuseppe Castiglioni, who shared these techniques with the artists who worked in the court of Emperor Qing Qianlong. The impact of these new representative practices resulted in a somewhat mixed production in which traditional themes of Chinese art coexisted with the modes of Western representation. In the 1920s and 1930s, the Academies Art Institute was created for young Chinese to learn the use of techniques widespread in the United States and Europe, practicing live painting, landscape painting, and the creative use of ordinary objects. The academies also dealt with the values of Western culture, and they did so both by using the "objectivist techniques to reproduce reality" (think of artists like Xu Beihong and Jiang Zhaoke) and by following the anti-realist and abstractist tendencies of Western modernism.

Between the end of the nineteenth century and the beginning of the twentieth Chinese social structure remained almost unchanged, anchored to the feudal and rural models. The Chinese educated classes gradually became aware of China's economic and social backwardness compared to the West: both the North American and the European economies were doing significantly better. As a result, a moment of profound cultural renewal began, guided by young educated people familiar with the cultures on whose models they wanted to change China. The May Fourth Movement, born following the student protest of May 4, 1919, triggered the majority of the most significant changes of those years, until May 1942, the year when Mao Zedong came to power.

Mao's view of the arts—as expressed during the conference on literature and the arts that took place in 1942 at the headquarters of the Chinese Communist Party in Yan'an—was very clear and precise: the artistic production had to be bent to the purposes of politics. It made no sense to think of art as autonomous from politics, or from the vision of the popular masses: art had to be committed to illustrating the point of view of the Chinese Communist Party. According to Mao, art had to be a tool of ideology. And yet, the regime culture failed in its intent of total control: as Plato knew very well, the arts can never be fully controlled, because they tend to lurk in the spaces left free by ideologies. And they often tend to use ideology itself—as indeed happened in the Maoist phase—to create new ways to overcome it.

The start date of the history of modern Chinese art is conventionally set in 1979, coinciding with the work of the Stars Group, founded by Ma Desheng and Huang Rui shortly after Mao's death and the end of the Cultural Revolution. On September 27 and 28, 1979, the group held its first major exhibition in the space adjacent to the National Museum in Beijing, without the permission of the institutions. The Stars Group's work went roughly in two directions: on the one hand the exploration of life and, on the other, took an interest in forms. The exhibition was closed by the police. It was then that the group decided to protest publicly.

In those years, there was a customary way to have one's voice heard in Beijing. At the end of the Cultural Revolution many people had moved from the countryside to the city to answer needs that had not been satisfied with the end of the revolution. However, it was not easy for them to understand the political interlocutors or the bureaucrats they had to talk to. So, they began to hang up their demands on a wall—which was called Democracy Wall—in the hope that someone would read their requests. The Stars Group's protest march therefore started from Democracy Wall, continued along Xidan Street and Chang-an Avenue, crossed Tiananmen Square, and ended at the Chinese Communist Party headquarters. It was a march for freedom of expression that, however, did not have the desired results. In the early 1980s the artists of the group dispersed all over the world because of the censorship. The activity of the Stars Group members was particularly significant in the Chinese context because of their political and social orientation. After all, they were the first artists to significantly mark the context of Chinese culture in those years.

Something very similar, but also embedded with careful research on the possibilities of collective production, was undertaken by the Northern Art Group, another important association of artists who worked in those years outside the government directives. The group was founded in Harbin, in 1984, by some young graduates. At first, the group expressed interest in all forms of art; however, after about a year of work and discussions, the members decided to concentrate on the visual arts. Unlike the Stars Group, the Northern Art Group—composed of artists such as Shu Qun, Wang Guangyi, Ren Jian, Gao Minglu, Li Xianting, Wang Xiaojian, Zhou Yan, and Huang Zhuan—developed part of their work collectively. Moreover, the group assumed a hierarchical structure: Shu Qun was the coordinator—and also author of the manifesto of the Northern Art Group (1985)—responsible for the general guidance and theoretical developments of the group, while Wang Guangyi was the vice-coordinator, in charge of their practices.

The Northern Art Group developed its work around three main ideas: first, the belief that the new cultural openings that gradually emerged in China had shifted their focus from traditional Chinese culture to Western culture. Secondly, the idea that North China was a more suitable environment for the development of strong people and ideas and, therefore, the needed cultural renewal could only come from that part of the country. In fact, especially from the climatic point of view, the North offered the perfect context for the development of a "Culture of the North" that would gradually replace that of the West and the East—thus both Western culture and traditional Chinese culture.

Finally, there was the idea that such profound cultural changes should go hand in hand with a technical renewal of equal magnitude. The group was conceived as an enlightened cultural elite that included the study of Western philosophers in their education: in fact, they read Hegel, Nietzsche, Gombrich and Kuhn. From Hegel and his philosophy of history they drew the idea that Western and Eastern cultures would be reabsorbed into a single culture—that of the Northern Group. From Nietzsche they derived the clear elitism underlying their work, while from Gombrich and Kuhn they took the idea that Northern culture would emerge as the new paradigm of reference for Chinese art. In the context of oriental culture, the group was influenced by the reflections of Confucius and Laozi and by several works of Buddhist inspiration.

Generally speaking, the group worked not only for the recovery of a metaphysics that aspired to independence from the political sphere—something that had been impossible during Mao's era—but also for a recovery of individualism, that is, for a valorization of the autonomy and role of the individual within Chinese culture. Shu Qun and Wang Guangyi, above all, developed a pictorial style that was in open contrast with traditional Chinese painting: the representation of emotions, for example, was reduced to a minimum or often totally absent. Reality, according to the Surrealist dictation, was often represented as a dream, and the idea was that this particular commingling between reality and dream could have political causal power.

Since the beginning of the 1980s, the work of Wang Guangyi has been particularly notable, also because of the themes he addressed: the reappropriation of iconic images (think of the icon of Mao) and the citationist reproduction of some masterpieces of Western art. In the reproduction of these works, inspired by Gombrich's intuitions, Wang overlays the original image with grids and other geometric patterns in such a way that the work cited somehow loses its aura. Once again, this is deconstruction and, once again, it is deconstruction aimed at construction.

## Wang Guangyi

Wang Guangyi 王广义 was born in 1957 in Harbin, in the northern Heilongjiang province, in a working family: his father was a railway worker. In the 1960s Wang participated in Mao's Cultural Revolution as a "little Red guard" and, at the same time, he began to cultivate his artistic talent by drawing the bulletins of his elementary school and by taking an art course at the Harbin Children's Palace. When the Cultural Revolution became harsher, Wang, like many of his peers, was sent for three years (from 1973 to 1976) to be re-educated in the countryside and was moved to the county of Zhaozhou (a municipality in Heilongjiang). It is in this phase of his life that he understood, as he would explain later, that individuals are insignificant and unable to change either the external world or their own destiny, embracing a profound fatalism and pessimism.

Despite his desire to pursue an artistic career, after the death of his father Wang returned to Harbin and became a railway worker himself. In this period, however, he did not neglect his artistic ambition and studied to pass the test at Zhejiang Academy of Art, where he was finally admitted in 1980. In the academy, Wang studied traditional art for the first two years and progressively approached contemporary art over the last two years. These are the years when, together with Shu Qun, Ren Jian, Liu Yan and other fellow students, he founded the Young Northern Artists Group, which was interested in thematizing and problematizing the meaning of traditional art and local traditions, and had the aim of inaugurating a new artistic season for China, or at least for the north of China.

The Chinese cultural atmosphere was very active in the 1980s, and many groups like the Young Northern Artists Group were born and spread throughout the region, so much so that the phenomenon acquired a national scope and took the name, coined by Gao Minglu, of the "1985 Art Movement."[12] The movement arose in relationship with Western art, toward which Chinese culture, again in the words of Gao Manglu, had the tendency of "importism": that is, "the borrowing, copying and outright theft of ideas from Western art."[13] The movement, therefore, intended to problematize not only traditional Chinese art and the way in which, together with Chinese culture as a whole, it had been bent by the Cultural Revolution, but also the reaction to this revolution. In the 1980s, in what could be defined as a "post-Cultural Revolution era," this reaction started to show in the development of innovative Westernized artistic techniques, while several young artists organized self-managed and controversial exhibitions that caused a sensation, in part because they defied the governmental cultural lines.

In 1985, Wang Guangyi wrote a manifesto of the movement titled "Us— The Participants of the '85 Art Movement,"[14] stating its main objectives: "Our purpose is to help humanity transcend the mire of a morose culture and to inspire the awe and vitality of the cultural spirit, and to uplift humanity and natural harmony in order to establish a new spiritual model." It is on the wave of this spirit of cultural renewal that the 1985 Art Movement came to life and grew, and Wang Guangyi took part in it with enthusiasm, in the conviction "that art had a duty to society, that art could lead people to rebuild their declining faith, so that this high-level thing could escape the grime of pathological human culture."[15] Those were the years of several major oil paintings: *Frozen North Pole* (1985), *Post-Classical* (1986), *Red Rationality* and *Black Rationality* (1988); the years of his first installation, "Inflammable and Explosive" (1989), and the years of international fame (in 1989, *Time* published his *Mao Zedong AO*).

In 1990, Wang Guangyi painted *Great Criticism—Coca-Cola*, the first of an extended series of oil paintings that would earn him fame both in China and abroad. In the following decade he produced numerous new installations. *Great Criticism* was exhibited in Italy, Australia, Hong Kong, Brazil, Japan, and Switzerland as well as many other countries, together with *International Politics, The Similarities and Differences of Food Guarantees under Two Political Systems* (1996), and *Origin of the Species—The History of European Civilization* (1996). Roughly in the same years, scholars started publishing critical texts on his work. In 1987, the journal *Fine Arts in China* dedicated a piece to Wang Guangyi entitled "New Wave Artist (II)—Wang Guangyi"; in 1991 *Beijing Youth Daily* devoted an issue to the artist, triggering a huge media debate; Wang Guangyi appeared in Gao Minglu's *A History of Chinese Contemporary Art—1985-1986*; and, in 1992, Yan Shanchun and Lu Peng published the first monograph entirely dedicated to his work: *Wang Guangyi within the Trends of Contemporary Art*. Since then, Wang's fame has only grown, and the publications dedicated to his work have multiplied.

Regarding the themes of his production, the question of social control emerged explicitly in the 1990s. Wang Guangyi continued to paint the canvases of *Great Criticism*, combining the style of Maoist propaganda posters with the great Western brands to indicate how Western consumerism and Maoist propaganda are different sides of the same coin. In addition, the 1990s series denounces the individual's passivity in the face of the state's capillary control, which affects every aspect of people's lives through educational, health, and economic policies. Wang Guangyi's position on the role of art also changed over time. At the time of the Young Northern Artists Group, he believed that art could change society and become a political tool. However, in the late 1980s, he became aware that there is no definitive hypothesis to be made about the role and function of art, which must always question its own meaning, its potentialities, and the issues it seeks to address—in addition to reality itself.

In his early years, Wang believed the artist should be guided by a given political vision of the future and by a particular social project. In the later stage of his production, he saw instead the artist as a sounding board for ideas and visions of the world expressed by the most diverse cultures, none of which is ever taken as absolute truth. For example, his readings of Nietzsche, Kant, Hegel, Gombrich, and other Western thinkers should not be understood as moments of rigorous and analytical study or as evidence of an interest in the creation of a constructive or deconstructive "system" or "theory" (be it social, political, or metaphysical). Instead, what Wang seeks in the texts of Western philosophers,

**Figure 0.1** Tiziana Andina and Erica Onnis in the studio of Wang Guangyi. Beijing, August 2018.

as well as those of classical Chinese thinkers, are *suggestions* and *inspiration* that, in the artist's hands, may become works of art.

For Wang Guangyi, "art happens. It is an accident,"[16] and this is the reason art is not a system or a philosophy, but a different language that draws material and lifeblood from philosophy, conveys it and is able to illuminate it, remaining, however, a profoundly different phenomenon. What we seek to analyze in this volume is exactly this complex relationship between philosophy and art in the work of Wang Guangyi. This is an intense, constant, and widespread dialogue: on the one hand, philosophy, namely a system of theories capable of mapping the universe with analytical depth; on the other, art, an investigative tool that—driven by the suggestions of philosophy—shows, focuses, and clarifies just some parts of this universe.

# Notes

1. Gladston, 2005, 2015.
2. Lyotard, 1979.
3. Especially Nietzsche and Hollingdale 1996, Nietzsche, Ansell-Pearson, and Diethe, 2007.

4 Nietzsche, 2009.
5 For an overview of some arguments related to the criticism of skepticism cf.: Moore, 1959: 32.
6 Danto, 2005.
7 Hegel, 1975.
8 Goldie and Schellekens, 2007, Danto, 2014.
9 Andina, 2014.
10 Andina, 2013: 51.
11 Gladston, 2015: 11.
12 Gao Minglu, 1986.
13 Ibid.
14 Wang, 1985.
15 Paparoni, 2013: 316.
16 Personal communication.

# References

Andina, T. (2013). *The Philosophy of Art: The question of definition from Hegel to post-Dantian theories*. Bloomsbury Studies in Philosophy. London and New York: Bloomsbury.

Andina, T. (ed.). (2014). *Bridging the Analytical Continental Divide: A companion to contemporary Western philosophy*. Leiden and Boston: Brill.

Danto, A. C. (2005). *The Philosophical Disenfranchisement of Art*. Columbia Classics in Philosophy. New York: Columbia University Press.

Danto, A. C. (2014). *After the End of Art: Contemporary art and the pale of history*. First Princeton Classics Edition, Lectures in the Fine Arts, A. W. Mellon (ed.). Princeton: Princeton University Press.

Gao, M. (1986). "Bawu meishu yundong," in *Meishujia Tongxun* (March 5): 15–23; English trans. "The 1985 New Wave Art Movement," in V. C. Doran (ed.) (1993). *China's New Art, Post-1989, with a Retrospective from 1979 to 1989*. Hong Kong: Hanart TZ Gallery, 104–7.

Gladston, P. (2005). *Art History after Deconstruction: Is there any future for a deconstructive attention to art historical discourse?* Auckland: Magnolia Press.

Gladston, P. (2013). "'Avant-garde' Art Groups in China, 1979–1989: The Stars—the Northern Art Group—the Pond Association—Xiamen Dada: A Critical Polylogue." Bristol and Chicago: Intellect.

Gladston, P. (2015). *Deconstructing Contemporary Chinese Art*. New York: Springer, Berlin, Heidelberg.

Goldie, P., and Schellekens, E. (2007). *Philosophy and Conceptual Art*. Oxford and New York: Clarendon Press; Oxford University Press.

Hegel, G. W. F. (1975). *Aesthetics: Lectures on fine art*. 2 vols. Oxford: Clarendon Press.
Hung, E. W. (2007). *Contemporary Chinese Art: Primary documents*. New York: The Museum of Modern Art.
Lyotard, J.-F. (1979). *La condition postmoderne: rapport sur le savoir, Collection Critique*. Paris: Éditions de Minuit.
Moore, G. E. (1959). *Philosophical Papers, Muirhead Library of Philosophy*. London and New York: Allen and Unwin; Macmillan.
Nietzsche, F. W., Geuss, R., and Nehmas, A. (2009). *Writings from the Early Notebooks*. Cambridge Texts in the History of Political Thought. New York: Cambridge University Press.
Nietzsche, F. W., Ansell-Pearson, K., and Diethe, C. (2007). *On the Genealogy of Morality*. Rev. student ed., Cambridge Texts in the History of Political Thought. New York: Cambridge University Press.
Nietzsche, F. W., and Hollingdale, R. J. (1996). *Human, All too Human*. Cambridge Texts in the History of Philosophy. New York: Cambridge University Press.
Paparoni, D. (2013). *Wang Guangyi: Works and thoughts*. Milan: SKIRA.
Wang, G. (1986). "Us—The Participants of the '85 Art Movement." In Zhongguo Meishu Bao, *Fine Arts in China*, 1986, 36.

Part I

# Defining the Human and Humanizing the Divine

1

# Gratings, Barriers, and Boundaries: Wang Guangyi's Transcendental Painting

Luca Illetterati 意泐

## Gratings and Strikethroughs

In *Red Rationality—Revision of Idols* (1987) or in the triptych *Mao Zedong AO* (1988) (see Figure 4.2), the figures and faces painted by Wang Guangyi are covered by a sort of grating: a geometric pattern that in some way hinders a free, full and direct vision of the images underneath. Something similar can also be seen, albeit in a different form, in *International Politics—Necessary Documents* and in other works of the 1990s (I am thinking for example of *Passport No. 2* (see Figure 1.1), where the reticular grating is significantly made up of the words saying who we are, where we were born, the time and place in which we are living).

In reality, what lies behind and underneath the grating is absolutely clear; the pattern does not really hide what exists in that sort of further space, beyond the grid. Whether what lies beyond is the trace of Michelangelo's *Pietà* or Mao Zedong's classic icon, or even the enlarged reinterpretation of a photo card, one that could appear in any kind of document, the object of representation is not really obliterated by the gratings—it is not hidden by the lines that cross it or by the signs placed above it. If anything, it is a bit as the Heideggerian expedient of striking-through the word *Sein* (Being) to indicate how it is both necessary and unattainable.

The word *Sein*, according to Heidegger, is at the same time the only object of thought (although the expression "object of thought" is inadequate in relation to Heideggerian philosophy) and its most radical obnubilation. The barred form S̶e̶i̶n̶ expresses both what must necessarily be said and the conviction that what is to be said cannot be said in the way we are able to say it. Likewise, in the images of Wang Guangyi, the observer must not make any effort to see what is beyond the grate. And indeed, just as in Heidegger's struck-through *Sein*, what lies beyond becomes even more visible thanks to its deferral to this form of pseudo-deletion.

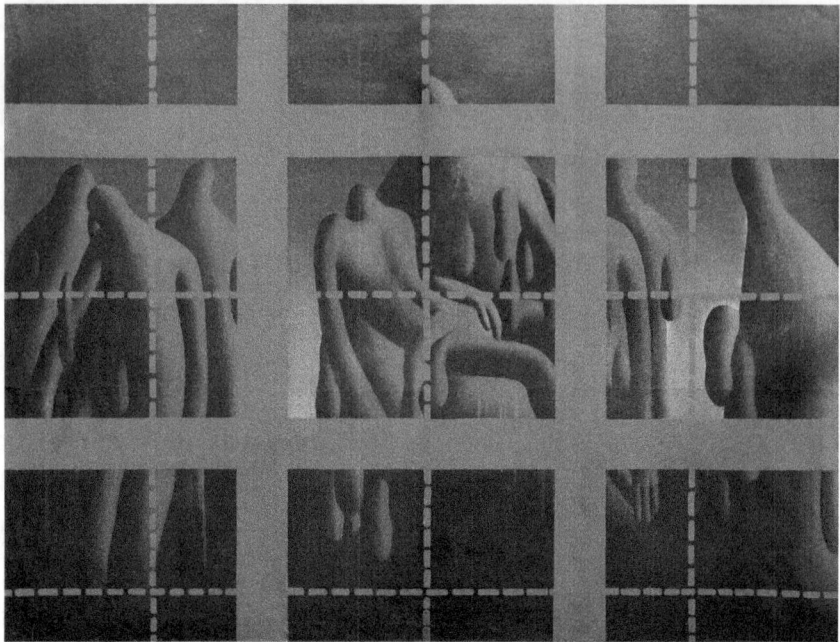

**Figure 1.1** Wang Guangyi, *Red Rationality—Revisions of Idols* (1987), oil on canvas, 160 × 200 cm.

As known, *Sein* is the word for "being," which in its verbal form is the all-pervasive and decisive part of any discourse and that, however, in our ordinary communicative practices, we perceive as requiring no explanation or definition of any kind. "Being" is in many ways the source of the meaning of most of our assertions and, yet (perhaps precisely because it is a condition of possibility of meaning), its meaning goes largely unquestioned.[1]

A separating and distancing sign—such as the Heideggerian strikethrough, but also the different forms of grid that characterize Wang Guangyi's works—actually clarifies what lies underneath it, submitting it to our gaze while making it both far and close, isolating it from the everyday context it is usually immersed in. The strikethrough, the grating, the lattice establish and bring to the fore the otherness of what lies beyond these forms of barrier.

## The Other Dimension

What the observer becomes aware of by experiencing these works, thanks to the barred image, is the fact that the latter exists *on the other side*, in a dimension *other* than the observer's; the image refers, so to speak, to a space of transcendence that is present to the gaze but also exists in a separate dimension with respect to the observer. What lies beyond the grating, what emerges behind the simple geometry that separates the observer from the image represented, are mostly ideal-typical figures, sometimes faceless (as in the case of *Pietà*), sometimes with a face that is so well known as to be basically a sort of icon (as in the case of Mao), sometimes with a face that is somehow standard, devoid of specific and peculiar characterizations, as in the photo card. In other words, what lies beyond the grating is never the representation of an individual concrete body— it is never really an embodied figure.

The image that lies beyond the grating is in some ways an image out of time, an image that stands out on a background that is radically alien to the concrete space of the world of life. The figures beyond the grating are, in short, overdetermined—so much so that their identification is immediate and does not require any particular effort—and yet abstract; they are individual, recognizable figures (Mao Zedong, the *Pietà* by Michelangelo, the face of a male on his identity document) and yet universal; they are specific historical figures and yet ideal figures, pure images, supra-historical icons.

The grating therefore establishes two dimensions of space, two experiences that are clearly separate and irreducible to one another, even if, in some way, they are each other's condition of possibility. On one side there is the observer: a concrete body, a singular body in movement and in becoming, a body forged by nature and history, always immersed in memory and tradition, and necessarily marked by peculiar emotional states. This body is therefore the result of a specific time-space.

On the other hand, there is a reality that is somehow frozen: the similarities between the figures of *Red Rationality* and those of the *Frozen North Pole* (Figure 1.2) and *Post Classical* (see Figure 4.1) series are evident in this sense, showing a universalized reality purged of temporal waste and placed within an ideal dimension, which is in many ways utopian (or perhaps dystopic) and supra-historical. The figure that lies beyond the grid is certainly Mao Zedong, but in such a typified form that it is, so to speak, *the idea* of Mao Zedong, a concept, an icon, as we have said, and therefore his representation in the form of disembodied universality. The same applies to the figure of Michelangelo's *Pietà*: what we see beyond the grating is the image of the *Pietà*, an almost abstract representation of it, a representation of its concept.

So much so that, in some ways, from the point of view of the content, it could also refer to one of the infinite reproductions of Michelangelo's sculpture

**Figure 1.2** Wang Guangyi, *Frozen North Pole No. 24* (1984–85), oil on canvas, 68 × 86 cm.

found in the stalls of trinket markets, because those kitsch statuettes embody not so much the specificity of Michelangelo's work but rather the idea behind it, its symbolic and iconic power. The *Pietà* beyond Wang Guangyi's grating is the opaque outline of the *Pietà*—one would almost call it the "Shroud of the *Pietà*." It is not coincidental—on the contrary, it is strictly consistent with Wang Guangyi's thought and artistic path—that he recently focused his attention on the theme of the Shroud (*Sindone*). The Shroud is the mark of transcendence, the shadow left in history by what is supra-historical, the footprint in the world of what is other than the world.

In the Catholic imaginary, the Shroud is the trace of eternity in time, the reflection of transcendence in life: it is the concrete, determined, material, and therefore perishable image of what is essential, ideal, and not subject to the laws of time; the image of an original reality that is destined to be experienced and presentified within the historical dimension only through its absence, as a reflection. It is necessary to understand the cult of the Shroud in the light of the great iconoclastic debate that marked so deeply the Western pictorial tradition. The Shroud bears in fact an image of what cannot have an image; it is a figure of what cannot be reduced to any specific or particular portrait; it bears a mark of the body and its negation at the same time. As the image of the Other, which cannot be represented without being radically betrayed and annulled, and therefore as a sign and representation of an absence, the Shroud is in many ways the obsession underlying the history of Western painting.

## Vorstellungen

But let us go back to the gratings. There are therefore two sides of the grid: one where we stand, with our bodies, our moods, and our memories; and one beyond, wherein lies the idea, the spirit, the essence. In the artwork, the grating activates a number of movements and passages that depend precisely on the grating and the space it occupies. So, the grid is what separates the dimension of transcendence from the ordinary one of the observer; it is the place that marks the border between time and eternity. However, it is also what leads us to the threshold of this transcendence, allowing us to cast our gaze beyond the place where we are and onto a space that—although through the grating—is open to us. Indeed, the dimension that presents itself as a sort of "beyond" becomes, in a way, what orients and gives meaning to the way we dwell in the world.

In fact, the otherness that lies beyond the grating is, as we have said, something immediately recognizable and identifiable. The otherness that is revealed there is not foreign. Far from it: this otherness presents itself in the form of the ordinary, the usual, the everyday. Everyone knows Mao Zedong's face; perhaps there is none better known, especially for a Chinese person. Even the most distracted person in the history of art can recognize Michelangelo's *Pietà* beyond the grating of *Red Rationality*: it is almost a universal icon of art, but also of a Christian religious feeling that, in it, becomes a universal and transcultural sentiment. And, again, everyone can recognize a photo card in the face of *Passport No. 2*: namely a photo that could be showing anyone, that could be anybody's photo.

Now, because of the deferral produced by the grating, this element of everydayness and familiarity becomes fraught with a symbolic value that radically transforms it and "transfigures" it, to use Danto's expression.[2] This transfiguration is also a disincarnation, a stripping of the historical and conditioned element that is proper to those faces. What lies beyond the grating is more than a face, more than a specific image irreducible in its singularity: once again, it is a Shroud, the trace of an idea, a kind of archetype, an idol. As Wang Guangyi repeatedly emphasizes, it is the representation of a concept.

In the introductory paragraphs of the *Encyclopedia of Philosophical Sciences* (1830), Hegel wrote that representations (*Vorstellungen*) "in general can be regarded as metaphors of thoughts and concepts" (§ 3 An.).[3] Now, the fact that Hegel describes representation as a metaphor of a concept underlines the idea that representations and concepts do not refer to different things, but rather are different ways to express the same thing. For Hegel, representations are *images* and generally modalities that are more immediate than conceptual articulation: they express what the concept expresses in the pure form of thought, without resorting to iconic constructs or sensible elements. In other words, representation is an image that is elevated to the form of universality and, yet, at the same time, does not take the form of the concept—that is, has not yet freed itself (in the Hegelian perspective) from the sensible element that is typical of the image.

Representation is therefore a sort of median and mediative structure between sensibility, which is determined in the singular, and thought, which is determined in the universal. In this way, representation is a universal determination expressed through sensible elements. And this is exactly what Wang Guangyi's images are: beyond the grating, they are universal and suprahistorical determinations expressed through determined historical elements. And yet these determinations cannot be reduced to concepts, as Hegel would like. In fact, their reduction to concepts would break their connection with time and history, which the representation preserves instead. The work of art is this ambiguous and necessarily contradictory status so that, as a concept, it tends to its own dissolution in a sort of immaterial universality and, as an artwork, it is always a historical, material, sensible incarnation.[4]

It is true that Mao Zedong is an icon, it is true that the *Pietà* appears here as its universal outline, it is true that the passport photo is the image of Pirandello's *One, No One, and One Hundred Thousand*; but Mao Zedong's icon is still a face that has existed in time, the outline of the *Pietà* is the outline of an artifact that has been brought to existence in a particular moment of history and that occupies a dedicated space in a specific place of the world, and the face of *Passport No. 2* is still a face that refers to a given specificity, to a point of time and space, to a certain memory and body.

## Daimon

The observer is brought to the edge that separates the historical, dynamic, carnal, and therefore always emotionally situated experience, from the ahistoric, frozen, ideal, and conceptual space that lies beyond. The work, and in some way the artist who produced it, seem to exist in an intermediate dimension, in a problematic "in-between" that denies *both* absolute universality, pure conceptuality, and abstract ideality *and* historical conditioning; both timeless purity and everyday banality, both eternity and fleetingness.

In this sense, contrary to the Platonic demiurge who shapes that magmatic and shapeless matter of the *chora* taking the pure form of ideas as a model, the artist—still according to Plato, whose metaphysics is undoubtedly influential in the work of Wang Guangyi—is more similar to the *daimon*. The latter is a way of being that for Plato stands as an intermediary between mortals and immortals: to carry out this activity of mediation, the *daimon* is neither mortal nor immortal and yet has, in some way—which is necessarily problematic, aporetic and contradictory—the nature of both. According to Plato, in fact, the *daimon* exists in the gap between the experience of mortals and the world of gods; precisely because it exists in this distance, it is also what allows for communication between these dimensions. To quote Plato, the *daimon* is the one who can "fill the space between the other two":[5] to be able to do so, it is certainly other than the dimensions it differentiates, but at the same time it also necessarily participates in both.

Wang Guangyi, in this sense, works within the interstitial spaces of experience, focusing his attention on the most diverse openings of transcendence that inhabit our lifeworld, in the conviction that the Shroud of the transcendent is also the only experience that we can have of it.

## Grenzen

From this point of view the gratings, the lattices, and all the signs and pictorial strategies that produce a differentiation and separation between a here and a beyond in Wang Guangyi's works perform a function similar to that which, in Kant's philosophy, is carried out by the limit or boundary (*Grenze*). The limit, for Kant, separates the experience that we can have of the world (which is necessarily phenomenal) from its noumenic foundation; in the perspective of Kant's transcendentalism, while playing a decisive role in our knowledge of the world, the latter can never be concretely experienced in it.

The limits of reason described in the "Transcendental Dialectic" of the *Critique of Pure Reason* are not only negative ones, showing reason where it must not venture, like a sort of no-trespassing sign. Indeed, the contradictions that reason encounters in its dialectical reasoning are not, for Kant, simple bumps in the road, nor are they random errors, which may deceive because of some argumentative trick. Rather, they are contradictions that arise and originate from the very nature of human reason: what is revealed, in the conflicting experience of dialectics and in the contradictions in which it incurs, is rather the *constitutive* limit of human reason.

In some dense and important paragraphs of the *Prolegomena of Any Future Metaphysics* collected under the telling title, "*On Determining the Boundary of Pure Reason*," Kant focuses on the conceptual implications related to the notion of limit. First of all, he clarifies two decisive points:

(a) *What* is the sphere within which we can know an object?
(b) *Why* is it that our reason, though aware of the limits that constitute it, *naturally* tends to go beyond the scope of the knowable and therefore to place itself beyond it?

As for the scope of our knowledge of an object (a) Kant highlights two apparently antithetical "impossibilities": the impossibility of knowing anything beyond the scope of possible experience (a1) and at the same time the impossibility of absolutizing experience as the only way of knowledge (a2). Regarding the first impossibility (a1) Kant writes:

> It would be an absurdity for us, with respect to any object, to hope to cognize more than belongs to a possible experience of it, or for us, with respect to any thing that we assume not to be an object of possible experience, to claim even the least cognition for determining it according to its nature as it is in itself.[6]

As for the second impossibility (a2), Kant is equally clear:

> But, on the other hand, it would be an even greater absurdity for us not to allow any things in themselves at all, or for us to want to pass off our experience for the only possible way of cognizing things—hence our intuition in space and time for the only possible intuition and our discursive understanding for the archetype of every possible understanding—and so to want to take principles of the possibility of experience for universal conditions on things in themselves.[7]

The awareness that the object we know is an object that is such *for us*, that it is a *phenomenon*, implies that there is a dimension, albeit inaccessible, in which the object is *in itself* and not for us, that is, the *noumenon*. And this in turn implies, according to Kant, that although we cannot have any concept of things in themselves, at the same time, "we are nevertheless not free to hold back entirely in the face of inquiries about those things; for experience never fully satisfies reason; it directs us ever further back in answering questions and leaves us unsatisfied as regards their full elucidation."[8]

This implicit reference of the phenomenon to the thing in itself—a *necessary* reference since the concept of phenomenon "contains" the concept of thing in itself—is what pushes reason towards the thing in itself, (b). In fact, by limiting the scope of possible knowledge to the phenomenon and implementing this therapeutic limitation towards itself, reason places itself somewhere that is not and cannot be part of phenomenal knowledge. In this act of delimitation, reason refers to the *noumenon* without being able in any way to determine it. It therefore stands on a level that is neither phenomenal—that is, within the scope that it defines as phenomenal—nor noumenal—that is, the sphere to which reason must refer to outline the phenomenal.

Likewise, Wang Guangyi's grids do not belong to the transcendence from which they separate us, but at the same time they do not fully belong to the phenomenal world, which is such precisely because it cannot access the transcendence to which, it is intimately and necessarily connected. The lattices that separate us from the face of Mao Zedong or from the essence of Michelangelo's *Pietà* found in *Red Rationality*, are precisely the limits that separate us from eternal ideas and that, through a historical representation of the supra-historic, put us in communication with them.

According to Kant, the tendency of reason to go beyond the scope of possible experience finds its foundation (1) in the fact that reason itself is what determines these limits, and (2) in the fact that, by placing itself on the boundary (*auf der Grenze*),[9] in its own peculiar way, reason is already always beyond the realm of what it defines as the scope of the knowable. Likewise, Wang Guangyi's gratings separate us from the concepts represented by making the gap between us and transcendence vivid and tangible. However, by showing us this limitation—that is, by highlighting this sort of grating that separates us from the reality that lies beyond—the grating itself becomes an experience of transcendence.

So, reason determines the phenomenal as the scope of the knowable, while outlining the realm of reality in itself as what we cannot know but must, however, consider to be implicit in the very concept of phenomenon. The boundary where reason sets itself when making this distinction, as Kant says in the final part of § 57 of the *Prolegomena*, "belongs just as much to the field of experience as to that of beings of thought."[10] What separates us from reality itself, that is, what keeps us away from the noumenon and makes us experience our difference from it—the lattice, the grid, the limit—is therefore necessarily both phenomenon and noumenon, on this side and beyond, history and eternity, temporality and its negation.

For Kant, reason lies *on the boundary*. And it is precisely its being on the boundary that allows reason to determine the scope of what it can know (i.e., the scope of the phenomenon), and what lies beyond its cognitive possibilities, that is, the noumenon. And yet, in this same act—namely in determining the phenomenon and its conditions of knowability—reason transcends it and arises in some way beyond the scope that it delimits. Indeed, experience is such that it cannot set a boundary for itself, because "From every conditioned it always arrives merely at another conditioned."[11] Therefore, experience finds its limit outside of itself, that is, precisely in the noumenal world, which it cannot access in any way. In this recognition—that experience cannot limit itself and that what determines experience is something other than it, and therefore the noumenon—reason therefore places itself neither on the level of experience, which is necessarily enclosed within the boundaries of conditioning, nor on some further level beyond those boundaries themselves, access to which is precluded to it. In this recognition, as we have said, reason exists on the limit itself, which is structurally characterized by belonging "to what is within it"[12] as much as "to the space lying outside."[13]

By placing itself on the boundary and demonstrating its non-trespassability, reason does not deny what Kant himself calls "the result of the entire *Critique*,"[14] that is, that reason has its own determining value only within what can be known in experience. This is an established point that is not affected by knowledge of the boundary (*Erkenntnis der Grenze*). Being on the limit (the fact that reason finds its place not simply *inside* or *outside* the boundary, but *on* the boundary itself, that is, on what separates and connects two areas) is what allows us to understand two things. First, reason, while aware that the knowledge it is given is knowledge of the phenomenon, is however pushed to retrace the conditions of the phenomenon itself and therefore also to address the noumenon that, however inaccessible, is involved in limiting the scope of the knowable to the phenomenon. Second, the reason what this is the case.[15]

Wang Guangyi's gratings, placing us in front of a "beyond" that becomes visible in its separateness and otherness, represented as a *Shroud*, places itself and us in a space that is interstitial and borderline between disembodied universality and embodied singularity; between history and that which, through its symbolic power, transcends it; between the space and time of the *here* and *now* and a dimension of frozen and supra-temporal spatiality; between the movement within which we are natural entities (*physei onta*, as Aristotle puts it) and the stability that is the negation of the movement, its denial, to which we tend through the actions of the spirit. These actions constitute the peculiar way—often aporetic and contradictory—of inhabiting the *physis* that is called being *ta metà tà physikà*.

The concept of limit is that which allows us to delimit the knowable (the scope of the phenomenon, or of *sense*, we could say referring to Wittgenstein) from the unknowable (the scope of the noumenon, that is, again according to Wittgenstein, of *nonsense*). Therefore, it is also the concept based on which it is possible to establish a connection between the phenomenal world and the noumenal world, between what we can speak of and what we cannot speak of, and of which we must therefore remain silent. In fact, given that the boundary both separates and connects two areas, Kant emphasizes that reason's "being on the boundary" is not only a condition that allows for a negative knowledge, leading reason to a situation of paralysis and sterility.

Since a boundary is itself something positive, which belongs as much to what is within it as to the space lying outside a given totality, reason therefore—merely by expanding up to this boundary—partakes of a real, positive cognition, provided that it does not try to go out beyond the boundary, since there it finds an empty space before it, space in which it can indeed think the forms for things, but no things themselves. But *setting the boundary* to the field of experience through something that is otherwise unknown to it is, from this standpoint, indeed a cognition that is still left to reason, whereby reason is neither locked inside the sensible world nor adrift out-side it, but, as befits knowledge of a boundary, restricts itself solely to the relation of what lies outside the boundary to what is contained within.[16]

We cannot say anything about what lies beyond the limit, according to Kant. Nevertheless, we can (and must) relate what we can talk about with what we cannot talk about. We can (and must) think of the difference between any of our discourses (which as such is always conditioned) and the knowledge of its conditioning (which is necessarily transcendental). In other words, in reference to Wang Guangyi's images, we must think about what it means to be on this side of the grate, a condition that cannot be overcome because it is rooted in our very way of being in the world, and therefore in history and time. We must experience this non-overcomeability and, therefore, *know* our conditioning and experience our finitude.

## Conclusions

Discussing critical philosophy and, in particular, taking cue from the Kantian question of the boundary, Hegel states, "Something can be known, even felt to be a *barrier* (*Schranke*), a lack (*Mangel*) only insofar as one has at the same time *gone beyond* it."[17] A little later, he goes on to say a barrier, a lack of knowing is determined precisely *to be* a barrier or lack only through a *comparison* with the *existing* idea of the universal, of what is whole and complete. Therefore, it is merely a lack of consciousness not to realize that the designation of something as finite or limited contains the proof of the *actual presence* of the infinite, the unlimited, that the knowledge [*Wissen*] of a boundary can exist only insofar as the unbounded exists *on this side,* in consciousness.[18]

Hegel's point, rather than a critique, is in fact a radicalization of what Kant says in his transcendental dialectics: a sort of path which, through transcendental philosophy, leads to the questioning of some of the basic assumptions of Kant's transcendentalism. The point is not to deny something undeniable, namely the finiteness and conditioning of our experience of the world, the perspectival and relative nature of our relationship with reality. Rather, the point is not to be contented with the haughty modesty of finitude, in the presumptuous and self-contradictory reduction of everything to a point of view and a perspective.

Setting us on the threshold that separates the transcendent from the everyday, that is to say, revealing the presence of transcendence in the known and the usual, Wang Guangyi represents the aporia of the limit, its being always and necessarily *here* and *there*, its belonging to *both* the dimensions between, in which it is placed and of which it marks the *difference* and reciprocal irreducibility: dimensions that therefore find in it, in the radical contradiction that the limit embodies, their very condition of possibility.

# Notes

1   Moro, 2018.
2   Danto, 1981.
3   Hegel, 2010: Part I, *Science of Logic*.
4   The work of art is a representation that resists the concept and can never be completely translated into it. This is the great theme that runs through all contemporary art. Even if art becomes conceptual, its sensible medium always says something that the concept as such cannot express.
5   Plato, 2008: §§ 202 and 6.
6   Kant, 2004: 102.
7   Ibid.
8   Ibid.: 103.
9   Ibid.: 108.
10  Ibid.: 108.

11   Ibid.: 111.
12   Kant, 2004: 111.
13   Ibid.
14   Ibid.: 112.
15   On the topic of the boundary in Kant, see Chiereghin, 1988: 469–93.
16   Kant, 2004: 111–12. For Kant, the fact that reason lies on the boundary between the knowledge of phenomena and the world of noumena is the condition that makes "cognition *according to analogy*" thinkable (Prol. 108. This cognition, in turn, makes metaphysics possible. On this point, cf. Faggiotto, 1988; Melchiorre, 1991; Marty, 1980.
17   Hegel, 2010: § 60 An.
18   Ibid.

# References

Chiereghin, F. (1988). "Die Metaphysik als Wissenschaft und Erfahrung der Grenze. Symbolisches Verhältnis und praktische Selbstbestimmung nach Kant." In R. P. Horstmann and D. Henrich (eds.) *Stuttgarter Hegelkongreß 1987. Metaphysik nach Kant?* Stuttgart: Klett-Cotta.

Danto, A. (1981). *The Transfiguration of a Commonplace. A Philosophy of Art.* Cambridge, MA: Harvard University Press.

Faggiotto, P. (1989). *Introduzione alla metafisica kantiana dell'analogia.* Milano: Massimo.

Hegel, G. W. F. (2010). *Encyclopedia of the Philosophical Sciences in Basic Outline.* Trans. K. Brinkmann and D. O. Dahlstrom. Cambridge: Cambridge University Press.

Kant, I. (2004). *Prolegomena to Any Future Metaphysics.* G. Hatfield (ed.). Cambridge: Cambridge University Press.

Plato. (2008). *Symposium.* Trans. M. C. Howatson and F. C. C. Sheffield. Cambridge: Cambridge University Press.

Marty, F. (1980). *La naissance de la métaphysique chez Kant: une étude sur la notion kantienne d'analogie.* Paris: Beauchesne.

Melchiorre, V. (1991). *Analogia e analisi trascendentale: linee per una nuova lettura di Kant.* Milano: Mursia.

Moro, A. (2018). *Brief History of the Verb to Be.* Cambridge, MA: The MIT Press.

# 2

# Wang Guangyi: Popular Study on Anthropology

Demetrio Paparoni 德沐

Between the years 1994 and 1998 Wang Guangyi created three series of works—*Passport*, *Visa*, and *Virus Carrier*—in which the figures of a newborn, a man depicted in the format of a passport photo, and a dog are accompanied by anagraphic and identificational information (Figure 2.1). On each image are the captions, in capital letters, "PASSPORT VISAS," "VISA," and "VIRUS CARRIER," like stamps affixed to documents, allowing or prohibiting individuals to cross a border. Requesting a visa involves willingly subjecting oneself to an investigation or profiling; providing photographs, digital fingerprints, and information regarding the reasons for travel. Classifying individuals through identity documents and registering characteristics for the sake of bureaucratic organization suggests that in each individual there is a hidden potential danger to the community (Figure 2.2).

Suspicion and fear have always played a decisive role in the collective unconscious, and they are instruments whose power has been used to convince the masses to agree to give up a considerable amount of liberty in exchange for protection. Raised and educated in China in the era of the Cultural Revolution, Wang Guangyi has been able to observe the effects of a society in which every individual feels under the watch of their neighbor, and his cited cycles of works certainly reveal such a climate. Viewed in the light of new geopolitical scenarios, the works in which Wang Guangyi deals with these themes remain widely applicable to present times, even when our attention is shifted to the democratic West. We might think of the restrictions and the introduction of new protocols for limiting entry into the United States to persons who have passed through or live in countries considered a threat.

In 2017 and 2018, with the cycle *Popular Study on Anthropology*, Wang Guangyi took on topics related to the classification of individuals or entire communities

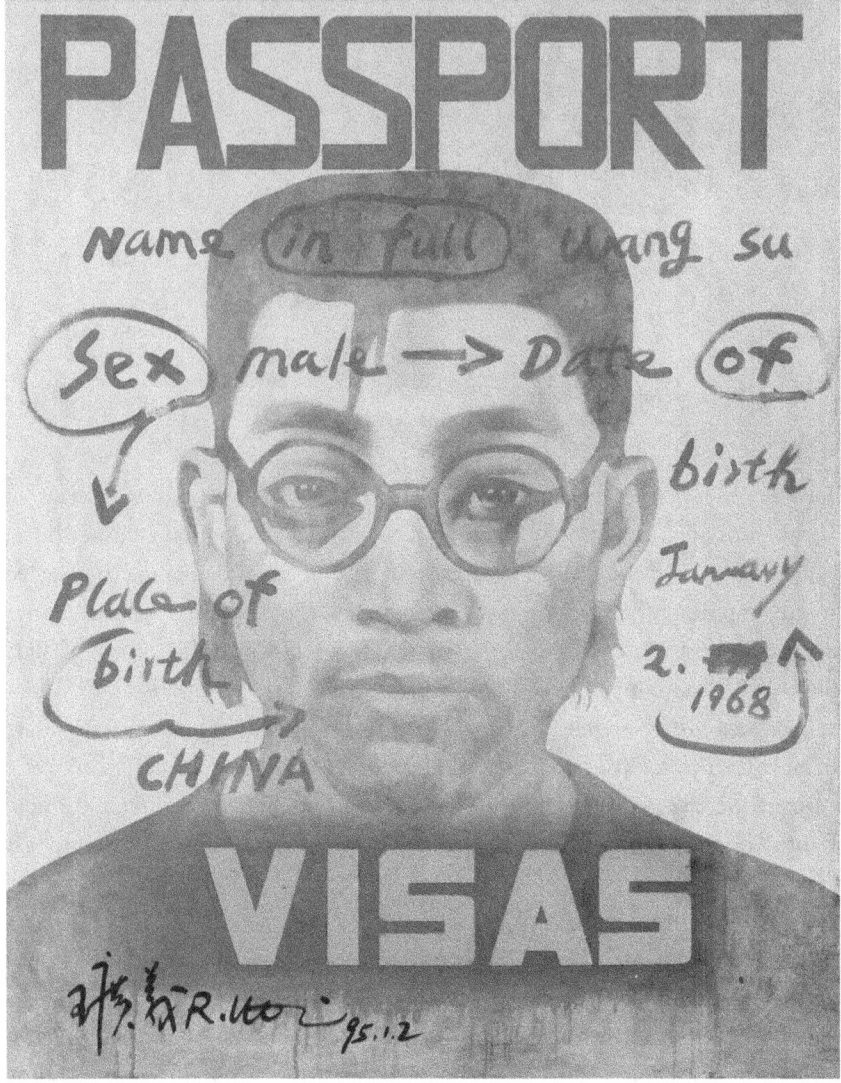

**Figure 2.1** Wang Guangyi, *Passport n. 2* (1995), oil on canvas, 150 × 120 cm.

based on morphological and physiological characteristics and in reference to the concept of race. The artist concentrated on the relationship between scientific and pseudoscientific theories of social anthropology and criminal anthropology, on current research in biogenetics and biotechnology, and on the consequences of their application for practical and political purposes. Wang Guangyi developed his research through three different series of works: *Race, Violence and Aesthetics* (2017), *Veil of Ignorance* (2018), and *Analysis on Races* (2018). Created with giclée printing on large sheets of paper (each measuring 160 × 320 cm) that were then

**Figure 2.2** Wang Guangyi, *VISA Project* (1994), installation with artificial fur, pictures, wooden boxes, screen printing, etc. 120 × 80 × 60 cm (33 pieces).

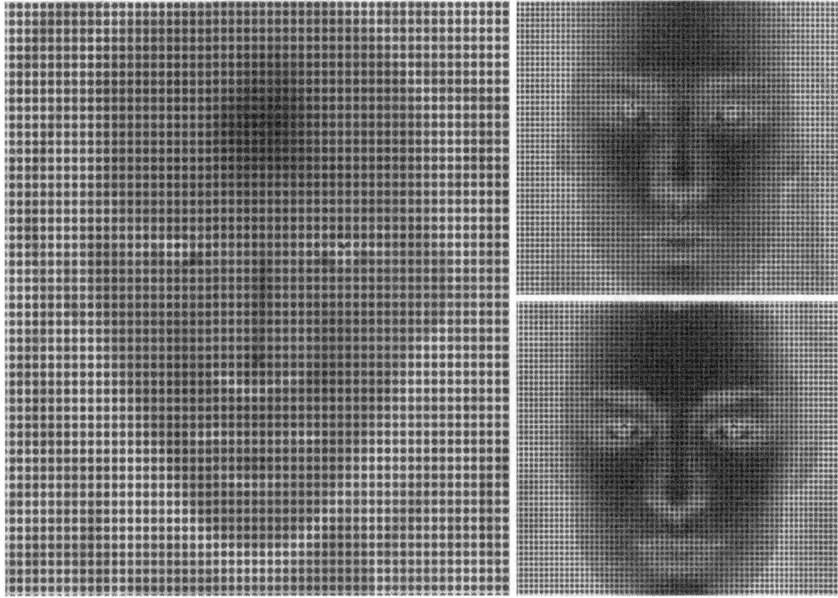

**Figure 2.3** Wang Guangyi, *Popular Study on Anthropology: Race and Aesthetics* (2017).

mounted on aluminum, the three works of the series *Race, Violence and Aesthetics* present human faces whose somatic characteristics have been associated with a particular ethnicity that the artist references in the caption, both in Chinese and in English (Figure 2.3). One of these works, marked precisely by the caption "Race and Violence," appropriates several illustrations from a book by Alfred Eydt entitled, *Schreibers rassenkundliche Anschauungstafel: Deutsche Rassenköpfe*, published in 1934 in Germany by Schreiber, a company in Esslingen am Neckar, known for the quality of its publications and its children's books. The author, Eydt, was a university professor from Dresden and a member of the National Socialist German Workers' Party—the party of Hitler—was considered to be an expert in racial politics, education, and psychology. In addition to dealing with themes such as the regulation of birth, mental illness, the diffusion of criminality, consanguinity, Jewishness, and the regulation of individuals who are considered parasites in society, Eydt's book summarizes the racial typologies that arranged the European population according to theories developed between the 1920s and the 1930s by German anthropologist Hans F. K. Günther.

Günther subdivided Europeans into Nordics, Gaelics, Westerners, Easterners, Slavs, and East Baltics and, based on physical and moral characteristics, established a hierarchy of these ethnic groups, placing the Nordics at the summit. Shifting the theories of Lamark and Darwin from biology to social anthropology, Günther reached the conclusion that, in order to obtain a population with the physical and moral characteristics of a superior race, it was necessary to increase the reproduction of individuals who, through their blood, could transmit these desirable characteristics. For the same reason, individuals whose blood was not worthy of reproduction were to be impeded.

Theories equally lacking scientific support, had developed in the two preceding centuries in other nations and led to the justification of colonial exploitation and slavery. Between the late nineteenth century and the early twentieth century there was a breakthrough in the way in which the theme of race was approached: by using craniometry, anthropometry, psychometry, and tests for measuring the intelligence quotient, several scholars of various nationalities paved the path for eugenics. Günther's pseudoscientific theories were related to this tradition and were in full harmony with the ideological view of the rising National Socialist Party, which would eventually base its own eugenics policies on them. These ideas had a devastating effect on millions of people because of the interest they elicited in those who at the time had the power to put them into practice.

In Eydt's book, as previously mentioned, the faces published were intended to recapitulate the elements characterizing the various races present in Europe.

Reintroduced by Wang Guangyi with a copy machine, enlarged, and made negative so as to accentuate the halftone effect, and portrayed with a dominating blue on a black background, the faces that we find in "Race and Violence" from *Popular Study on Anthropology* inspire us to contemplate the difference that is created between an individual's exterior appearance and his intrinsic identity. In other words, according to the artist, in people just as in things, what an individual really is can be barely distinguished; it eludes rational understanding. To be more exact, in relation to the spiritual dimension and to the realm of the sacred, what truly defines the essence and the uniqueness of an individual is always shrouded by something that conceals it.

The portraits recovered for the works included in the *Popular Study on Anthropology* cycle are not only imbued with historical, political, social, and ideological implications, but they draw upon the theme of faith, which traverses Wang Guangyi's entire body of work. In fact, in his various cycles of works he has emphasized the conviction that an individual cannot do without faith, even when it is founded on mythical traditions, conditioning by ideologies or the market, and on superstition. Theories on race supported by Nazi–Fascist anthropologists were presented as scientific evidence in order to consolidate the faith of an ideology in a population searching for new idols. *Popular Study on Anthropology* thus reconnects with an entire body of work by an artist who, from the beginning, has directed his research toward the essence of phenomena, in the direction of what Kant called "thing in itself." Wang Guangyi operates with the awareness that beyond the duality between appearance and hidden reality there is something that cannot be precisely defined insofar as it places itself outside of our possibility of understanding. Therefore, *measuring* man cannot restore his essence, contrary to what was believed, for instance, by Italian anthropologist Cesare Lombroso (1835–1909) who, even before Günther, was convinced that people prone to socially deviant behaviors presented physical characteristics that were scientifically traceable in the shape of the skull.

This is the theme to which Wang Guangyi dedicates his cycle *Analysis on Races*, comprised of photos featuring faces printed as negatives and placed alongside sketches that simplify the shape of the skull and emphasize it. Subverting the conclusions of these pseudoscientific studies, Wang Guangyi remarks how the analysis of differences in faces and in skulls is a testament to the complexity and the wealth of original appearances in the human species.

Due to the negative, these portraits resemble images of x-rays. By revisiting an expressive-conceptual expedient he had used in his work since 1987, the artist superimposed a red grid onto the images, a method that is reminiscent of a technique taught in art academies in order to recreate an image in enlarged or reduced dimensions. In the Maoist period the grid was an instrument used to make gigantic enlargements of the image of the president. Once it was covered by the finished painting, the grid was concealed, along with the trickery that transformed the image of a political leader into a gigantic image of a divinity who dominates ordinary human beings.

The fact remains that nineteenth-century positivist pseudo theories according to which individuals can be divided into different races have in the last fifty years been largely dismissed on paleontological and biological grounds. Today we know to be false the notion that the color of one's skin and one's somatic traits can allow for human beings to be classified into homogeneous groups.

The picture that stands out in the central part of *Race and Violence* is a famous old photograph that shows Nazi students applying the pseudo-scientific system of measuring an individual's face in order to determine his ethnic lineage. However, it invokes theories that have been dismissed on all scientific grounds, not only involving Nazi Germany. Nonetheless, being a well-known image, we tend to take it for granted and set it aside without scrutinizing its many implications, which are still current, or we forget that part of history that concerns us personally. When describing his works, Wang Guangyi emphasizes how, even in China, phenomena of racism were experienced during the transition of power between dynasties of different origins. The artist specifically calls to mind those of past centuries, when the government of Mongolian ethnicity replaced that of Han ethnicity and, when, subsequently, the dynasty of Manchurian ethnicity came into power.

In the other two works created for the *Popular Study on Anthropology* cycle, captioned "Race and Aesthetics," the focus shifts to aesthetics. These works present photographs of faces, found on Chinese websites, and accompanied by captions indicating their ethnicity or geographical place of origin. Here, too, the artist introduces them through the effect of the photographic negative, preserving the original caption while adding the English translation. The artist, hence, wishes to underscore the arbitrariness of all interpretations and classifications based on physical characteristics.

The way in which similar images are published in magazines and newspapers, or travel the Web, make them come off as neutral, without suggesting the intent to affirm one ethnicity as superior over another. Yet, more often than not, these sequences of faces offer an ideal model of beauty, often based on algorithms. These portraits carry with them a subtext that are inclined to establish parameters of identity that, presented as objective, tend to condition our collective imagination. Reintroduced by Wang Guangyi through the effect of the photographic negative, they express the way in which the mind tends to instrumentally codify the complexity of an unknowable reality—the true essence of humanity and its spirituality—a reality whose true meaning, according to Wang Guangyi's Kantian interpretation, resides in the noumenon, which underlies the phenomenon. Human essence, therefore, is not codifiable based on somatic or cultural traits.

The photographic negative image is not a novelty in the work of Wang Guangyi, who had already experimented with it in several oil paintings from his cycles, *Great Criticism* (1990–2007), *Shining Forever* (2003) and, more recently, *New Religion* (2011). *New Religion* (see Figure 3.1) depicts great political and spiritual leaders (including Lenin, Stalin, Mao, Christ, and John XXIII), influential philosophers (Marx and Engels), and masterpieces of Western art (Andrea Mantegna's *Lamentation of Christ* and Leonardo's *Last Supper*). In this series the artist questions the fascination exerted by great utopias and why people feel the need to single out figures to whom they entrust their spiritual or material salvation.

For the artist, the use of photographic negative images in *New Religion* translates into impairing the spectator's familiarity with well-known images, urging him to consider them, not as predictable, but as capable of eliciting new reflections on their meaning. Nevertheless, the images remain identifiable as they represent universally known subjects. The same cannot be said for the faces found in the works of the cycle *Popular Study on Anthropology*: by not featuring well-known faces, the grainy negative reproductions make of these individuals simple imprints. The captions are thus what attribute the depicted person to a geographical area, which constitutes the driving motive for the artist to appropriate the image.

Yet again, the use of the reproduction of negative images in the work of Wang Guangyi becomes a critical act toward those who allow appearance and reality to coincide. In fact, the photographic negative entirely eliminates any possibility to brand a subject: skin color is eliminated, and somatic traits lack definition. What is most impressive in the photographic film is not a defined image that corresponds to the reality of the subject, but rather the subject's imprint. Just as in the Shroud of Turin, another theme taken on by Wang Guangyi, here the subjects transcend their appearance.

The third cycle of *Popular Study on Anthropology*, entitled Veil of Ignorance, is comprised of prints of faces for which the artist used acrylic paint. The image, covered by a colored veil and by spots that prevent the traits from being brought into focus, is presented as a deteriorated fresco. As the artist himself explained, the blurriness of the images does not allow for the subjects' area of origin to be identified. Since we are unable to attribute "racial properties" to these faces, we can only recognize them as what they truly are: individuals.

Here the artist embraces the concept of the "veil of ignorance": the mental experiment found in "A Theory of Justice", the most famous work of the political philosopher John Rawls (1921–2002). In a Socratic fashion, Rawls asks himself what justice is and arrives to the conclusion that justice is fairness. How, therefore, can a fair society be established *ex novo*? By putting legislators in a condition of ignorance regarding their future: behind a veil. If legislators did not know what position they would fill in the embryonic society that is being established, they would not assign privileges to any class or person, due to the possibility that they would not be included. In order to avoid the risk of falling into a disadvantaged class, they would develop laws that treat all people fairly. According to Rawls, mental experiments (such as the ship of Theseus, the evil genius, and the veil of ignorance) can be powerful philosophical instruments if used properly.

Underlying the topic dealt with in *Popular Study on Anthropology* are ethical and political matters related to experiments in biogenetics and biotechnology. Though these experiments do not currently aspire to transform human intelligence into superintelligence, in a very distant future, developments in this field could be aimed at enhancing the operations of the brain through selective reproduction and reproductive cloning by copying the genomes of highly talented individuals, with exceptional characteristics. Still fresh in the minds of Europeans is Aktion T4, the scientifically cloaked Nazi program that carried out the suppression of ill individuals who were considered "lives not worth living". Nick Bostrom notes in his book "Superintelligence. Paths, Dangers, Strategies" (2014) that every reproductive practice that aimed to improve the genetic patrimony was avoided in postbelic Germany. Yet, there is always a chance that it might not be opposed in other countries that may be inclined to promote the use of genetic selection and engineering with the intention of enhancing the intelligence of their populations. The risks involved in genetic experimentations are countless. As previously mentioned, an eerie reminisce of past eugenic practices lingers. The consequences are not always entirely predictable. Modified genes, for instance, could bring about madness, resulting in unforeseeable outcomes.

As for the enhancement of intelligence, the matter is made more complex due to the fact that there is no intelligence gene, hence it is still unknown what memory, imagination, and fantasy are at a biological level. DNA can be worked on in order to modify physical traits—to make humans more resistant or immune to an illness, for instance—but cognitive processes cannot be intervened with. Wang Guangyi also reflected on this while creating the works of *Popular Study on Anthropology*, once again considering his work as an attempt to direct attention to the essence of the individual and to spirituality, which cannot be defined.

# Part II

# Duplicating the Scene

# 3

# Wang Guangyi's "Material Spirit": A Religion Embodied in Art

Tiziana Andina 安提强

## Art and Philosophy

"The profession of art still exists. Therefore, I am not a thinker, nor am I a philosopher; I am an artist with ideas" (see pp. 250-1). Considering Wang Guangyi's works and statements,[1] what emerges is a very important point in order to understand today's complex art world: the irreducibility of philosophy and art. In other words, contrary to what is posited by many artists and philosophers alike, art has a unique function within the sphere of human knowledge and practice. Creating art and being an artist is different from being a philosopher or a scientist. This is why Hegel's famous prophecy did not come true.[2]

Contrary to what is believed by some philosophers (exemplarily, Georg Wilhelm Friedrich Hegel and Arthur Danto), philosophy cannot take the place of art because, unlike art, it uses concepts and organizes them into arguments. Likewise, contrary to what is believed by many contemporary artists (exemplarily, Joseph Beuys and Joseph Kosuth),[3] art cannot hope to dismiss philosophy because, while making use of representations, it also requires that these be somehow incorporated in the work. I believe this issue is particularly relevant to the visual arts which, more than others, have undergone an identity crisis during the twentieth century: if it is true that Joseph Beuys would have been happy to be called a philosopher and certainly thought of himself as an educator, no musician or poet has ever seriously taken into consideration the Hegelian thesis of the death of art, at least not for what pertains to music or poetry.

Like it or not, visual art is a representation incorporated into a medium, and the latter is important for the work to be what it is. Even when visual arts make use of language, they do so in ways that are completely different from those used in philosophy: in art, language reveals a highly metaphorical component that, for the most part, is foreign to philosophy. Moreover, the representation of art is not the same as that of philosophy. The latter is bound to a relationship of correspondence with the reality that it intends to capture through thought and, at least ideally, has to take responsibility for its truth. On the other hand, art concerns the dimension of fiction, of the fable, of myth or, also, as in the case of Wang Guangyi, the dimension of spirituality. It follows that art entertains a constitutively different relationship with the truth compared to philosophy.

From this perspective, it is not surprising that Wang Guangyi should not see the artistic practice as the development of the retinal perspective: art is not a form of knowledge like the others, such as humanistic knowledge and science. It is neither a form of knowledge of the sensible world, nor a special kind of naive physics that considers the reality available to perception. It is not even a simple reflection on its own means of expression—perspective, color theory, modes of representation, chiaroscuro, and so on. Rather it is a revisitation of the world, at least the part of it we can observe and understand, from the point of view of its most sensitive observers: artists. However—and this is the second salient aspect of Wang Guangyi's poetics—the artist, rather than paying attention to the visible or retinal properties of things, is particularly sensitive to the properties that the eye cannot see, but which are just as real and binding as traditional aesthetic or formal properties. It seems that the point is exactly this: to make the invisible visible, in an effort that does not require a faithful rendition of reality. What the artist really wants is for his work to reveal something that escapes from the *lògos*.

In the *Birth of Tragedy* (1872), discussing the origin of art, Friedrich Nietzsche proposed a very similar idea. He suggested answering the question about the essence of art ("What is art?") through the genealogical method, that is, by retrospectively determining the origin of the "thing" that we call art: in this way we will find that at the basis of art there is simply an instinct. This instinct, however, has not always been expressed in an artistic form. In fact, during the Hellenistic period, the human instinct for transcendence and sacredness found expression in music and theater. Music and theater, in the Nietzschean interpretation, are the ways in which human beings show their access to the sphere of sacredness. When the actor becomes aware of not being a body lent to the expression of the spirit but, more properly, of being part of a representation of the divine, then—and only then—there is a shift from the religious dimension to the artistic one.[4] In other words, there is a very subtle line separating art from religion. In essence, these are two different stages of our ability to represent the world: two different stages of representation, based on the same instinct.

I believe that Wang Guangyi would entirely agree with Nietzsche on this point: in their perspective, art and religion belong to the same dimension—they are one the evolution of the other. Religion and art belong to the sphere of myth and emotions, while philosophy belongs to that of *lògos*. And yet there is something that distinguishes art and religion: Nietzsche clearly identifies this something in representation. Artistic representation must be recognized as such by the spectator: this point is essential for the representation to be deemed artistic. In order for the spectator to understand the spectacle, he must be aware of the fact that what he sees is indeed a spectacle. In other words, he must know that he is dealing with something that concerns some aspects of reality, not with ordinary reality pure and simple.

Picasso pointed this out, in his own way, when he placed a real label on a (drawn) bottle of Suze. Already in the *Poetics*, Aristotle had underlined the importance of clearly grasping the difference between reality and fiction from the cognitive point of view, so that artistic fruition may be structured in the modalities that are proper to it. This point is very clear for what concerns the emotions we experience in the artistic relationship: "Objects which in themselves we view with pain, we delight to contemplate when reproduced with minute fidelity: such as the forms of the most ignoble animals and of dead bodies."[5] For this relationship to exist and be effective, so as to allow for artistic enjoyment, the viewer must have some awareness of the object that is part of the relationship. Otherwise it would be as if a child riding a broom like a horse thought he was really riding a horse: it would not be a game, but a misunderstanding.

To sum up, one could therefore consider the topic as follows: art has traditionally had the task, among others, of representing reality. In the *Birth of Tragedy*, Nietzsche shows how to identify the characteristics and meaning of artistic representation. One of the earliest known forms of representation has to do with the sacred and consists in the idea that the tragic actor is the vehicle by which the divine concretely appears through a human body (the actor's). Therefore, in this framework, the divinity *re-presents* itself, in a space and in a time that are human. The evolution of the practice of tragic theater has allowed for the refinement of both the concept and the practices of representation: the god is not incorporated into a living body; rather, the actor's body refers to our concept of divinity. This is how representation, also in art, operates a shift between fidelity and fiction.

In this context, it is certainly possible for philosophy to invade the "territory" of art and vice versa but, on the whole, the domains of the two disciplines remain distinct. That said, it is also true that art and philosophy share at least one thing: the fact that both represent their contents, albeit in ways that are typically different. This, in my opinion, is the element that Wang Guangyi manages to grasp so well, and this is why he is one of the key figures of contemporary art.

## New Contemporary Art

The interpretation Wang Guangyi offers of the contemporary world must therefore be brought back to this context, starting from the idea that the questions that arouse reflection on art generate new art (see Chapter 14, Yan Shanchun's conversation with Wang Guangyi). Ideas are not born out of nothing, rather they belong to a historical narrative that favors their development and determination. Therefore, every idea, even the most original, breaking with all that preceded it, can only derive from, and be understood based on, the general meaning of that narrative. In art, all things, even the most significant breaks, are necessarily part of the history of art. "Contemporary" art is therefore linked to the history of art and, at least in the case of Wang Guangyi, relates to it in terms of continuity rather than rupture. In many of his works, Wang Guangyi fully embraces the link with the past expressed by the history of art and, thanks to this choice, significantly enhances the representational scope of his works.

Let us consider some examples. Wang Guangyi implements this strategy in many works, but two cycles seem to me to be particularly significant in this regard. I am referring to *New Religion* and *Great Criticism*. *New Religion*, a series of oils on canvas, clearly intends to emphasize the pervasiveness of the religious sentiment that exists even where we would least suspect it. Religion, in this sense, is new, but only for what concerns its forms of manifestation, whereas the spirit that drives it is very ancient. The subjects are political leaders such as Mao, Lenin, or Stalin, spiritual leaders such as Christ and Pope John XXIII, and philosophers, in particular Marx and Engels. The fact that Wang Guangyi chose a particular rendering for the works of the cycle—the "negative" effect of photographic film—serves to guide the viewer towards a precise meaning common to all the paintings of *New Religion*. The negative effect has mainly the objective of eliminating the details of a face, of a body, of a context, while leaving the object of the representation perfectly recognizable. This is the same effect that we find in *Last Supper* (2011), a work openly inspired by Da Vinci and that, perhaps to make the citationist game even more acrobatic, could have been titled "This is not *Last Supper*"—alluding to Warhol rather than to Leonardo's original (Figure 3.1 see p. 45). Indeed, the reference to Warhol's interpretation

**Figure 3.1** Wang Guangyi, *New Religion—The Last Supper* (2011), oil on canvas, 400 × 1600 cm.

of *Last Supper* (1986) is certainly evident; in a sense, Wang Guangyi radicalizes Warhol's vision, making it even more powerful. Warhol doubles his last supper, exactly as if we put two snapshots, taken sequentially, next to each other, and uses color (black and yellow) in an extremely expressive way. The game of the double painted scene, in addition to recalling the idea of two successive frames, insists on obvious metaphysical allusions. In a strongly secularized world, such as the one that forms Andy Warhol's cultural and artistic horizon, it makes no sense to speak of monotheism: there are many values and gods. And, above all, less clearly than in Wang Guangyi's *Last Supper* but expressing exactly the same kind of intuition, Warhol blurs the details of the work, leaving the observer to face the full symbolic weight of the event. In Western and Christian traditions, that is the supper par excellence: the artist does not need to resort to formalist strategies to recall that event and its meanings.

By engaging in an even more openly symbolic poetic, Wang Guangyi uses color—in this case only the color red—to draw the outlines of shapes, objects, and people. Not only does the work need no narrative details, it does not need a title either: such is the power of the outline of those figures that the artist would have achieved his goal anyway. In fact, the observer, at least the Western one, cannot fail to recognize and complete the artistic narration. Even more than Warhol, Guangyi seems to want his art to exhibit a character of an affectivity, so much so that the viewer's attention is entirely directed to the power of the symbolic, that is, to what is represented in the work—to its meanings.

*Great Criticism*, the cycle that made the Chinese artist world famous, is a powerful variation of the same stylistic character. The works of *Great Criticism* present a double symbolic choice: they use some of the most widespread and powerful symbols of the Western world (and here, again, the influence of Warhol's Pop Art is evident), and link them to the images used by Chinese political propaganda (Figure 3.2 see p. 46). We see are peasants, soldiers, workers,

**Figure 3.2** Wang Guangyi, *Great Criticism—Marlboro* (1992), oil on canvas, 175 × 175 cm.

portrayed in standardized ways, therefore deeply rhetorical and stripped of any personal characteristic. Even more clearly than in *Last Supper*, characters take the place of people, and are presented as symbolic powers. In this way, Wang Guangyi achieves a contrast between two myths: the people—the embodiment of the Chinese spirit—and the individualism embodied in the symbols of the Western market: "In my view, the central point I want to express in the *Great Criticism* series is the ideological antagonism that exists between Western culture and socialist ideology. The significance of this antagonism has more to do with issues in cultural studies than simply art in and of itself."[6]

Yet I think *Great Criticism* is more than the opposition of two worlds: it is the creation of a kind of meta-mythology, a synthesis of two worlds that, in Wang Guangyi's vision and particular reinterpretation of Pop Art, come to a synthesis of extraordinary symbolic power. Perhaps because of censorship, Wang Guangyi's work appears as a deconstruction—carried out according to the grammar of visual art—of the myth of consumerism fueled by North American culture. However, his stylistic choice to use Pop Art should not be underestimated, also in terms of the meaning embedded in the work. Wang Guangyi appropriates what is perhaps the best-known language of twentieth-century Western art to deconstruct the culture that produced it: in so doing, though, he places his own art in the wake of that culture, de facto recognizing its supremacy. In some ways it is also possible to go further and consider *Great Criticism* as the construction of a new mythology that has the same virtues—and therefore the same vices—as the Warholian mythology.

I will try to explain myself better. Let us go back to the parallelism between Wang Guangyi and Andy Warhol. The latter's works are certainly perfect examples of how art can engage, in a clever and deep way, with populist attitudes and inclinations. Warhol was universally known for having magnified American populism and for making it an interpretative lens through which to read the reality of his time. So, *Mao*, painted by Warhol in 1973 (see Figure 7.1), represents Mao Zedong in the same pop style with which Warhol had eternalized Marilyn Monroe, making her an icon. If there is no difference between an actress and a political leader like Mao—that is, if both are symbolic figures, authors of and actors in two different cultural mythologies—the artist can emphasize this aspect, representing them with the same style: Pop. Warhol could probably have named his portrait *Demythologizing Mao*. Indeed, Warhol was a deconstructor, but he was also the creator of that mythology, mythologizing mass culture and American society of the twentieth century. His extraordinary *Coca-Cola*, which is a symbol of the North American lifestyle, is simply perfect as it is and, perhaps for this reason, Warhol chose to represent it without any redundancy or stylistic refinement. It is as though he wanted to say, "This is Coca-Cola: this is America. Nothing else is needed: both are perfect the way they are."

Wang Guangyi's goal in *Great Criticism* was akin to Warhol's: he used Warhol's style to deconstruct what Warhol had mythologized and magnified. He demythologized the mythologist. Having said that, are we sure that *Great Criticism is* only a major act of cultural and artistic deconstruction, a criticism of Western culture and market? I don't think so, and Wang Guangyi himself often leaves clues in his works to lead us in the right interpretative direction, so as to understand the conceptual and semantic difference between him and Andy Warhol.

As the latter had done with American culture, Wang Guangyi is mythologizing Chinese culture, using a narrative model that is itself a little populist. In other words, Wang Guangyi's art is to Chinese culture what Warhol's is to Western culture, but there is difference. If Warhol recognizes the world that he mythologizes as the best of all possible worlds—exemplifying a perfect ideal of democracy, where both the President of the United States and the average American citizen can drink the same Coca-Cola—Wang Guangyi, using the telling elements disseminated in his works (letters, numbers, grids: see, e.g., *Hand-waving Mao Zedong with Black Square*, or *Great Criticism—Coca-Cola*), warns us that his mythology refers to a higher universe. It is the "true" universe, the space of the sacred that Wang Guangyi sees as the core of reality—the origin and the ultimate *télos* of the world that he is mythologizing and, at the same time, describing so well.

With any great deconstruction project, it makes sense to ask to what end it has been undertaken, because no deconstruction makes sense or is more than sophistry, albeit very elegant and sophisticated, if it does not aim at a reconstruction. It seems to me that Wang Guangyi's reconstruction is essentially about the transcendental dimension, and that his deconstruction is almost a pretext to constantly remind us of the sacred—which is very clear if you consider the origin of the art, described at the beginning of this chapter.

If the original dimension of art is that of the sacred, which the developments of representation have been able to diminish through all possible media, it is clear that transcendence is what the artist looks for and seeks. But how can one—as Kant noted so acutely—express narratively and symbolically something that cannot be understood through the tools of reason, or that escapes any attempt at incorporation? Kant reminded us that the thing, in itself, marks the horizon that defines the very possibility of human existence and action. Beyond that limit we can intuit the presence of a boundless domain that is fundamental for our lives, but to embody that domain—to express its meanings in a concrete body—is something that lies on the edge of what can or cannot be done. This is why Wang Guangyi often resorts to graphic and symbolic tools that interrupt and occlude the presence of a perceptual datum or refer to a presence that is given only through absence, as in the case of the shroud. Wang Guangyi's shroud bears no sign of the body—perhaps there is a trace of it in the folds of the fabric, but the artist seems to tell us that there is no point in looking for it: all we would see is the trace of the human dimension, something that brings us back to what a body once was.

The space of the human and that of transcendence are circumscribed by strong boundaries: they are like solid thick walls, built with jute bags (see *Things-in-Themselves*, Figure 8.2 see p. 162). It is unthinkable to be able to circumvent those walls, but perhaps if we try we will be able to catch a glimmer of light that shines through the rough canvas. After all, Wang Guangyi is giving us the same suggestion that Plato had already offered us: if we cannot enjoy the real world by observing it in full light, at least we must try to recompose the fragments we can find in its shadows.

## Notes

1  Paparoni, 2013.
2  Hegel, 1807.
3  Goldie and Schellekens, 2007.
4  Nietzsche, 1872.
5  Aristotle, 1978: 48b, 9–12.
6  AA.VV., 2002: 28.

## References

AA.VV. (2002). *Wang Guangyi*. Hong Kong: Timezone 8 Publisher.
Aristotle (1978), *On Poetics*, trans. D. Ross, in *The Works of Aristotle*, vol. 1, Franklin Center, Pa., Franklin Library.
Goldie, P., and Schellekens, E. (2007). *Philosophy and Conceptual Art*. Oxford, NY: Clarendon Press.
Hegel, G. W. F. (1973). *Phänomenologie des Geistes* (1. Aufl. ed.). Frankfurt (am Main): Suhrkamp.
Nietzsche, F. W. (1872). *Die Geburt der Tragèodie aus dem Geiste der Musik*. Leipzig: E. W. Fritzsch.
Paparoni, D. (2013). *Wang Guangyi. Works and Thoughts 1985–2012*. Milan: Skira.

# 4

# The Tears of Pictures: Duplication and Inflection in Wang Guangyi's Oeuvre

Enrico Terrone 容恒

Pictures are special things. When we see a picture, we do not limit ourselves to seeing a colored surface before us. We also see something *in* this surface. Richard Wollheim,[1] in developing Ernst Gombrich's[2] account of depiction, calls the colored surface the *medium* of the picture and what we see *in* this surface the *object* of the picture. He writes:

> If I look at a representation as a representation, then it is not just permitted to, but required of, me that I attend simultaneously to object and medium. So, if I look at Holbein's portrait, the standard of correctness requires me to see Henry VIII there; but additionally I must—not only may but must—be visually aware of an unrestricted range of features of Holbein's panel if my perception of the representation is to be appropriate. This requirement upon the seeing appropriate to representations I shall call "the twofold thesis."[3]

In sum, the appreciation of a picture involves two key elements, namely *twofoldness* and the *standard of correctness*. While *twofoldness* allows us to visually attend to both object and medium, the *standard of correctness* allows us to correctly identify the object that we see in the medium. For instance, in viewing Holbein's portrait, twofoldness allows us to visually attend to both a colored surface and a person, while the standard of correctness allows us to identify this person as Henry VIII of England.

According to Wollheim, twofoldness is the hallmark of the pictorial experience, namely *seeing-in*, which is made of two experiential "folds": one directed to the pictorial medium, the other to the object depicted. In a later essay, Wollheim[4] calls these two folds "configurational fold" and "recognitional fold," respectively. In Wollheim's framework, the standard of correctness supplements the recognitional fold with a cognitive element, namely, a stock of information concerning the picture's history of production that allows us to properly experience the objected depicted: "What the standard does it to select the correct perception of a representation out of possible perceptions of it."[5] The title of a picture often provides us with some basic information about that picture's standard of correctness.

On the one hand, naturalistic paintings (not to mention photographs) usually tend to draw the viewer's attention to the recognitional fold.[6] On the other hand, art critics such as Clement Greenberg[7] have criticized pictorial naturalism, arguing that painters should instead draw the viewer's attention to the picture's surface, which is the content of the configurational fold. Interestingly, Wollheim provides us with an account of depiction in which, in principle, both folds are relevant so that the viewer's attention is disseminated between them. Thus, drawing the viewer's attention to one fold or the other is not a matter of all or nothing. It is just a matter of degree.

In this chapter I will use Wollheim's framework as a source of conceptual tools for a philosophical journey through Wang Guangyi's paintings. I will follow a chronological order, beginning with the cycle *Frozen North Pole* (1984–5) and ending with *Daily Life* (2014). I will show that, in several paintings by Wang Guangyi, duplication plays a key role in both the configurational fold and the recognitional fold of the pictorial experience. More specifically, duplication provides us with a pleasant experience of formal equilibrium in the configurational fold as well as with an uncanny experience of duplicated existence in the recognitional fold. I suggest that much of the fascination elicited by these paintings lies in the contrast between the two folds. Furthermore, I will show that duplication often intervenes, also in the standard of correctness of Wang Guangyi's paintings, especially when titles invite us to see these paintings as a duplication of other images.

Still, duplication is not the whole story. Wang Guangyi does not limit himself to accurately building up duplication in his paintings: he also breaks the perfect duplication he himself has built. In order to explain this phenomenon, I will use another conceptual tool that has been introduced and discussed in the debate about depiction.[8] This is the concept of *inflection*, which designates an interference of the configurational fold in the recognitional fold: "what is seen in a surface includes properties a full characterization of which needs to make reference to that surface's design."[9] If inflection occurs, one can appreciate the features of the object depicted only by making reference to some features of the picture as a colored surface. In short, one cannot help but see some features of the configurational fold also in the recognitional fold. I will argue that inflection plays a key role in breaking perfect duplication in Wang Guangyi's paintings. In so doing, I will highlight a special kind of inflection that I will call "the tears of pictures."

## *Frozen North Pole*

*Frozen North Pole* (see Figure 1.2) is a cycle created by Wang Guangyi between 1984 and 1985. Cycles in art raise an interesting ontological issue, namely, whether a cycle is a unitary work of art that has the individual paintings as its components or, instead, whether we should treat each painting in the cycle as a self-standing work. Here, I limit myself to addressing this issue in an irenic manner, assuming that both the cycle as a whole and the paintings that constitute it can be treated as works of art, and I will focus on some paintings of the cycle. I will do the same for the other Wang Guangyi cycles or series.

In *Frozen North Pole No. 24* (1985), we see two human beings walking on the left, in the foreground, and an animal, arguably (albeit quite surprisingly) a sheep, in the background (on the right, on the horizon line). That is what we see at first in the recognitional fold. The standard of correctness provided by the title allows us to identify this place as the North Pole. The adjective "Frozen" in the title strikes us as redundant, since the North Pole is, so to speak, analytically frozen—frozen by definition. This suggests that the choice of the adjective "frozen" does not have the function of providing us with more information. Rather, this term has the function of orienting our experience: we should recognize the North Pole and focus on its being frozen, on its constitutive frost.

If we focus on the configurational fold, we see a rectangular surface (68 × 86 cm) in which there are just three colors, namely, white, blue, and light brown (chromatic parsimony, as we will see, is one of the hallmarks of Wang Guangyi's style). The distribution of the colors on the surface is simple: two thirds is filled by a blue rectangle, which depicts the sky, while the lowest third is occupied by a white rectangle, which depicts the ground. The white clouds in the sky create a sort of visual dialogue between these two areas, and so does the sheep, which looks like a piece of ground that has penetrated into the sky. This polar landscape exhibits a perfect stasis, it is really *frozen*, as if it did not need action. Such a stasis is somehow contrasted by the two human beings in the foreground. They introduce action in a frozen landscape. Yet, the frost bears on their movements, which appear extremely slow and laborious. Their bodies express a sense of heaviness, which seems to come from the furs, coats, and boots they need in order to face the frost. They appear quite clumsy compared with the simple elegance of the ship and, more generally, of the polar landscape. They look like two walking bells that introduce two heavy vertical volumes moving diagonally in a space dominated by simple horizontal shapes: the ground, the sky, the clouds, the sheep. Furthermore, the humans are almost indistinguishable each from the other. They appear as each the duplicate of the other, in contrast with the absolute uniqueness of the sheep.

Still, in *Frozen North Pole No. 24*, exact duplication is broken by a detail, namely, the left hand of the person on the left. While the person on the right looks like a perfect bell, the person on the left exhibits a distinctively human feature. Interestingly, this crucial detail is also the location on the picture in which inflection shows up. In looking at this hand, one cannot help but see also the brush strokes that correspond to the fingers. The painting makes us feel the concreteness of its surface precisely in the location in which the perfect duplication of the depicted subject is broken. In this respect, *Frozen North Pole No. 24* is sharply different from other paintings belonging to the same cycle, for instance *Frozen North Pole No. 28*, in which the duplication of the two human figures—viewed from the back just as in the paintings of the contemporaneous cycle, *The Back of Humanity* (1985)—is absolutely perfect, without any inflection bearing on it.

## Post-Classical

Wang Guangyi created the *Post-Classical* cycle between 1986 and 1988. Here, I will focus on one painting of this cycle, namely, *Post-Classical—Death of Marat A* (1987) (Figure 4.1). The title clearly states the core of the standard of correctness. In order to properly appreciate this painting, we should treat it as a creative duplication of Jacques-Louis David's *La Mort de Marat* (1793). The idea of a duplication is embodied in the painting itself, which uses the panel's vertical axis of symmetry to duplicate the scene depicted. Thus, on the right we see a scene that has a structural correspondence with the scene depicted by David, whereas on the left we see the same scene as if reflected in a mirror.

In fact, Wang's painting does not exactly replicate David's; rather, Wang's aims at grasping its structure, its essence. In David's there are several colors and many details; in Wang's, only gray volumes on a black background. While David painted Marat as a human being in flesh and bones, Wang painted him rather as a pure human form, which can, as such, have several instances (and actually

**Figure 4.1** Wang Guangyi, *Post-Classical—Death of Marat A* (1987), oil on canvas, 116 × 166 cm.

has two instances in this picture). David's painting reminds us of Greek and Roman statues; Wang's seems to be closer to the quasi-abstract bodies sculpted by Brancusi. Arguably, this is what "Post-Classical" means in the title of the cycle. Picasso's "post-classical" duplication of Velázquez's *Las Meninas* also is a key reference in this respect.

One might say Wang's Marat is frozen in a timeless space, as if it were, in turn, part of the frozen North Pole cycle. Furthermore: a frozen North Pole in which not only life but also light has disappeared. In fact, in looking at *Post-Classical—Death of Marat A*, one has the impression of enjoying nothing but pure volumes in the recognitional fold and shades of gray on a back background in the configurational fold. The volumes are so sharp and robust that the pictorial experience is dominated by the recognitional fold, and one finds it hard to pay attention also to the configurational fold. Yet, this is not the whole story. There is an element in the painting that, in spite of belonging to the recognitional fold, draws our attention back to the configurational fold, to the picture as a surface. Here is where inflection shows up. The inflecting element consists in the vertical lines that fall from Marat's tub. These lines represent Marat's blood in the recognitional fold, and yet one cannot help but see them as paint dripping down onto the painting's surface. These lines are Marat's blood and the painting's tears at the same time. They introduce movement in a frozen scene, as well as asymmetry in an otherwise perfectly symmetrical composition. In fact, the lines of blood on the left are not the mirror reflex of those on the right. Thus, these tears of paint break the perfect duplication of the scene depicted.

It is worth noting that Wang did not limit himself to duplicating *La Mort de Marat* in *Post-Classical—Death of Marat A* (1987). He also created another duplicate, namely, *Post-Classical—Death of Marat B* (1986), which in turn embodies a duplication of the scene depicted by David. In sum, Wang gives us two *Death of Marat* paintings and four scenes depicting the death of Marat. If the hallmark of the classical is uniqueness, the hallmark of the post-classical, as suggested by Walter Benjamin,[10] is multiplicity through duplication. Yet, from Wang's perspective, duplication and multiplicity do not mean absolute identity of replicas. In fact, there are relevant differences between version *A* and version *B* of *Post-Classical—Death of Marat*. They are both based on vertical symmetry but, in version *B*, the scene having a structural correspondence with the scene depicted by David is on the left, instead of on the right. As a consequence, the two Marats are facing each other, whereas in version *A* they turn their backs on each other. But the difference that I find most striking is that in version *B* there is no blood, no tears of paint, no inflection. Version *B*, unlike version *A*, presents us the scene of Marat's death as absolutely frozen in a pure three-dimensional space.

## *Mao Zedong AO*

A portrait is, as such, a duplication of a person. Thus, the duplication of a portrait is absolute duplication: it is duplication all the way down. In this sense, Andy Warhol's "multiple portraits" of icons such as Marilyn Monroe, Elvis Presley, Che Guevara, and Mao Zedong are the triumph of Benjamin's technical reproduction. In a Warholian vein, Wang Guangyi triplicates Mao Zedong's portrait in his triptych *Mao Zedong AO* (1988) (Figure 4.2). Yet, Warhol's multiple portraits of Mao are variously colored, whereas Wang Guangyi's triptych exhibits a rather austere black and white palette. The inflection element that characterizes this painting is a black grid superimposed on the triple portrait. The viewer cannot help but seeing this as both a grid on the surface in the configurational fold and as a barrier separating Mao from the viewer's space in the recognitional fold. In this case, inflection does not break duplication (or, better, *triplication*) but rather reinforces it. In fact, the grid implacably covers all the three instances of Mao. The presence of two Latin alphabet letters in the four corners of each portrait

**Figure 4.2** Wang Guangyi, *Mao Zedong AO* (1988), oil on canvas, 150 × 360 cm.

contributes to the sense of repetition, and also to inflection, as far as this forces us to treat the grid not only as a barrier in the recognitional fold but also as something superimposed onto the painting's surface in the configurational fold. The very title of the triptych calls our attention to these letters and to the peculiar twofoldness that they enable: *Mao Zedong AO* means we encounter Mao in the recognitional fold and the two last letters of his name, namely "A" and "O," in the configurational fold (as well as, because of inflection, the grid in both folds).

In the ultimate version of the painting, the letter "O" has been replaced by the letter "C." The original painting containing the letter "O" can still be seen in some photographs but is no longer available *as a painting*. The reason for that was censorship, as Wang Guangyi explains: "They didn't care what I changed," he recalls, "but it had to be something, so I made the simplest change. With one line of paint through the right side of the O, I changed it into a C, and they seemed satisfied. The government controlled everything; they just wanted to show their power."[11]

## Chinese Tourist Map: Beijing

The portrait of Mao comes back in *Chinese Tourist Map: Beijing* (1989), but in a different context (Figure 4.3). The title of the painting is allusive and only gives us a clue of the standard of correctness. The place we see actually is in Beijing, as the title states, but it does not tell us which place. Still, in order to properly appreciate this painting, one should know that this place is Tiananmen

**Figure 4.3** Wang Guangyi, *Chinese Tourist Map: Beijing* (1989), oil on canvas, 120 × 150 cm.

Square and that Wang Guangyi executed the painting after the bloody military suppression of a pro-democracy movement that occurred in this square in June 1989. He portrays the main building of the square (namely the entrance of the Forbidden City) in a quite naturalistic manner emphasizing the vertical symmetry of the building (vertical symmetry, as seen above, is a recurrent feature in Wang Guangyi's paintings; it is his basic way of introducing duplication into paintings). Yet, this naturalistic depiction is significantly inflected by several elements.

While the recognitional fold focuses on the square and the building, the configurational fold is characterized by graphic signs, namely, the word "weather" in the lower right corner and the digits "-5 → 7" in the upper left corner (together with icons of sun and storm and Chinese ideograms). Wang Guangyi uses weather as a metaphor of history. The storm turns a cold, sunny day into a warmer, rainy one, just as the Tiananmen Square protests of 1989 changed the history of China. That is to say, the storm in the painting stands for the massacre in history. The rain falling from the clouds stands for the blood of the victims. Here inflection plays a fundamental role since what we see as rain (in the recognitional fold), and recognize as blood (by grasping the standard of correctness), appears to us also as paint dripping down, as the tears of the picture (in the configurational fold).

Furthermore, inflection also affects the portrait of Mao on the facade of the building. A spot of paint turns Mao's face into a sheer stain. He no longer has eyes to see or a mouth to speak. It is as if the rain had irredeemably damaged his image.

## *Great Criticism*

Most paintings of Wang Guangyi's cycle *Great Criticism* (1990–2007) combine images of communist workers with logos of capitalist firms. For instance, in *Great Castigation: Coca-Cola* (1993) (see Figures 6.1 and 6.2) three workers are holding one large fountain pen "whose nib lies just above the second C in the white letters 'Coca-Cola,' and whose length appears to be the pole of a red flag. If the first C is communism, then the second, the one threatened by the pen's nib, is "capitalism." Book and pen replace hammer and sickle."[12]

The three workers have the same posture and resemble each other. They seem to be the result of a triplication, just like Wang Guangyi's triple portrait of Mao in *Mao Zedong AO*. Such an iteration effect is increased by the mechanical reproduction of the same numbers (e.g., 965, 4213) on the surface of the painting. This suggests that both Western capitalism and Eastern communism rest on mechanical reproduction. The former reproduces merchandise, the latter manpower.

Focusing on the configurational fold, we notice the painting has just four colors: black, white, yellow, and red. The background consists in a red strip in the lower third of the panel and a yellow rectangle in the upper two thirds. Red and yellow are the colors of the Chinese flag, red and white are the colors of the Coca-Cola logo. In this sense, red is the key color of the painting, since it establishes a chromatic correspondence between Western and Eastern ideologies. Thus, the red strip of the Coca-Cola logo on the right matches the red book (in the hand of the first worker), the red star (on the cap of the third worker) and the red strip (having the pen as its pole). Yellow is not only the dominant color in the background, but also the color of the skin and the clothes of the workers, just as of the pen they hold. These workers are yellow figures on a yellow background. Therefore, their visibility depends on an almost-continuous black pattern that starts from the suit of the first worker at the lower left and ends in the pen at the upper right.

This black pattern introduces inflection in the painting, inasmuch as one cannot help but see it both as a thick contour in the configurational fold and as a grouping of people and things in the recognitional fold. Interestingly, the black pattern is very sharp in its left part in which it depicts the heads and the torsos of the workers, but its style changes at the right end, where it depicts the hands holding the pen. Here some paint drips down from the hands and from the pen. If in the recognitional fold this may represent the pen's ink running down, in the configurational fold we are faced, once again, with the tears of the picture.

## The Guides

*The Guides* (2001) is a work constituted by five portraits that depict, left to right, Marx, Engels, Lenin, Stalin, and Mao. Wang Guangyi portrays the five "guides" of communism in chronological order, from the earliest to the most recent, along a timeline that runs from left to right. In this sense the work is more than a sheer series of portraits: it is a historical narration. On one hand, Marx and Engels, those who conceived communism, clearly look toward the right of the timeline, that is, toward the future. On the other hand, Lenin, Stalin and Mao, those who applied communism, look toward the center of the timeline, with a slight inclination toward the left. They are interested in the past, but especially in the present. If we focus on the configurational fold, we observe that all five guides are depicted against a black background by means of red and gray marks. The red marks draw the main contours of the figures, while the gray marks contribute to providing these figures with shades and volumes.

The depiction is strongly inflected. We cannot help but see the shapes of the figures (in the recognitional fold) also as brush strokes (in the configurational fold). Inflection is especially striking in the portraits of Marx and Engels, in which the stylistic element that I have named the picture's tears is dominant. These two portraits have tears all the way through. In part, this depends on the aspect of the subjects depicted. In fact, Marx and Engels have quite long beards, Lenin only a goatee, Stalin only a mustache, and Mao is completely shaven. And the depiction of beards surely can favor the emergence of the picture's tears. But this is not the whole story. The decrease of the picture's tears along the timeline seems to suggest that something has changed, not only in faces, but also in history. The picture's tears even increase in moving from Marx to Engels, but then significantly decrease in moving from Engels to Lenin, and further decrease, albeit without disappearing, in moving from Lenin to Stalin and finally to Mao. Interestingly, this decrease of the picture's tears is somehow compensated by an increase in the numbers that, just as in *Great Castigation*, Wang Guangyi superimposes on the depicted subject. The decrease on the picture's tears and the increase of the picture's numbers along the timeline suggests that, in the passage from theory to practice, from philosophy to politics, communism has thereby lost something vital and fluid (the picture's tears also evoke blood and life), quite paradoxically, becoming something more cold and abstract, something too far from real life.

It is worth comparing *The Guides* with a coeval painting, namely *The Last Supper* (2011) (see Figure 3.1), which has a similar style (red figures on a black background) but a different subject: religious instead of political. The "guide" depicted in this painting is, in fact, Jesus Christ. In the wake of his *Post-Classical* cycle, Wang Guangyi duplicates another masterpiece from the history of Western art, namely, Leonardo's *The Last Supper*. Once again, the duplication goes hand in hand with an alteration based on Wang Guangyi's hallmarks: the reduction of the palette to a few colors (here, black, gray, and red) and the tears of the picture, which, as in *The Guides*, vertically drip, in contrast with the horizontal alignment of the depicted subjects.

## *Death of the Guide*

Just as *The Guides* and *Last Supper*, *Death of the Guide* (2011) and *Pietà* (2011) modulate the same pictorial idea in a political key and in a religious key respectively. In *Death of the Guide*, Wang Guangyi portrays Mao's body in its coffin. The painting uses just a few colors: black for the background, yellow for Mao's body and for the surface where it lies, dark blue for the top of the coffin, light blue for the contours of both the body and the coffin. The tears of the picture drip from these blue contours. They introduce a vertical movement in a painting dominated by a horizontal rest (Figure 4.4). In *Pietà*, Wang Guangyi uses a similar palette to depict a similar subject, namely Jesus's body laid down on the Stone of Unction and covered by the Shroud. Once again, the religious subject is depicted through the duplication of a masterpiece of the history of Western art, which in this case is Mantegna's *Lamentation of Christ*. The body of Christ is painted in yellow just as is Mao's body in *Death of the Guide*, and the Stone of Unction and the Shroud are painted in blue as is Mao's coffin. Yet, there are two important structural differences between these two paintings.

First, Mao is completely alone whereas Christ is watched over by the Virgin Mary and Saint John (in Mantegna's painting Mary Magdalene is also there, but she is unrecognizable in Wang Guangyi's duplication). Interestingly, Wang

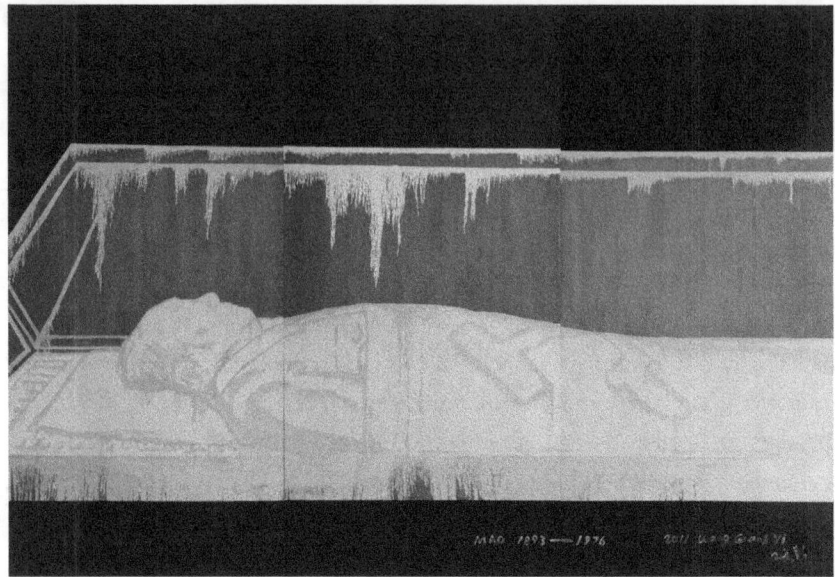

**Figure 4.4** Wang Guangyi, *Death of the Guide* (2011), oil on canvas, 400 × 600 cm.

Guangyi painted these figures in blue, not yellow. This suggests that their living bodies do not belong to the same category as the bodies of Christ or Mao. Rather, if we take colors as clues of categories, they belong to the same category as objects such as the stone, the shroud, the coffin. The dead bodies seem to have a unique sacredness that is beyond the reach of both living beings and inanimate objects.

Secondly, Mao's body is depicted as lying along the horizontal dimension of the pictorial space whereas Christ's body, following the structure of Mantegna's painting, is depicted as lying along the depth of the pictorial space. Yet, in both cases, the tears of the picture drip along the vertical dimension, orthogonal to the dead body.

The pictorial idea shared by *Death of the Guide* and *Pietà* also characterizes a later Wang Guangyi painting, namely *Man Taking His Afternoon Siesta* (2014). The eponymous man lies along the depth of the pictorial space, just as Christ in *Pietà*, but he is completely alone, as is Mao in *Death of the Guide*. The tears of the picture keep dripping along the vertical dimension, but in this case inflection is strengthened by the superimposition of a grid such as we found in *Mao Zedong AO*. The title suggests that this man, unlike Christ and Mao, is not dead, just sleeping. Nevertheless, the similarity that connects this painting to *Death of the Guide* and *Pietà*—especially to the latter—is striking. In this sense, *Man Taking his Afternoon Siesta*, as a secularized reenactment of Mantegna's *Lamentation of*

*Christ* reminds us (as Western viewers) of the *tableau vivant* set up by Pier Paolo Pasolini in the finale of his film *Mamma Roma* (1962).

I do not know whether Wang Guangyi knows Pasolini's work. I guess he does not. Still, both Wang Guangyi and Pasolini have a similar attitude toward Mantegna's masterpiece: they both acknowledge that Christ in this painting is much more human than divine—or maybe he is divine in virtue of being so human. Thus, they both reenact Mantegna's painting replacing Christ with a humble human being. More generally, Wang Guangyi and Pasolini share the attempt to reconcile Christianity, and its representation in Western art, with communism. The difference is that Wang Guangyi also aims at including Western pop culture in an exhaustive synthesis, whereas Pasolini conceives of both Christianity and communism as the opposite of—and as absolutely irreconcilable with—Western pop culture.

## *Holy Sindone*

Christ's shroud, which we have just encountered as a crucial component of Wang Guangyi's *Pietà*, becomes the absolute protagonist in *Holy Sindone* (2013). Focusing on the recognitional fold of this painting, we are faced with a minimal landscape with the ground painted in black and the sky, the color of which changes from gray to blue moving from the horizon line to the top of the painting (Figure 4.5).

The Holy Shroud appears twice in the picture, in conformity with the rule of duplication that characterizes many of Wang Guangyi's paintings. More specifically, the Shroud appears once in the sky and once on the earth. In the sky, the Shroud is completely clean, perfectly white and accurately folded. By contrast, on earth, we see it as dirty and wrinkled. The tears of the picture, which drop from the sky to the ground, provide us with the link between these two different instances of the Shroud. In fact, the Shroud in the sky is surrounded by a black rectangle from which the tears of the picture drop down on earth. This suggests that the tears of the picture in the configurational fold correspond to Christ's blood in the recognitional fold. Yet, even if the viewer recognizes these as bloodlines, she cannot help but also see them as paint lines in the configurational fold. In this sense inflection is crucial to the appreciation of this painting.

The Holy Sindone appears as the eponymous subject also in a coeval work by Wang Guangyi, namely the black and white triptych *How to Define Sindone to Human Beings?* (2013). Here, the Shroud is depicted in the central panel. It

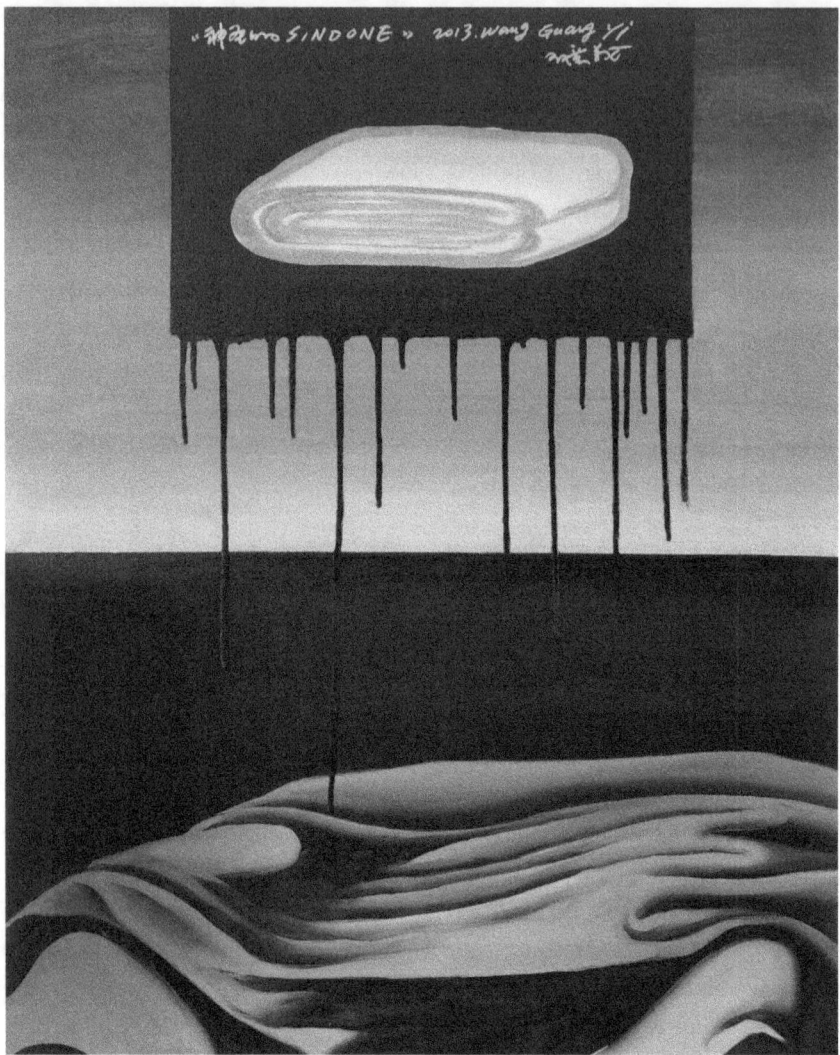

**Figure 4.5** Wang Guangyi, *Holy Sindone* (2013), oil on canvas, 100 × 70 cm.

is accurately folded just as in *Holy Sindone*, but now it lies on a chair, instead of being suspended in the sky. Furthermore, the Shroud is no longer painted in white but in dark gray; it only has white contours.

The lateral panels of *How to Define Sindone to Human Beings?* are two portraits that face each other. In the left panel, Wang Guangyi, in the wake of his *Post-Classical cycle*, duplicates Velazquez's *Portrait of Pope Innocent X*, the obsession of Francis Bacon, who duplicated it in *Study after Velázquez's Portrait of Pope Innocent X* (1953) as well as in more than forty other paintings. The right panel also is a sort of duplication, since it portrays (a photograph of) Joseph Beuys during his performance *How to Explain Pictures to a Dead Hare* (1965), from which the title of Wang Guangyi's triptych derives. While the central panel of *How to Define Sindone to Human Beings?* shows the Shroud lying on a chair in its pure form, this right panel shows it on Beuys's left leg, drenched with the dead hare's blood. In fact, Beuys is "protectively cradling the deceased hare in a manner akin to the Madonna in a pietà" (Antliff, 2014). In this way, Wang Guangyi depicts the Shroud twice, one time as immaculate and the other as bleeding, just as he did in *Holy Sindone*. But in *How to Define Sindone to Human Beings?* there is also a third element, namely, the portrait of Innocent X in the left panel. There is no Shroud there, only the draping of the Pope's sumptuous garb, and a parchment he holds in his left hand. While the central panel represents Christ as a divine entity, and the right panel represents him as a dying living being, this left panel rather focuses on Christianity as an institution, as worldly power. Yet, the tears of the picture show up in all three panels of the triptych.

## *Daily Life*

The Holy Sindone also appears in Wang Guangyi's *Death of Jesus* (2013). Here, Jesus's body lies horizontally on the Stone of Unction, just as Mao lies on his coffin in *Death of the Guide*. On Jesus's left, the Virgin Mary raises the Shroud from his body. The scene is painted in yellow and blue on a black background. The tears of the picture drip from both the Sindone and the Stone. They seem to represent Mary's tears and Jesus's bodily fluids. The tears dripping from the Sindone are painted in pure blue, while in those dripping from the Stone the blue is combined with the yellow of the Stone's surface to produce a kind of green. On the bottom of the painting, the green tears dripping from the Stone are supplemented with black tears dripping from the very background of the picture, as if the scene as a whole expelled its fluids. Thus, the tears of the picture introduce a strong sense of corporeality in the domain of sacredness.

In *Daily Life* (2014) (see Figure 13.1) this sense of corporeality becomes the absolute protagonist of the painting. Instead of the Stone of Unction and the Holy Sindone, we see a toilet bowl and a roll of toilet paper. Instead of Jesus and Mary, a man standing in the toilet and putting a finger in his mouth. This scene seems to be aimed at eliciting disgust rather than pity. The tears of the picture drop from the toilet bowl, but also from the ceiling and even from the floor. One has the impression that the whole space of the scene is decomposing.

Yet, as suggested by the sense of depth provided by the perspective, some bits of sacredness remain even in this crude piece of daily life. Just as *Man Taking His Afternoon Siesta* was a secularized reenactment of *Pietà*, *Daily Life* can be seen as a secularized reenactment of *Death of Jesus*. Bodily fluids drip from the toilet bowl just as they dripped from the Stone of Unction and the Holy Sindone. The tears of pictures reconcile the most sublime with the humblest.

## Notes

1 Wollheim, 1980.
2 Gombrich, 1960.
3 Wollheim, 1980: 142.
4 Wollheim, 1998.
5 Wollheim, 1980: 137.
6 Cf. Lopes, 1996.
7 Greenberg, 1961.
8 Podro, 1998; Lopes, 2005; Hopkins, 2010.
9 Hopkins, 2010: 158.
10 Benjamin, 1936.
11 See Cohen, 2012.
12 Wiseman, 2007: 112.

## References

Antliff, A. (2014). "Why Joseph Beuys and His Dead Hare Live On." Available online: http://fr.phaidon.com/agenda/art/articles/2014/march/03/why-joseph-beuys-and-his-dead-hare-live-on/ (accessed June 17, 2017).

Benjamin, W. (1936). "L'œuvre d'art à l'époque de sa reproduction mécanisée," *Zeitschrift für Sozialforschung*, 5: 40–66; "Das Kunstwerk im Zeitalter seiner technischen Reproduzierbarkeit," in R. Tiedemann and H. Schweppenhäuser, eds. (1980). *Gesammelte Schriften*, I:2. Frankfurt am Main: Suhrkamp, 431–69; in M. W. Jennings, B. Doherty, and T. Y. Levin, eds. (2008). *The Work of Art in the Age of its Technological Reproducibility and Other Writings on Media*. Cambridge, MA: Harvard University Press.

Cohen, A. (2012). "Reasoning with Idols. Wang Guangyi." *ArtAsiaPacific*, 77. Available online: http://artasiapacific.com/Magazine/77/ReasoningWithIdolsWangGuangyi (accessed June 17, 2017).

Gombrich, E. (1960). *Art and Illusion*. London: Phaidon.

Greenberg, C. (1961). *Art and Culture: Critical Essays*. Boston: Beacon Press.
Hopkins, R. (2010). "Inflected Pictorial Experience: Its Treatment and Significance," in C. Abell and K. Bantinaki (eds.) *Philosophical Perspectives on Depiction*. Oxford: Oxford University Press, 151–80.
Lopes, D. (1996). *Understanding Pictures*. Oxford: Clarendon.
Lopes, D. (2005). *Sight and Sensibility: Evaluating Pictures*. Oxford: Oxford University Press.
Podro, M. (1998). *Depiction*. Cambridge, MA: Harvard University Press.
Wiseman, M. B. (2007). "Subversive Strategies in Chinese Avant-Garde Art." *Journal of Aesthetics and Art Criticism*, 65(1): 109–19.
Wollheim, R. (1980). *Art and Its Objects* (2nd ed. revised). Cambridge: Cambridge University Press.
Wollheim, R. (1998). "On Pictorial Representation." *The Journal of Aesthetics and Art Criticism*, 56 (3): 217–26.

# Part III

# Bridging the Cultural Divide through Pop

# 5

# On the Meanings of Propaganda

Erica Onnis 欧雯

## The Historical Context

The role and identity of the twentieth century have been and will be debated for a long time. Some historians consider it the "short century"[1] for the frenzied acceleration that marked its social and technological development, while others call it the "long century" for its indissoluble link with the nineteenth century. In any case, the impressive legacy of the twentieth century is undeniable, and today potentially difficult to manage. For China, the twentieth century was the century of the fall of the empire, of the republic and of communism. In a few decades the country experienced epochal changes that exacerbated its contradictions: backwardness, poverty, and illiteracy in rural areas coexisting with modernity, productivity, and renewal in some provinces of central and southern China.

Following the Wuchang insurrection of 10 October 1911, which led to the secession of numerous regions, the revolution against the Qing monarchy was triggered, leading to the abdication of Emperor Xuantong (Pu Yi) in February of the following year. In November 1911, Yuan Shikai, commander of the powerful Beiyang Army, was appointed prime minister by the empress dowager, Longyu, mother of Pu Yi, who hoped, by so doing, to maintain political stability in Beijing. After the events of Wuchang, however, the revolutionary league, led by Sun Yat-sen, declared the birth of the Republic of China, and numerous provinces joined this new political entity, of which Sun Yat-sen was elected temporary president in December of the same year, 1911.

Given the capillarity of the uprising led by Sun Yat-sen and the power of the Beyang Army led by Yuan Shikai, the two leaders decided to come to terms and, in 1912, Longyu declared the abdication of her son, the last emperor of the Qing dynasty. Sun Yat-sen formally took office as president of the Republic of China at the beginning of 1912, to be replaced by Yuan Shikai shortly thereafter. The ambition to unify the country, however, vanished at the death of the latter, when his old collaborators took control of the provinces they governed and gave way to what is historically known as the "Warlord Era" (1916–26).

While new parties, trade unions, peasant leagues, protest groups, and criminal gangs (such as the Green Gang) threatening republican stability flourished all over the country, the warlords' struggles made the new China ever more fragmented, violent, poor, and restless. This period lasted until the "Northern Expedition" of 1926, when the nationalist republican forces (the newborn Guoming Tang), led by General Jiang Jieshi (Chiang Kai-Shek) and allied with the communists, succeeded in defeating most of the warlords. The aim of the nationalists was the unification of Chinese territory and the creation of the new modern and international cultural identity that the monarchy had not been able to provide and which, as we shall see, would be the same objective of the Communist Party and Mao Zedong.

For this reason, from the cultural point of view, twentieth-century China radically revised its traditional values and Confucian ideals, recovered by the intellectuals only in the 1980s. In fact, since the establishment of the Republic of China, Sun Yat-sen has tried to modernize the country by, for example, imposing the Western solar calendar. This process was amplified in the following years and led to profound transformations: that of the educational system, with the abolition of imperial exams; that of the legal system, with the establishment of modern courts and professional regulations based on Western and Japanese models; the famous transformation of the linguistic system, with the reform of language, whose first phase dated back to 1915, with the "New Culture Movement," and ended in the 1960s with the introduction of simplified characters (jianhuazi 简体字), a simplified standard language (putonghua 普通话), and a character transliteration system aimed at combating illiteracy (hanyu pinyin 汉语拼音).

With regard to shared values, a genuine anti-Confucian revolution started at the beginning of the twentieth century, with a strong polemic against Confucian values such as filial piety (xiao 孝), the cult of ancestors and rites (li 礼), and respect for the past and for traditions. As we will see, speaking of Mao Zedong, the twentieth century in the new China was essentially the century of innovation, change, reform, and progress.

Following the ongoing fighting and a bloody civil war between nationalists and communists, Republican strongholds fell one after the other and, in 1949, Chiang Kai-shek and other nationalist authorities took refuge on the island of

Taiwan, permanently leaving the Asian continent. On 1 October, in Beijing's Tiananmen Square, the People's Republic of China was founded, with the definitive consolidation of the powerful figure of President Mao, who exasperated the desire for political and cultural renewal in the Cultural Revolution.

## Destroying the Four Olds!

About twenty years later, in 1962, during the Eighth Session of the Tenth CCP Plenary Meeting, Mao declared: "If we want to overthrow an authority, we must first make propaganda, and do work in the area of ideology."[2] In the years ranging from 1966 to 1976, Mao guided the impressive ideological and political movement known in the West as the Great Proletarian Cultural Revolution or, more simply, the Cultural Revolution: an anomalous phenomenon, which was described as "one of the most bizarre events in history."[3] The revolution was *cultural* because "Mao conceived of it in Marxist terms as a thoroughgoing revolution in ideological spheres and at superstructural levels."[4] It was an imposing propaganda movement aimed at eradicating every form of traditional culture: a culture that according to Mao consisted of "four olds" (四旧 si jiu) that were to be replaced with the "four novelties" (四 新 si xin):

> The Proletarian Cultural Revolution is going to thoroughly eliminate all the old ideas, old culture, old customs and old habits of the exploiting classes, which have corrupted the people for thousands of years, and to create and construct the proletarian new idea, new culture, new customs and new habits among the masses.[5]

So it was that, in the name of the motto "破四旧!" (po si jiu), translatable as "Destroy the Four Olds!" hordes of students wearing the uniform of the Red Guards sacked, destroyed, and vandalized buildings, archaeological sites, books, artifacts and artworks of incalculable value, as well as shops and public buildings such as schools and universities, emblems of the culture that Mao wanted to eradicate.

If we look at the Maoist Manifesto shown in Figure 5.1, we can see the portrait of President Mao in the upper left corner. Next to it are four characters 造反有理 (zao fan you li) meaning "Rebellion is justified"; the Little Red Book is held by the Red Guards (紅衛兵, hongjiebing, the three characters repeated several times on the right); the symbols of the traditional culture are trampled by their feet, and the sign at the center of the poster reads 破四旧立四新 (po

**Figure 5.1** Maoist Era Posters. Above: 破四旧 *Pò sì jiù* (Destroying the "four olds," 1966). Below: 无产阶级文化大革命万岁; *Wúchǎnjiējí wénhuà dà gémìng wànsuì* (Long Live the Great Proletarian Cultural Revolution).

si jiu li si xin), "destroy the four olds, build the four novelties." The four olds, as explained, were the old ideas, culture, customs, and habits of the exploiting classes, which Mao could annihilate thanks to the obsessive and urgent rhythm of propaganda.

The power of Chinese propaganda lied in a political language that became everyday language, a family vocabulary that crept into every interstice of the citizens' private life, making it inevitably unreal and paroxysmal:

- Serve the people! Comrade, could I have two pounds of pork?
- The revolution is not a gala dinner! It will be one yuan and 85!
- ... But then it is right to rebel!
- And be frugal when you implement the revolution. Here are your meat and your change.[6]

In 2000, the novelist Gao Xingjian was the first writer of Chinese origin to be awarded the Nobel Prize for Literature. Born in 1940 in Ganzhou, Jiangxi, Gao now has French citizenship and has resided in Paris since 1998. He is *persona non grata* for the People's Republic of China, where his works were banned after he published *Escape*, a play inspired by the June 1989 Tiananmen Square protests. Gao has known the Maoist regime, the senselessness of the Cultural Revolution, and the immense contradictions of a continent-wide nation—a nation he had to leave after the scandalous events of Tiananmen Square. Upon accepting the Nobel Prize, he said these words: "Language is the ultimate crystallization of human civilization. It is intricate, incisive, and difficult to grasp, and yet it is pervasive, penetrates human perceptions and links humanity, the perceiving subject, to its own understanding of the world."[7]

After all, the human being is a social being, and the ability to shape social reality is a fundamental characteristic of language. Andy Clark asserts that "Language is in many ways the ultimate artifact: so ubiquitous it is almost invisible, so intimate it is not clear whether it is a kind of tool or a dimension of the user."[8] Maurizio Ferraris, in his *Documentality. Why it Is Necessary to Leave Traces,*[9] argued that nothing social exists outside the text, where "text" is to be understood in a broad sense as a trace, that is information expressed and delivered to the world. For Ferraris, the text—written, repeated, remembered, or handed down—allows for recording, thanks to which the ineffability of social reality and truth is fixed in memory and history:

> Society is not based on communication but on registration. Because nothing social exists outside the text, papers, archives, and documents constitute the fundamental elements of the social world. Society is not based on communication but on

registration, which is the condition for the creation of social objects. Man grows as man and socializes through registration. Naked life is nothing but a remote starting point, and culture begins very early making for a clothed life, which is manifested in registrations and imitations: language, behaviors, and rites.[10]

It is therefore no coincidence that numerous propaganda posters portrayed the Red Guards with fountain pens and brushes, as well as clubs, hammers, shovels, and other work tools. The message conveyed was that next to material deconstruction, an authority can be destroyed through the imposition of a new lexicon and new linguistic formulas. As we will see, Wang Guangyi will use brushes and pens in many of his works belonging to the *Great Criticism* cycle, as well as in other works of the *Materialist* series (see Figure 14.1) or in *Small Criticism* (see Figure 11.1).

For humans, *to grow* means to improve physically and psychologically,[11] and this happens within a linguistic-relational dimension that affects any acquisition of meaning. If the interpersonal communication adopted is able to influence the individual's gaze on the world—that is, if speech shapes thinking—it will be easy to understand the meaning and role of the propaganda that overwhelmed the Chinese people in the 1950s and 1960s. During those decades, in China, language became *exclusively* political and the consequences of this became evident in the short and the long terms.[12]

The Chinese government focused particularly on children, whose consciousness was the most malleable, forcing them to become familiar from an early age with a form of life that was at one with the seriousness of politics. Lampooning or joking about the Party, no matter how young one was, was not allowed, and half a word could trigger the accusation of being a counter-revolutionary, the most dangerous and feared label, capable of ruining any family forever, no matter how high-class.

In his multilayered fresco *China in Ten Words*,[13] the popular Chinese writer Yu Hua says that the first characters he learnt to read as a child were 毛主席 (Mao zhuxi), "President Mao," and 人民 (renmin), "people," which he knew even before his own name and those of his parents.[14] Another valuable testimony comes from writer Ji Li Jiang, born in Shanghai in 1954 and currently residing in Hawaii, whose famous *Red Scarf Girl*[15] portrays her life as a teenager during the years of the Cultural Revolution. Jiang's text opens with these words:

> I was born on Chinese New Year.
>
> Carefully, my parents chose my name: Ji-li, meaning lucky and beautiful. They hoped that I would be the happiest girl in the world.

And I was.

I was happy because I was always loved and respected. I was proud because I was able to excel and always expected to succeed. I was trusting, too. I never doubted what I was told: "Heaven and earth are great, but greater still is the kindness of the Communist Party; father and mother are dear, but dearer still is Chairman Mao."[16]

During the Cultural Revolution, every child was encouraged and even required to monitor their family members strictly and report any behavior that even just seemed counterrevolutionary or contrary to the Party's guidelines, summarized in Mao's omnipresent *Little Red Book* and repeated as mantras day after day in school. The children constituted little armies ready to grow up and fight for the Party, for the country and for their president:

We had often been sorry that we were too young to have fought with Chairman Mao against the Japanese invaders, who tried to conquer China; against the dictator Chiang Kaishek, who ruthlessly oppressed the Chinese people; and against the American aggressors in Korea. We had missed our chance to become national heroes by helping our motherland. Now our chance had come. Destroying the fourolds was a new battle, and an important one: it would keep China from losing her Communist ideals. Though we were not facing real guns or real tanks, this battle would be even harder, because our enemies, the rotten ideas and customs we were so used to, were inside ourselves.[17]

Wang Guangyi himself, talking about his relationship with Mao, states:

In this sense, Mao is my idol, the most important memory I have because I have seen his image every day. My first paintings on paper were portraits of Mao. At the time, painting Mao, according to my vision, was like painting a saint. It was something very sacred. Even today, inside me, I still feel that Mao is a sacred figure. I think that the idols and mystical images that a person has seen in childhood leave a profound mark. This impression has its repercussions on me even today. Although today I can see Mao Zedong more rationally, I can not erase the mystical sentiment that he evokes.[18]

It was therefore according to these lines that the radical change that led China from the Confucian *Weltanschauung* to the communist, materialist, and atheist ideology was produced.

An example of the radical nature of this turning point was the change in the structure of family relationships, which had always been fundamental to traditional Chinese culture. One of the cornerstones of Confucian China was the aforementioned filial piety, which is the respect that the son owes to his father. In Chinese, the character that identifies filial piety 孝 (xiao) is composed of the character 子 (zi), which means *child*, below a derivative of the character 老 (lao) or *elderly*, to indicate, graphically, how the child should submit to his parent's authority. Yet, in the Maoist era, this relationship lost meaning and the children began to monitor and report their parents, driven by a single and insatiable desire: to please and obey the timeless, great President Mao Zedong, whose ruddy and benevolent face appeared in official portraits in every public or private space.

However, if the Maoist ideology was monolithic and undeniable, its application was always arbitrary depending on the president's personal interests, with constant changes of direction and consequent extreme social instability. At the time of the Cultural Revolution, any citizen could be turned into a public enemy from one day to the next[19]. A paradigmatic example is the case of Liu Shaoqi, Mao's close collaborator and second president of the People's Republic of China, who was jailed following a difference of opinion with Mao in the years of the Great Leap Forward and left to die of diabetes in prison, in anonymity and with no medical treatment. The death certificate, next to "profession," said "unemployed." Another famous case is that of the painter and calligrapher Shi Lu (pseudonym of Feng Yaheng), author of a famous painting entitled *Fighting in Northern Shaanxi* (1959). Today the picture is at the Museum of the Chinese Revolution and is considered his masterpiece, but back when it was made it was received very differently. Unlike traditional iconography, which placed Mao's face in the center of the image, Shi Lu's painting depicted Mao standing in the Shaanxi mountains, fighting the nationalist troops of the Guomintang. Mao is portrayed from the back in the center of the painting, but his figure is small, almost lost in the mountains. Shi Lu paid a very high price for his break from tradition: he was imprisoned, denigrated and condemned to a miserable fate. He died in the 1980s, without knowing that the very work that had caused his ruin would then be exposed, a few years later, in one of the most imposing buildings of Tiananmen Square.

Yu Hua provides a characteristic description of this unstable political climate:

> In popular idiom it was a matter of "flipping pancakes": everyone was just a pancake sizzling on the griddle, flipped from side to side by the hand of fate. Yesterday's revolutionary became today's counterrevolutionary, just as today's counterrevolutionary would become tomorrow's revolutionary.[20]

After Mao's death in 1976, the Congress of the Party declared the Cultural Revolution over, and Deng Xiaoping, Mao's successor as president, pushed the country toward a period of profound economic reform. For the umpteenth time the Chinese people were the involuntary protagonists of epochal transformations that in a few decades changed the face of the country. Deng's motto, borrowed from his collaborator, Liu Bocheng, is well-known: "It doesn't matter whether a cat is black or white, as long as it catches mice." With the end of the Maoist hegemony, the importance of ideology faded. Now there are no more leaders to be idolized, and values, whether Confucian or not, seem to be devoid of meaning. At the turn of the third millennium, China is on the eve of a new gold rush: now, only "wealth is glorious."[21]

## Political Control and Lost Transcendence

It is in this context of confusion and ideological instability that, in my opinion, one should read and interpret the work of Wang Guangyi, an artist who is very skilled in resuming an old game while changing its fundamental rules.

Wang Guangyi has always been a very prolific artist, but his celebrity is particularly linked, in China as well as abroad, to the series called *Great Criticism*, a pictorial cycle that was created between the 1990s and early 2000s. The works that make up the series are oils and acrylics on canvas and use the style of propaganda posters of the Cultural Revolution along with a series of Western elements such as, for example, the brands of big corporations like Pepsi, Coca-Cola, Marlboro, Sony, Rolex, and so on (see Figures 3.2, 6.1, and 6.2)

Thanks to *Great Criticism*, Wang Guangyi won a place in the world art scene, but this success came at the price of a misunderstanding of his works: in China, as well as in the West, the cycle was understood as "the emblem of Chinese Pop Art."[22]

In the words of critic Li Xianting:

> Since 1989, one after the other, many significant artists of the 85 Movement abandoned their metaphysical characters and, each their own way, they all began to walk the path of Pop, devoting themselves largely to the satirical deconstruction of the most important Chinese subjects and political events.[23]

Yet, in the intentions of its author, *Great Criticism* should not be a work of denunciation, nor of political satire, but an attempt to push the observer to ask questions about existence, reality, and transcendence. By combining the Maoist propaganda style with Western brands, which appear in most of the paintings that make up the *Great Criticism* cycle, Wang Guangyi produces an alienating effect in the observer, especially if she is Chinese. The uncanny derives from the juxtaposition of a prosaic element, that is, the symbols of Western, hectic consumerism, to an almost sacred element, that is, the language of the Party and Chairman Mao who, for a long time, was perceived to be more divine than human.

As far as this last point is concerned, numerous propaganda posters of the 1960s and 1970s wished longevity to President Mao, using the usual formula "毛主席万岁, 万万岁" (Mao Zhuxi wansui, wanwansui) often translated as "Long live President Mao." Literally, however, the formula 万岁,万万岁 (wansui, wanwansui) means "ten thousand years, ten thousand of ten thousand years." Since the Tang dynasty, this wish had only been reserved to the emperor, who in China represented the "Son of Heaven" and was endowed with transcendent characteristics. Starting from the twentieth century, the expression was then combined with the name of Mao and his revolutionary mission, as shown in Figure 5.1. Mao itself, in Wang Guangyi's opinion, fluctuated between two opposite desires: on the one hand, being a different, modern guide for a different, modern China and, on the other, being a sort of last emperor. These opposing ambitions are exemplified by the case of the Dongfeng CA71,[24] in 1958 the first car built in China on Mao's request. The car was completely hand crafted, its ornaments were in gold and it was decorated with a dragon, which is the symbol of the emperor. Wang said: "This dragon, however, showed the feudal desire to continue to venerate imperial power. Sometimes the spirit goes beyond matter. I think that Mao, when accepting that car, felt like an emperor accepting a tribute."[25] Wang Guangyi, who is about the same age as Ji Li Jiang, bears witness to having undergone President Mao's mythological influence. In a 2014 interview with art critic Demetrio Paparoni and Italian artist Mimmo Paladino, he stated:

> From when I was born and for many years thereafter Mao was all that I saw. He was always the subject of conversation. Everyone spoke of him. I was raised to believe what he said, without questioning his words. [...] When I was a child, Mao was already a legend, from a human being he had already become much more of a mythical figure, he had become a god.[26]

Such a juxtaposition between Mao's sacredness and the triviality of Western consumerism may at first glance appear disrespectful: the Maoist posters praising Coca Cola or cigarettes seem to be an attempt to ridicule a political system that, for decades, has prohibited any freedom of expression and was embodied by a man who could not be challenged by anyone and in any context.

Wang Guangyi's goal, however, is not to ridicule Mao, but to desacralize him and bring him back to a human dimension, placing him next to the relics of a prosaic everyday life such as that of consumerism.

This process of desecration, after all, can be seen in several other works by Wang Guangyi. In 1988 Wang produced a series of works such as *Mao Zedong in the Yan'an period*, *Mao Zedong—Red Grid* (1 and 2) (see Figure 7.3) and the triptych *Mao Zedong AO* (see Figure 4.2), where Mao's face appears under a thick grid, either black or red. Here, Wang refers to the grid technique (九宫格 jiugongge in Chinese), a widespread artistic method used in the art academy. You draw a grid on the drawing to be copied, then you draw another one with the same number of squares on the sheet or on the white canvas and use it as a reference to reproduce the proportions of the original. After having drawn the figure, the grid is erased or covered with paint, so that the working tool disappears. In these works, however, Wang leaves the grid, indicating the technical expedient behind the aesthetic representation: a warning of how every truth is a knowingly and artificially constructed lie. President Mao's divine figure is a good example of this. Quoting Wang Guangyi, "If the grid used to reproduce his figure comes to the surface, Mao becomes once again a man."[27]

However, making use of political themes such as the portrait of Mao does not necessarily mean making political art or political pop. Wang Guangyi does not use the themes of the Cultural Revolution for their political value, but for the existential meaning that was attributed to politics and its protagonists, above all Mao. Furthermore, the choice of associating consumerism with propaganda is not accidental. Although the two phenomena may seem very different, Wang's work sheds light on how they are in fact attributable to the same political mechanisms: the search for consensus and the production of homologation, that is the inability, actively induced in the individual, to take anti-conformist or antithetical positions compared to those of the mass. Maoism and consumerism, however distant, seem equally capable of producing truths that are not challenged, but are passively accepted by ordinary people. In Wang Guangyi's words, they are two different ways of brainwashing individuals.

Stylistically, the paintings of *Great Criticism* immediately recall the 1950s and 1960s: they adopt the style of Maoist propaganda posters, as well as their stereotypical images and their bright reds. Yet one of the most significant elements of this work is its seriality. Wang Guangyi has worked on *Great Criticism* for 17 years, prompting the negative judgment of some critics who considered this serial repetition excessive. However, in my opinion, it is exactly this obsessive and pounding repetition of the same theme that best represents the core of the propaganda machine.

If we turn our attention to Wang Guangyi's entire artistic production, without focusing solely on *Great Criticism*, it appears evident that the theme of control is omnipresent. Political control—which in the Maoist era was embodied by the ubiquitous propaganda manifestos and the slogans repeated like mantras in every social, public, or private context—re-presents itself in a softer, but still pressing form at all levels of contemporary Chinese society. Wang Guangyi, through a deep artistic analysis, examines the most various social phenomena by identifying them as the many declinations of political control. Starting from *Passport* and *VISA* (see Figures 2.1 and 2.2), up to *Virus Carriers* and *Blood Test—Everyone Is a Potential Virus Carrier* (1996), through *The Similarities and Differences of Food Guarantees under Two Political Systems* (1996), *Quarantine—All Food Is Potentially Poisonous* (1996) (see Figure 12.1), *24-hour Food Degeneration Process* (1997) (see Figure 11.2) and *Basic Education* (2001), Wang highlights how the government holds widespread control over all aspects of the individual's life by means of the bureaucratic system, the health system, the educational system, and even the food system. Propaganda and control: propaganda *is* control—of lifestyles, of choices, of ways to look at the world.

Wang Guangyi does not want to reverse the direction of the river, so to speak, but manages to divert its course, appropriating the instrument by which the New China erased the critical sense of its citizens and using it to stimulate a renewed critical gaze, demonstrating that propaganda can have a new constructive power, completely opposed to the repressive one exploited by the government. The deconstruction of ideology that Mao had encouraged by transforming Chinese social reality into a page of his *Little Red Book* becomes a possibility of metaphysical redemption in Guangyi's art.

Entering the universe of *Great Criticism*, we are gradually sucked into a surreal dimension and a meeting of cultures that is also a clash between ages. *Great Criticism* recreates the atmosphere of the Cultural Revolution, but fills it with disturbing elements and uncanny details that create cognitive dissonances, like a Freudian *Unheimliche*:[28] a "strangerness" which is, nevertheless, familiar. What the posters are promoting today, are the fake needs of well-to-do Western consumerism: this keeps the observer in the present and allows him to see the phenomenon of Maoism from a historical and cultural distance.

What Wang Guangyi wants to trigger in the observer is a reaction, a feeling of estrangement that is almost a nuisance. The political theme fills his work because politics was the daily bread of the Chinese people in the 1960s and 1970s, and the artist wants to break this addiction by causing a reaction that corresponds to a critical stance: "To break the inveterate semantic expectations and the consolidated aesthetic judgments that this iconography [that of propaganda] aroused in the observer."[29]

However, Wang Guangyi limits himself to indicating a new way, without predetermining its development or walking this path with the observer. This is the artist's task: "Why do artists exist? They exist because they offer a different point of view, an original view different from that of ordinary people."[30] This different point of view on reality that the artist claims to seek consists precisely in arousing questions and doubts, without providing predetermined solutions. Wang's art is an invitation to change paradigms—a pressing invitation, derived from the evaluation of the consequences that a dictatorship of language and thought left in individual consciences, and dictated by the need to reconstruct lost metaphysical structures.

This lack of references that the Chinese people have inherited from the Maoist era, however, is a void that constitutes an important potential, and what Wang's art wants to offer is a sort of metaperspective, a "non-point of view" that it is equivalent to the acceptance of multiple points of view from which to see reality. During the twentieth century, the Chinese people underwent a lot of brainwashing and lost contact with traditions, breaking away from their millennial capacity to reach for transcendence. In Ai Weiwei's words: "The history of modern China is a history of negation, a denial of the value of humanity, a murder of individuality. It is a history without a soul."[31]

This is what Wang Guangyi wants to offer: the ability to look beyond the flow of preconceived meanings in which his people have been immersed in recent decades. The goal is to go further, toward a transcendence that modernity seems to have given up, but that man cannot do without: "What I want to do now is engage in the work of clearing out. That is, clearing out the 'flood of meaning' that has resulted from the illogical tendencies of human passions. This clearing out must begin with myself. I think that the essence of contemporary art is a blind-spot of meaning."[32]

However, the idea of reaching a point of view alien to the consolidated meanings of which reality is imbued is, after all, but the umpteenth brainwashing, albeit more refined and with an opposite purpose. As the artist put it: "I have been brainwashed many times. For one, I was brainwashed by the Western art history [...] Then there was my education by socialism, by Mao Zedong [...]. And then, China's opening and reform brought Western materialism. I was brainwashed by fetishism. Today, after all these brainwashings I find that they have left an emptiness in my mind."[33]

*Great Criticism* highlights and thematizes a void so that it can be filled, without however suggesting how to fill it. It expresses the urgent need for China to rediscover an identity that is truly its own, overcoming the arbitrary indications of a political system and rejecting the fake models borrowed from the West. This, for Wang Guangyi, is the most pressing issue for the Chinese cultural world today: the path that everyone must take to become a conscious individual and not a number or an anonymous piece of a hypnotized, comatose society such as the one described by the Chinese novelist Ma Jian is his masterpiece *Beijing Coma*.[34] This is the path the artist himself took in the effort to find a place in the history of art and in the world, as "a vector of his own personal theology."[35]

# Notes

1. Cf. Hobsbawm, 1994.
2. AA.VV., 2004: 89.
3. Fairbank, 1997: 316.
4. Guo, Song, Zhou, 2015: 1.
5. Chen, 1966: 1.
6. Example of dialogue typical of the period of the Cultural Revolution, reported in Stafutti and Ajani, 2008: p. IX.
7. Gao, 2001: 7. The English translation is available at https://www.nobelprize.org/nobel_prizes/literature/laureates/2000/gao-lecture-e.html.
8. Clark, 1997: 191.
9. Ferraris, 2012 (the original text was published in Italy in 2005).
10. Ferraris, 2012: 319.
11. On these topics, see Prochiantz, 1989.
12. Wang Guangyi's words in Paparoni, 2014:158. "Mao was seen as a myth since I was born, thus, even today at more than fifty years of age, I cannot judge him in an objective way."
13. Yu Hua, 2012.
14. Ibid.: 3.
15. Ji Li, 1997.
16. Ibid.: XV.
17. Ibid.: 28–9.
18. Cf. *infra*, Cohen's conversation with Wang Guangyi, 181.
19. Yu Hua, 2012: 171.

20  Ibid.
21  Quote attributed to Deng Xiaoping.
22  Huang, 2013: 28.
23  Xianting in Huang, 2008–12: 29.
24  The car is now preserved at the *Beijing Classic Car Museum*. This car is interesting as it highlights another ambiguity of Maoist Era and its relations with the West. While the car is obviously similar to European and American models, the name "Dong Feng" (东风) means "East wind" and it is inspired to a Chinese saying. In Mao's words: «There are two winds in the world today, the East Wind and the West Wind. There is a Chinese saying, "Either the East Wind prevails over the West Wind or the West Wind prevails over the East Wind." I believe it is characteristic of the situation today that the East Wind is prevailing over the West Wind» (Mao, 1972: 80–1).
25  For Cohen's conversation with Wang Guangyi, see p. 183.
26  Wang Guangyi in Paparoni, 2014: 158.
27  For Cohen's conversation with Wang Guangyi see p. 179.
28  Freud, 1919.
29  Huang, 2013: 33.
30  Wang Guangyi in Paparoni, 2014: 156.
31  Ai, 1997:10. English translation in Barmé 1999: 363.
32  Wang Guangyi in Paparoni, 2013: 317.
33  Wang Guangyi, quotation from the film CHIMERAS, 2013.
34  *Beijing Coma* (Ma, 2008), settled in the 2000s and banned since its publication by Chinese government, tells the story of Dai Wei, a biology student shot during Tiananmen protests and remained in a coma since then.
35  Huang, 2013: 111.

# References

AA.VV. (2004). 九評共產黨: 一份對中國共產黨的判決書; Engl. tr. *Nine Commentaries on the Communist Party*. New York: Epoch Times.

Ai, W. (1997). 作出選擇 (Making choices). In Zeng, X. and Ai, W. (eds.) 灰皮书 (Grey Cover Book). Beijing: Published independently.

Barmé, G. R. (1999). *In the Red: On contemporary Chinese culture*. New York: Columbia University Press.

Chen, B. (1966). *Hengsao Yiqie Niugui Sheshen* (*Sweep Away All the Ox-demon and Snake-spirit*), Renmin Ribao (People's Daily), June 1.

Clark, A. (1997). *Being There: Putting brain, body and world together again*. Cambridge, MA: MIT Press.

Fairbank, J. K. (1986). *The Great Chinese Revolution, 1800–1985*. London: Harper Perennial.

Ferraris, M. (2012). *Documentality. Why it is necessary to leave traces*. New York: Fordham University Press.

Freud, S. (1919). Das Unheimliche, in "Imago," *Zeitschrift für Anwendung der Psychoanalyse auf die Geisteswissenschaften*, 5(6): 1.

Gao, X., and Yang, L. (2001). *Il pane dell'esilio. La letteratura cinese dopo Tiananmen*. Milan: Medusa.

Guo, J., Song, Y., and Zhou Y. (2015). *Historical Dictionary of the Chinese Cultural Revolution*. Lanham: Rowman & Littlefield.

Jiang, J. (2007). *Burden or Legacy: From the Cultural Revolution to the Chinese Contemporary Art*. Hong Kong: Hong Kong University Press.

Jiang, J. L. (1997). *Red Scarf Girl. A memoir of the Cultural Revolution*. New York: Harper Collins.

Hobsbawm, E. (1994). *Age of Extremes: The short twentieth century, 1914–1991*. London: Michael Joseph.

Hua, Y. (2010). 十个词汇中的中国; Engl. trans. A. J. Barr (ed.), *China in Ten Words*. New York: Vintage Books (2012).

Huang, Z. (2013). *Politics and Theology in Chinese Contemporary Art: Reflections on the work of Wang Guangyi*. Milan: Skira Editore.

Ma, J. (2008). *Beijing Coma*. New York: Random House.

Mao, Z. (1966). 毛主席语录. Beijing: People's Liberation Army Daily. Engl. tr. *Quotations from Chairman Mao Tsetung*. Beijing: Foreign language Press.

Paparoni, D. (2013). *Wang Guangyi. Works and thoughts*. Milan: SKIRA.

Paparoni, D. (2014). *Wang Guangyi. Viaggio in Italia*. Napoli: Tramontano Arte.

Prochiantz, A. (1989). *La construction de cerveau*. Engl. trans. W. J. Gladstone (ed.) *How the Brain Evolved*. New York: McGraw-Hill (1992).

Stafutti, S., and Ajani, G. (2008). *Colpirne uno per educarne cento*. Torino: Einaudi.

# 6

# A Critique of Wang Guangyi's *Great Criticism: Coca-Cola*

Xian Zhou 周宪

As a leading figure in Chinese contemporary arts who has drawn much attention from global art circles, Wang Guangyi had been committed to the project of the *Great Criticism* series from the early 1990s to 2007, a trail-blazing endeavor in the pop art of contemporary China that laid the cornerstone for his idiosyncratic "Wang style." One piece of his series, *The Great Criticism: Coca Cola*, published in the Italian magazine *Flash Art* in 1991, made quite a stir among the world artists by presenting the distinct artistic iconology of "Political Pop" in China's contemporary art. The present chapter is meant to examine *The Great Criticism* series with a view to shedding some light on the intricate correlations between *Great Criticism* and the recent social transformations in China and doing so from perspectives as diverse as cultural sociology, psychology, and image-rhetoric.

## The Strategies of *Great Criticism* and Its Different Explanations

Hampered by social closure and cultural isolation since 1949, Chinese contemporary art tends to imitate, borrow, and convert different artistic languages, styles, and themes from Western modernism. When most Chinese artists were preoccupied with copying Western art, Wang Guangyi took the world by surprise with his *Great Criticism* series. The seemingly simple pop images captured the Western imagination and, in turn, boosted "the domestic sales of exported commodities," namely, the phenomenal promotion of Wang's status and influence as an artist in China through earning symbolic capital in the Western art circle.

This shortcut for Chinese artists to acquire symbolic capital is noteworthy whose spirit is well encapsulated in a Chinese idiom that "the fragrance of blooming flowers can only be appreciated by outsiders beyond the garden walls." What Wang and like-minded artists usually do is to adopt the style and vocabulary of Western art with an eye on the Western criteria of aesthetic evaluation. After obtaining recognition and reputation in the West, the artist usually returns to the domestic art circle and transforms the foreign symbolic capital—including exhibitions, professional critiques, social reception, and auction performance—into his personal art resources back home. The most successful contemporary Chinese artists, the so-called "F4" or Flower Four (Zhang Xiaogang, Yue Minjun, Wang Guangyi, Fang Lijun), all followed the same route. Successful examples of a similar kind can also be found in other art fields such as literature, architecture, music, and drama. This strategy has, to a great extent, altered the contemporary terrain of Chinese arts since the New Culture Movement in the early twentieth century. Chinese artists are no longer passive imitators; instead, they are now able to ride the wave of international arts. Wang Guangyi apparently discovered, utilized, and benefited from this shortcut. Of course, I am not intending to make a normative value judgment here, but merely a descriptive statement. That is to say, whether or not this strategy implies post-colonial subtleties across different cultures is not discussed here.

In this light, an intriguing question arises: Why does the Western art circle take a shine to Wang Guangyi and give his *Great Criticism* series so much attention and recognition? Are there any differences between the work's acceptance in China and in the West?

The chapter selects two representative views among Western scholars that reveal similar judgments and different focuses. In general, these views outline the mainstream opinion on the *Great Criticism* series.

The first opinion comes from the Italian critics with whom Wang has a close connection. Demetrio Paparoni said:

> In the early 1990s, Wang Guangyi was already well-known in the west for his *The Great Criticism* series which combines the worker-peasant-soldier (WPS) images from propaganda posters of the Mao era with logos of western commercial brands. Such a juxtaposition expresses the artist's desire to picture two kinds of preaching that serve to hone people's mind: socialist nations are dedicated to maintaining the political propaganda of the press, and western capitalist nations try to create a satisfactory design of products. Wang Guangyi particularly chose the western commercial logos in order to indicate the consumerist fetishism in this society.[1]

Another opinion is raised by American scholar Mary Bittner Wiseman, who specifically commented on the value and significance of *Great Criticism* in her review of the characteristics of Chinese contemporary art:

> Political themes from the Cultural Revolution joined Pop Art in a series of oil paintings by Wang Guangyi, one of which, *Great Castigation: Coca-Cola* [1993], combines the image of three workers lined up side by side with the soft drink logo. Only the heads and raised left arms of the second and third workers can be seen. The first clutches a red book and all the three hold one large fountain pen whose nib lies just above the second C in the white letter "Coca-Cola" and whose length appears to be the pole of a red flag. If the first C is communism, then the second, the one threatened by the pen's nib, is "capitalism," [...] The conjunction of the two reduces the revolutionary workers and the logo of China's most popular company to kitsch, trivializing the ideologies of Maoism and Western economies. To reduce Maoism to kitsch is to subvert its authority over the people's beliefs and values.
>
> *Great Castigation: Coca-Cola* is nothing more than an exemplification of materialism, historical and consumer, where "nothing can escape being material.[2]

For Paparoni, the purpose of *The Great Criticism* is to criticize the two kinds of propaganda that are seemingly different but, in effect, similar. One is Chinese socialist preaching, and the other is advocacy of Western materialism and commercial culture; both are a method of "brainwashing" designed to instigate some concept or mode of behavior. Wiseman also found a subversion of authority in Wang's *Great Criticism*, for she interpreted the two capital Cs in Coca-Cola respectively as "communism" and "capitalism," Although the huge brush is pointed toward the second C (capitalist), she stressed the work's criticism of the authority in Maoist political pedagogy (as in the first C), which by reverting to kitsch, vulgarizes Maoism and the Western economy.

The distinct iconological feature of *Great Criticism* is the juxtaposition of socialist propaganda from the Cultural Revolution and famous Western commercial brands. The brainwashing function identified by Paparoni and Wiseman's interpretation of the subversive import represent the prevailing views on the series in the West. Based on this understanding, Wang Guangyi has been favorably reviewed by many Western critics and thus accumulated considerable volumes of symbolic capital, which not only established his status in the West, but also catapulted him to the apex of Chinese contemporary art.

Nevertheless, it must be noted that the interpretations of the same series in China is completely different from those in the West. The discrepancies and differences uncover some key issues regarding how to take hold of Wang's *Great Criticism*. Here we may quote Chinese critic Gao Minglu, who says:

> Even though Wang Guangyi and some other artists' political pop acquired popularity abroad, but not at home, the social mentality reflected in their political pop, the aesthetic character and even the commercial value are in tune with the "Mao fever." Most political pop painters share an ambivalent attitude towards the Cultural Revolution. This ambivalence combines love and hate, and they even admire the power of Mao's discourse and its aesthetic features … More than that, Mao's power to control and create media is worshipped as well. … If the political pop of the early 1990s was ironically intent upon deconstructing something, it is the utopian illusion of Mao's myth of Cultural Revolution as well as self-mockery and repudiation of the painters' own humanistic sentiments in the mid-1980s. However, this does not indicate a complete opposition to Mao's aesthetic values or the way in which Mao's political discourse went popular, nor does it express an ironic twist on some kind of illusory myth as believed by some western critics. Instead, these artists still worship power. This is because in a society with a pyramid-shaped power hierarchy, any social group that resides within the structure and is subject to its shaping force, yearns for the rulership at the top of the pyramid. And avant-garde art makes no exception. It is just in these terms that Maoist revolutionary popular art, the 1985 Art Movement, and political pop are all embedded in the same historical totality and proceed from the same origin of utopian logic. … They know it at heart that despite being the opposite and opponent of the power, they also crave for it. And as the descendants of the utopia, they collude with what has already become their own tradition. The love-and-hate mentality of varying degrees can be found with the new generation of artists since the 1985 Movement.[3]

In domestic cultural and historical contexts, Chinese critics made a conclusion that is totally different from the Western critics. Gao Minglu saw the ambiguous relationship between Wang's works and the authority, especially the "love-and-hate" relationship, that potential complicity between avant-garde artists and the authority. Gao's judgment that "Maoist revolutionary popular art, the 1985 Art Movement, and political pop are all embedded in the same historical totality and proceed from the same origin of utopian logic," evidently different from the views of Western counterparts, deserves further contemplation. Suspending the existing conclusions and current mode of thinking, we are capable of arriving at some new ideas or conclusions by delving into *The Great Criticism* series more critically. In what follows I will try to give a reinterpretation of the series in close connection with the artist's career development from an integrated perspective of psychoanalysis and iconographic rhetorics.

## The Social Context and Individual Experience of *Great Criticism*

I would like to first review Wang's life experience since his early years. In 1957, Wang Guangyi was born into a poor worker's family in Harbin.[4] From 1966 to 1968, when the Cultural Revolution was in full swing, Wang was at the Freudian "latency stage." The year 1978 saw China ushered into the new era of opening up and, in 1980, he was admitted into the Department of Oil Painting of the China Academy of Art in Hangzhou, where he completed his BA degree program in 1984. At a stage of "identity crisis," as termed by Erik H. Erikson, Wang was embarking on his *North Pole* series. In 1985, he left Harbin for Zhuhai in Guangdong Province, and perhaps since Guangdong was the earliest test area of China's opening-up policy, the new movement prompted a sharp change in his artistic style. Wang soon completed the *Post-Classic* series followed by the *Red Reason* and *Black Reason* series. It is noteworthy that, in both series, he creatively painted Mao's images upon a gridded background, the practice of which according to himself, was first started at the end of 1986.[5] It can be argued that there would be no *Great Criticism* series without the *Mao Zedong* series because, from a psychoanalytical perspective, there lies a hidden subtext of collective memory: the Cultural Revolution, which has left an indelible mark on Wang Guangyi's adolescence. Although the revolution had long ended, the memory of it has stayed in Wang's subconscious.

As indicated by Wang's interviews, *The Great Criticism* series was created by chance but, in fact, it was not. He left Zhuhai for Wuhan under immense pressure since his work *Mao Zedong* was published in *Time* magazine. Later, he met his close friend Zhang Peili in Hangzhou, and their conversation sparked the original inspiration for *The Great Criticism* series. Wang Guangyi said:

> I went to Hangzhou, and at Lao Zhang's place he found me a book about mastheads during the Cultural Revolution. Later Liao Wen also looked for these materials in Beijing. Because I hadn't read that for a long time, I felt excited when Lao Zhang handed me the book, so I started this after I came back. At first I did not think of doing stuff like Coca-Cola; I just wanted to enlarge the picture

in the beginning, so I can decide after one piece was finished. The size was one meter by one meter, and done through gridding because there was no way to get it done but to paint exactly the same. Still, I thought it was a problem as it subtly suggests some kind of cultural mode. At that time, I just had some foreign cigarettes and cokes, and cokes were still a luxury back then, those in bigger cans. I placed the coke beside the canvas when I painted, and coincidentally found that this was good. I could not make out where to put it, but I felt "that's it!" when the painting was finished.

"Coca-Cola" brought me good fortune because the Italian magazine *Flash Art* unexpectedly published this piece of work on the front cover of an 1991 issue.[6]

Wang's words call for special attention here. First, his excitement at the sight of the Cultural Revolution mastheads means that these images used to be very familiar to him but had faded out over time. We can presume that Wang was already learning how to paint during the Cultural Revolution when such images were ubiquitous and became the raw materials of his iconographic memories. This is like bumping into an old friend you have not seen in years. I think the personal pictorial memories, by shaping the latent psychological impetus for the works of similar type to appear in Chinese contemporary art, were vital to the creation of *The Great Criticism*. Second, Wang initially applied the gridding method to achieve a vivid imitation of the original images of the Cultural Revolution. The artist's intention invites reflection. It stands to good reason that given his professional training at the China Academy of Art, he is fully capable of reproducing a copy of the original image. For one thing, he had used gridding to paint the *Mao Zedong* series, and, for another, enlargement upon gridding—though necessary for the duplication of a portrait that entails precision of detail and proportion—is actually superfluous for copying a coarsely crafted masthead by unprofessional people in the revolution. I think it more or less reflects Wang's complicated attitude toward images of the Cultural Revolution when he found "there is no way to get it done but to paint exactly the same" and intuitively discerned "a problem as it subtly suggests some kind of cultural mode." Based on the understanding of the "cultural mode," he thought it would be a failure if the duplicate was not exactly the same. Why did Wang not use the gridding method to paint other pieces of *Great Criticism*? My guess is that once the gridding method had incorporated those images into his visual–conceptual experience and formed what he called "the cultural mode" (in Gombrich's terms, a "schemata," to be explained later), he was able to reach an "accustomed and proficient" stage, just like an experienced potter who can draw various patterns on a greenware at will. Therefore, even though Wang Guangyi created many pieces of *Great Criticism* from the 1990s to 2007, he never again mentions the gridding method. The schemata of *Great Criticism* have completely established themselves as the signature of the "Wang style," and as an iconological model of the political pop in Chinese contemporary art. Third, the appearance of a Coca-Cola in the painting is said to be a sheer accident because of its physical closeness to the canvas and "chance" of being put into the painting. But, in my opinion, there is an inevitability underlying the seeming contingency. There is certainly a purpose to serve for the artist to paint the typical images of WPSs, who hold red flags, pens, the "Red Book" (*Quotations from Chairman Mao*), and dominated Cultural Revolution mastheads. Likewise, the presence of the Coke can in the painting is by no means without a purpose. In the late 1980s, China's economy and society had obviously progressed, and the trade-oriented economy made it possible for foreign products—from common soft drinks to expensive luxuries—to enter the daily life of the Chinse people. So much so that foreign brands have melted into the background of the daily life of artists like Wang Guangyi, and adding the logo of Coca-Cola to the painting is simply beyond a "convenient" move dictated by chance. When Wang was working on the first piece of *Great Criticism*, he had to find some current counterparts for the quotidian mastheads of the revolution. A picture that shows only a duplicated masthead of the Cultural Revolution with no connection to the present day, would probably lose much of its attraction to the contemporary audience. Some contemporary clues would be necessary to form a comparative graphic structure. The logo of Coca-Cola therefore became a sensible choice under the circumstances as Wang happened to find a can of Coke near at hand, and this is the inevitability underlying the contingency.

Another question that interests me is why did Wang Guangyi feel excited when he saw the Cultural Revolution mastheads? Why did he immediately decide to put these image into paintings, and what drove him to make such a decision? Sometimes the decision made by an artist can be emotional and hasty, but what prompted Wang Guangyi to the decision to image the Cultural Revolution and Coca-Cola seems even more intriguing. In order to clarify this question, I would like to start with Gombrich's theory of schemata. Wang Guangyi is familiar with the theory for he attended the China Academy of Art when this art historian and his theories had found many followers there. When comparing the differences in the graphic design of the paintings of Derwent Water by Chinese artist Jiang Yi and an anonymous British artist, Gombrich made a philosophical comment:

We see how the relatively rigid vocabulary of the Chinese tradition acts as a selective screen which admits only the features for which schemata exist. The artist will be attracted by motifs which can be rendered in his idiom. As he scans the landscape, the sights which can be matched successfully with the schemata he has learned to handle will leap forward as centers of attention. The style, like the medium, creates a mental set which makes the artist look for certain aspects in the scene around him that he can render. Painting is an activity, and he artist will therefore tend to see what he paints rather than to paint what he sees.[7]

According to this theory, Wang's excitement about the mastheads is what Gombrich called "matching," a correspondence between what he sees and what he is looking for, or he sees what he is going to paint. This is a process of "sieving," that is, "a selective screen which admits only the features for which schemata exist" and, in this way, "the sights which can be matched successfully with the schemata he has learned to handle will leap forward as centers of attention." Then, what are the schemata in Wang's visual experience? No doubt, the four-year undergraduate training has shaped many professional schemata, especially an iconographic model of oil painting. But I especially want to point out that, in Wang's individual psychological development, he has experienced the Freudian latency stage (from five to adolescence) and, subsequently, the Eriksonian stage of "identity crisis" (twelve to nineteen), largely coinciding with the ten-year time span of the Cultural Revolution. On the one hand, he felt small due to his family's poverty but, also, his family's worker background left him and his family unscathed in the Cultural Revolution. His memories of the revolution therefore were very different from those of the persecuted artists. At the same time, Wang had a burning passion for art and studied extremely hard; he was not only familiar with the popular Cultural Revolution mastheads, but he actually drew some of them himself. In the post–Cultural Revolution era, when the reform and opening up were launched, Wang tried to seek out new iconographies from past cultural memories, and always looked for "matching" images from the existing schemata, among which are mastheads of the Cultural Revolution. On the one hand, they evoked the old memories of the Cultural Revolution, and offered a possibility for Wang to get over his "identity crisis." Therefore, the mastheads of the Cultural Revolution awakened his complex visual experience and filled him with heightened excitement.

Simply put, "identity crisis" is the crisis of not knowing "who I am," a common question in the arts circle, particularly striking with young artists who have not yet established their distinctive artistic style. For every artist, the question of "Who am I?" is more often rephrased as "What is my style?" The second question, symptomatic of the identity crisis, constantly baffles and even torments the artist. Wang has on different occasions expressed that *The Great*

*Criticism* brought him good fortune and established his status in domestic and international art circles. Such acknowledgement undoubtedly confirms the resolution of his identity crisis. *Mao Zedong* to *Great Criticism: Coca-Cola* marks an important transitional period for Wang who, freed from his previous identity crisis, just began to establish his identity as a political pop artist in art circles home and abroad, with *Great Criticism* being his stylistic symbol.

Both the 1990s and the ten-year Cultural Revolution (1966–77) have seen earth-shaking changes in China. Fraught with traumatic memories, these mastheads certainly invite different responses from different people. The artists who suffered in the Cultural Revolution would voluntarily stave off or even reject these images linked to their miserable memories. However, born into a worker's family, Wang Guangyi did not suffer for his family background, so these images were not repulsive to him. Furthermore, dislocated from the historical context in which they were created, their political significance and cultural violence have been much subdued. And yet they do revive the artist's visual memories of the past; in Wang's words,

> the Cultural Revolution to me is not what it is to the general public (in a politico-economic sense) [...] For an average man, he may care more about the facts and outcomes of a historical event; but for an artist, he cares more about the visual complexity within a visual pattern that can be brought by a historical event. [...] When I put together the "Great Criticism" and "Coca-Cola", its spirit points to the relationship between fetishism and utopia.[8]

I think the first half of Wang's quote is credible; he explicitly expressed that the visual complexity within the visual pattern of the Cultural Revolution has an influence on him. However, the second half is not as convincing, since it was difficult for him to consciously criticize "utopia" and "fetishism" when he started to create *The Great Criticism: Coca-Cola*. Just as he confessed, he had discussions with some critics after this work was completed, and these discussions to a great extent encouraged him.[9] Perhaps the so-called double criticism of utopia and fetishism was inspired by the interpretation of critics. Wang Guangyi himself admires a saying of Derrida: "Writing precedes thinking," from which he has developed his own motto: "Working precedes thinking."[10]

## Oxymoron in *Great Criticism: Coca-Cola*

In the early 1990s, Wang Guangyi's visionary mind captured the complicated meanings of mastheads of the Cultural Revolution and, more creatively, he made a connection between the mastheads and the logo of Coca-Cola and set the basic iconological pattern for his *Great Criticism* series, which brought him immediate fame. As for the mastheads of the Cultural Revolution, they sank into oblivion in the new era of China's reform and opening-up policy, and their reappearance in Wang's paintings evokes different reactions in different viewers. But in the increasingly stratified and commercialized West, these political and utopian revolutionary images, like the portrait of Che Guevara, have been invested with some new visual magic. The reason why Wang Guangyi chose these rebellious WPS images, I think, is that they seemed strikingly Chinese, simple, and historical. More importantly, these images were born with characteristics very much in keeping with the iconology of pop art. It is easy to presume that if Wang Guangyi followed Warhol's paradigms of Coca-Cola bottles or Mao Zedong, he would never have achieved his current success. His sagacity lies in his full awareness about the necessity to apply Warhol's techniques to genuine Chinese images for the invention of a new kind of Chinese pop art. The combination of the utopian revolutionary images and the most popular Western commercial symbols gives birth to Chinese contemporary pop art distinctively different from Warhol's American pop.

Among Wang's *The Great Criticism* series, the most famous is *The Great Criticism: Coca-Cola,* the cover piece on the Italian magazine *Flash Art*. In order to analyze *The Great Criticism*, I would like to draw two lines here. First, the following discussion is focused on those juxtaposed foreign commercial logos; as for other series—such as those about the World Trade Organization (WTO), *Time* magazine, artists, museums—are not considered in this discussion. Second, I will narrow down the scope of these works to the Coca-Cola series, for they are the most representative. Roughly estimated, from the 1990s to 2007 Wang Guangyi painted no fewer than 22 pieces of *The Great Criticism: Coca-Cola*.[11] The time span is long, and the images, colors, and compositions vary from one to another; but one symbol remains constant, that is, the logo of Coca-Cola (see Figures 6.1 and 6.2).

There are several iconographic aspects about Wang's *The Great Criticism: Coca-Cola* series. First, the center of the painting is occupied by a number of people (ranging from two to dozens) who form a group portrait. But the grouping method, ambience, relative surroundings, and manners of these people in each painting are very different. Second, the characters' actions are highly exaggerated and dramatized, like a stage performance. In other words, the scenarios do not come from real situations in everyday life but are deliberately posed for enhanced impact and attraction. Apparently, there are two concerns

**Figure 6.1** Wang Guangyi, *Great Criticism—Coca-Cola* (a. 1990, oil on canvas, 200 × 200 cm; b. 1999, oil on canvas, 200 × 180 cm; c. 2002, oil on canvas, 200 × 200 cm; d. 2003, oil on canvas, 120 × 150 cm; e. 2006, oil on canvas, 200 × 300 cm).

**Figure 6.2** Wang Guangyi, *Great Criticism—Coca-Cola* (a. 2005, oil on canvas, 150 × 120 cm; b. 2005, oil on canvas, 60 × 70 cm).

underlying such rendition, namely, the origin from the necessary visual features of the Cultural Revolution propaganda, and the iconological requirement of pop art to be succinct and impressive. Third, the images obviously carry the style of a poster, which is also the most common styling approach in pop art. *The Great Criticism: Coca-Cola* can be put on exhibition in museums and decorate domestic space, too. It seems very proper to apply Hamilton's classic conclusion about the secret of pop art to *The Great Criticism: Coca-Cola*: "Popular, transient, expendable, low cost, mass produced, young, witty, sexy, gimmicky, glamorous, big business."[12] For instance, there are no neutral colors or transitional colors, only the contrastive matches among red, yellow, black, and blue, highly suggestive of the features of advertisements and posters. However, these features fall short of the full manifestation of pop art style, and the streamlined typeface of Coca-Cola, either foregrounded or figured in the background, becomes the linchpin. This involves the fourth aspect, the logo of a product. One major characteristic of Western pop art is the direct incorporation of daily commodities or advertisements. Artists from Hamilton to Warhol all did the same. So, using commercial logos in paintings is nothing new. But, in my opinion, the most innovative aspect of *The Great Criticism* series is the juxtaposition of the well-known Western commercial logos and stereotypical WPS images, which brings in a special tension. As I have mentioned before, mere duplication or appropriation of the Cultural Revolution mastheads is not innovative, and can hardly draw attention in the art circles home and abroad. It is exactly through the introduction of Western commercial logos into the artwork that a unique strategy of visual rhetoric falls in line. This involves a complicated phenomenon in contemporary Chinese society and culture: the relationship between the culture of the utopian revolution and the ecstasy of consumerism.

Myriad discussions have taken place about the pairing of these two entirely different or even antithetic subjects. Some believe that both result from the seemingly opposed yet essential same "brainwashing" phenomena that are the two dominant ideologies of contemporary society. Some find this juxtaposition "a criticism against the western commercial culture prevailing in China."[13] Some consider these works highly parodical and game-like, which inadvertently reduces their critical thrust to a minimum and infinitely raises their humorous effects.[14] Still others see Wang's efforts to integrate two entirely different artistic forms. I would like to approach *Great Criticism* from a new perspective, that of the visual rhetoric.

A fundamental visual rhetorical strategy that runs through the *Great Criticism* series is the use of the oxymoron. In order to explain this strategy, I borrow the idea of rhetoric from historiography. Nearly all analyses of *Great Criticism* have mentioned the binary opposition in the combination of images, that is, the combination of highly political and revolutionary images of the Cultural Revolution at home and the typical commercial brands of Western capitalist society. In terms of the principles of pictorial composition, Wang adopts juxtaposition, which is very common in Western pop art. Though juxtaposition in artwork is commonplace in the West, as we can see in Hamilton and Warhol, Wang Guangyi's way of doing juxtaposition differs from the Western style with two obvious features. The first is the sharp opposition between the revolutionary images of *Great Criticism* and the consumerist commercial logos—promotional iconography that originally belong to two entirely different ideologies and discursive systems. So, when they are framed in the same piece, an oxymoronic effect comes into being. Oxymoron is "a figure of speech in which apparently contradictory terms appear in conjunction."[15] In terms of rhetoric, oxymoron reveals the distinction of the composition of the image, while juxtaposition, as mentioned by many art critics, is just a neutral explanation that is unable to clarify the true characteristics of the visual rhetoric of *Great Criticism*.

In general, the key to an oxymoron is the syntactic combination of two antonyms, and this is a common rhetorical phenomenon in language. For example, Shakespeare used this figure of speech many times in *Romeo and Juliet*. Romeo says, "O heavy lightness! Serious vanity! Mis-shapen chaos of well-seeming forms! Feather of lead, bright smoke, cold fire, sick health! Still-waking sleep."[16] Nearly every phrase is a combination of antithetic words, which seems illogical for they form a paradoxical semantic structure. Another example is the oxymoronic description of a "black sun" in Sholokhov's *And Quiet Flows the Don*. The basic structure of an oxymoron is the combination of two semantically antithetical words, which builds up a special structure of semantic tension, like Romeo's "heavy lightness" or "cold fire," Oxymoron originates from the deeply rooted mindset of binary opposition because polarized concepts like true and false, good and evil, and beautiful and ugly provide the most convenient pattern of thought. Wang Guangyi has expressed on several occasions that he was deeply influenced by such a thought pattern. As he admitted, "people who grew up in a socialist country like China tend to see the world in binary opposition. I don't want to make a judgment about the existence of such a mindset. But I would like to remind the audience of a vision and mindset which represents another value system and is on the verge of oblivion."[17]

According to Foucault, the mindset of binary opposition is essentially a form of power because there will always be the dominator and the dominated, implying some kind of "will-to-knowledge" or "will-to-truth" and hence manifesting a power relation. For instance, the denial of falsehood by truth, goodness's dominance over evil, beauty's transcendence beyond ugliness. These are all realized through this discursive strategy.[18] In fact, art is one of the important ways to implement these discursive strategies. The history of art is replete with various models of binary opposition, and the juxtaposition of images is not a simple comparison between two different objects, but the recognition and reinforcement of a certain power relation. Ever since modernism, especially in the era of postmodernism, art has often been mobilized to deconstruct the long-entrenched discourse of binary opposition. This is true of avant-garde art, and also true of pop art, as it erodes upon the barrier and opposition between fine art and mass culture or commercial culture. One interpretation of *Great Criticism: Coca-Cola* is that Wang bridged the gap between the revolutionary discourse and the commercial discourse, thus establishing a new form of discourse. I doubt this interpretation. Can we make an assumption that *Great Criticism: Coca-Cola* implies a simultaneous confirmation and negation of the utopian revolutionary images of the Cultural Revolution and the logo of Coca-Cola? Or is it possible that he has a negative attitude toward them both?

I think Wang is more likely to have adopted the "double mindset" of oxymoron. The so-called "double mindset" means absorbing two opposed ideas in a unified thought mechanism without taking an affirmative or critical stance. Wang is probably one of those artists who work with the "double mindset," for he has many times expressed that he did not intentionally stick to one concept or stance when he was creating *The Great Criticism* series, and that he intended to be more "neutral." He said, "I think the reason why people remember *The Great Criticism*—even if they don't like it, they remember it anyway—is that I have no 'stance' ... a neutrality shapes it. Everyone thought I was 'attacking' something, as if I had a specific stance, but in fact people came to see that I did nothing, or maybe it's just all sorts of contingent factors that gave meaning to my *The Great Criticism*."[19]

In order to clarify this paradoxical phenomenon, let us break down the oxymoron in *The Great Criticism: Coca-Cola*. For an oxymoron, there is not only one standard structure, but multiple, with varying degrees of opposition. At least we can categorize three types of oxymoronic structures that are different in their degree of opposition: (1) Complete opposition and contradiction, in which A and B are in sharp opposition, causing an intense situation of mutual denial, that is, A is a clear negation of B and vice versa, like "the black sun" and so forth; (2) relative opposition and contradiction, in which A and B are in mild conflict and no obvious mutual negation can be found: this gives rise to a relatively stable tension, such as "dim dawn"; (3) a peaceful structure of differences, in which A and B are not in obvious opposition or contradiction; they are just different, but this difference is not negative and mutually exclusive, as in the neutral concept of "juxtaposition."

Most reviews on *Great Criticism* series are concerned about the first type of conflict, that is, complete opposition and contradiction. Through my interpretation of many of Wang Guangyi's works, I think the aforementioned three types are all present in the series, and the first type is arguably not as common as the second or the third. Therefore, *Great Criticism: Coca-Cola* also has three degrees of oxymoronic structures. Figure 6.1a is the work that first brought Wang Guangyi fame, and it has a complete, contradictory structure in which the WPS wave the red flag high and hold the pen tightly with it tilting to the logo of Coca-Cola, and this reflects the sharp opposition of two different discourses. But upon closer examination of his other works, we find pictorial structures with entirely different tensions. For instance, in Figure 6.1b, the WPS adopts the composition of Soviet Union propaganda pictures. The three WPS characters uphold the hammer, the sickle, and the Red Book, which stand for workers, peasants, and the Cultural Revolution respectively. But the treatment of the relationship between the group portrait and the logo is very different from Figure 6.1a. The three characters in Figure 6.1b are beaming, in sharp contrast with the serious and dramatized visages in Figure 6.1a. The hammer, the sickle, and the Red Book, which are held high by the three characters, are on the same level with the logo, as if the characters are also holding up Coca-Cola.

Figures 6.2a and 6.2b utilize the stage photo of the "model opera" during the Cultural Revolution. Figure 6.2a uses the stage photo of ballet, *The Red Detachment of Women*. Two female soldiers dance gracefully, their movements smooth and joyful, and the Coca-Cola logo is just like part of the stage backdrop, outlining the merriment of the female soldiers, as if their happiness comes from drinking Coca-Cola. So the painting shows no sign of "great criticism," Figure 6.2b borrows a stage photo of *Taking Tiger Mountain by Strategy* for the same effect. If Figure 6.1a is the complete opposition and contradiction, then Figure 6.1b is the relative opposition and contradiction, and Figures 6.2a and 6.2b clearly show a peaceful structure of differences. Considering the paintings in *The Great Criticism: Coca-Cola* series were created over nearly two decades, from 1990s to 2007, and Wang's explicit expression of his "neutral stance" or "lack of stance," the relationship between the artist's intention and the themes in his works cannot be reduced to a double negation of two ideologies as some critics suggest.

## *The Image-Text Intertextuality of* Great Criticism: Coca-Cola

There is yet another iconological feature of the *Great Criticism* series that is worth analysis: the images of different characters from the mastheads of the Cultural Revolution plus the textual logos of Western commercial brands. When joining the two different cultural symbols, Wang Guangyi did not choose the images of the Western products, but consistently used the textual logo. Why so? This is an intriguing question.

The practice of incorporating a "word-image" is widespread in Western pop art. For instance, Robert Indiana's *LOVE* (1968) is a simple combination of two letters on top and two below. Another example is Warhol's *Close Cover Before Striking* (Pepsi-Cola, 1962), which portrays a Pepsi-Cola bottlecap with a phrase at the center: "say 'Pepsi Please.'" Another common combination of pictures and words is the textual narrative of cartoons or comics, such as Roy Lichtenstein's *M-Maybe* (A Girl's Picture, 1965). Wang Guangyi handles the images and words in a way that is different from the image-word blending in the Western pop art, in that he only uses the textual logos of commodities, not their actual images. Warhol's Coca-Cola series, such as *Green Coca-Cola Bottles* (1967) consists of three Coca-Cola bottles in the middle and the textual logo at the bottom, exemplifying such cross-reference and mutual explanation of the image and the text. But only a few works of *The Great Criticism* series use the actual images of Western commodities, and these were all created in the early 1990s. For instance, *The Great Criticism: Tang* (1990) features three cups containing different volumes of Tang, a beverage; and *The Great Criticism: Marlboro* (1990) presents a facsimile of a Marlboro pack at the center. From then on, the images of commodities rarely appear in Wang's paintings; only textual logos are featured. What does this suggest? A reasonable speculation is that Wang believes the images of real products affect the simplicity of the painting and do not contribute to the pure opposition of the graphic and textual symbols, while simple contrastive patterns are often found with pop art.

Next, the theory of intertextuality in deconstruction can be employed to analyze this phenomenon.

Intertextuality originally refers to a literary work in which one text constantly mentions, alludes, or refers to another, thus setting up a complex dialogic relationship between the texts. The situation is somewhat different for *Great Criticism: Coca-Cola* because first, this is a graphic text, not a linguistic work; second, it has both images and text, constituting the intertextuality between words and images, and this is what I am concerned about.

According to the Western art theory, images and words belong to two completely different domains. Lessing's *Laocoon* specifically discusses the differences between painting and poetry. However, the development of art often ignores boundaries, and artists love to break down conventional artistic categories to bring together what has previously been separated and kept apart. This is all too common in art since modernism, and postmodernism sees its growing popularity in hybridity. As American critic Leslie Fiedler's slogan goes, "Cross the Border, Close the Gap," it is possible to mix anything together.

In *Great Criticism: Coca-Cola* series, "the great criticism" consists of two sides: the images from the Cultural Revolution mastheads and the text of Coca-Cola, two elements of the oxymoron, together representing two entirely different cultures and ideologies. From the perspective of intertextuality, we have reason to take the images of the WPSs in the foreground as the center of the painting, and the logo of Coca-Cola as the background. Viewed in this way, these two elements form a "quotation": the textual logo of Coca-Cola in the back is like a quotation made by the main body of the painting, the images of the WPSs. The image quotes the text as its background and brings in an oxymoronic effect. According to linguist Stefan Morawski, there are three types of quotations in an intertextual relationship: the authoritative quotation, the erudite quotation, and the ornamental quotation. If we take the logo of Coca-Cola as a quotation of the visual text, it is topologically similar to the third type, the ornamental quotation. Morawski pointed out that the authoritative quotation is the "leading actor" in a text, while the rest of the text takes a supporting role. The Scriptures or quotes of a great leader fall into the erudite type of quotation just as the saying goes, "I annotate the canons." The erudite quotation aims to convince people. The quote and its context act upon each other, such as the quotation in scientific studies. The ornamental quotation, emerging as the opposite of the authoritative quotation, is not independent, but furnishes an explanatory account for the main text, in a spirit of "the canons annotate me."[20] However, in *Great Criticism: Coca-Cola*, the text as a quotation is not exclusively cast in a supporting role. In a sense, it is a textual logo quoted by the main image and also a self-referential object of reference. Based on this understanding, we can add the fourth type of quotation, that is, the contrastive type. Coca-Cola as a quotation of the painting is in a contrastive relationship with the group portrait of the characters. In fact, the logo "Coca-Cola" has no special meaning whatsoever; it is just a symbol of a brand. However, when put in the frame of *Great Criticism: Coca-Cola*, this quotation is invested with delicate subtlety and complexity, whose referential function makes it both the background and the foreground, the ornament and the subject.

Primarily, the image–text intertextuality calls forth a tensile structure of Chinese and Western cultures. The contrast of local images and Western texts reveals the complicated connection between China and the West. Ever since the Opium War, China had been on deeply troubling terms with the West. The Western powers forced their way into China with their warships and cannons. From the invasion of the Eight-Nation Alliance and the reckless burning and looting of the Old Summer Palace, the establishment of concessions in Shanghai and other coastal cities, and down to the Korean War, the West had been regarded as a hostile force against China. On the other hand, since the late Qing dynasty, China has been learning from the West and trying to catch up with its Western counterparts in areas ranging from modern education, science and technology, social institutions, ideology, and culture and, of course, to literature and art. The craze for learning from the West can be best encapsulated in Wei Yuan's remark: "Beat the foreigners by learning from their advantages." The love-and-hate mentality has essentially shaped Chinese people's conflicted opinions of the West. Such is the historical context of *Great Criticism: Coca-Cola*, hidden in the contrast between the image and the text.

Second, this series pits the home-grown revolutionary tradition against the Western commercial culture. In terms of themes and mode of expression, they are two totally different ideological symbols. *The Great Criticism* stands for an idealistic culture, an ascetic culture of privation similar to Puritanism. However, Coca-Cola stands for the culture of materialism, which advocates the pleasure of consumption. A mere glance at the slogans of Coca-Cola over the years will reveal its consumerist culture and pursuit after pleasure and comforts: "Enjoy Thirst" (1923), "Makes Good Things Taste Better,"(1956), "We've Got a Taste for You"(1985), and "Open Happiness"(2009). Two entirely different ideologies contrast with, refer to, negate, or coexist, which in fact demonstrates the profound transformations that contemporary China has been going through.

Last, the image-text intertextuality also suggests the contrastive relationship between history and current development. The Cultural Revolution that *Great Criticism* represents has already been stored away in people's memories. However, even if the era is long gone, popular trends like "Red (revolutionary) Songs," "Mao Fever," and "Revival of the Culture of the Educated Youth" clearly show that the past culture still claims an intangible and potential sway over Chinese society today. On the other hand, Coca-Cola, a symbol of the American consumerist culture, has already blended into the everyday life of Chinese people, as cola drinking is a common among Chinese youths. *Great Criticism: Coca-Cola* bridges the historical and the contemporary. But Chinese viewers of different generations will have different responses. For those who have experienced the Cultural Revolution, the visual experience of *Great Criticism* refreshes their memory as if it were only yesterday, and they must have some secret apprehension for the extensive infiltration of Western commercial culture. Those who were born in the 1980s and 1990s, after the opening up, tend to have a much weaker response to the strong contrast. The images of WPSs or the model opera of the Cultural Revolution, feeling so much like a parody, are strange to them. On the other hand, they are too familiar with Coca-Cola to actually pay attention to it. The historical distance in the painting compounded by the cultural gap between different generations in Chinese society necessitates a highly complicated reception of the artworks.

## Conclusion

As a trendsetter of Chinese contemporary art, Wang Guangyi has initiated and led the development of pop art in China. Shaping the iconology of Chinese pop art, *The Great Criticism* series has been hailed as a classic model in the history of Chinese contemporary art. From the intentions of the artist, to *The Great Criticism* series and the different comprehensions and interpretations of Chinese and Western critics, we can see the complexity of Chinese contemporary art. Wang Guangyi himself embodies the idea of complexity because on the one hand he stresses the role of artists as the critics of society and culture, and on the other hand he professes to have a "neutral stance" or "no stance." He believes artists cannot make out their own intentions when they create their works, but he also cares most about "the politics of art" and its deconstructive function. All the above underscores the necessity of a reconsideration of every aspect of Chinese society and culture that has conditioned Wang's paintings. Any simple and biased explanation may fail to wholly grasp the complexity of *The Great Criticism* series. Therefore, it is necessary to focus on the "field" where various forces converged and entwined, from the Cultural Revolution to the era of opening up, and to examine the "field" where Wang Guangyi's personality and psyche came to be fully developed; and, finally, to the "field" where *The Great Criticism* series was produced. The complex relationships between the three fields hence demand a correlation analysis of various forces instead of fixing upon any of them at the cost of missing the rest.

## Notes

1. Paparoni, 2015: 143.
2. Wiseman, 2007: 112–13.
3. Gao, 2007: 100.
4. In a talk with a friend, Wang mentioned his family background: "My family was very poor in my childhood. My father was a simple and honest road builder, and my mother was a kindhearted and introvert housewife. My father's paltry wages were the only income for a family of seven or eight people. My family background and plain appearance made me feel below others in society." See Yan, 2015: 35.
5. Li, 2015: 237.
6. Ibid.: 239–40.
7. Gombrich, 1996: 107.
8. Qtd. in Huang, 2015: 178.
9. Li, 2015: 240.
10. Qtd. in Lü Peng, "A History of Criticism—Wang Guangyi's Artistic Experience," ibid.: 91.
11. According to "The Portfolio of Wang Guangyi, 1984–2014," in *The Art and Thoughts of Wang Guangyi: A Collection of Critiques and Interviews*, ed. Wang Junyi (Beijing: China Youth Publishing Group, 2015), from 1991–2007, there are 22 paintings themed *The Great Criticism: Coca-Cola* collected in the book.

12   Hamilton, 2012: 344.
13   Li Xianting's remark, qtd. in Lü, 2015: 93.
14   Ibid.
15   Pearsal, 1998: 1237.
16   Shakespeare, ed. 1974: 1060–61.
17   Merewether, 2015: 232.
18   See Foucault, 1986: 148.
19   Qtd. in Huang, 2015: 100.
20   See Morawski, 1970: 690–705.

# References

Foucault, M. (1986). "Discourse on Language." In H. Adams and L. Searle (eds.) *Critical Theory Since 1965*. Tallahassee: Florida State University Press.

Gao, M. (2007). Kitsch, Power, Complicity, Political Pop. Qtd. in Wang, N. (2007) "The Battle between Gao Minglu and Li Xianting." *Art Observation*: 6.

Gombrich, E. H. (1996). "Truth and the Stereotype." In Richard Woodfield (ed.) *The Essential Gombrich*. London: Phaidon.

Hamilton, R. (2012). "Letter to Peter and Alison Smithson." In Kristine Stiles and Peter Selz (eds.) *Theories and Documents of Contemporary Art*. Berkeley, CA: University of California Press.

Huang Z. (2015). "The Classical World in Contemporary Art—On Wang Guangyi." In Wang Junyi (ed.) *The Art and Thoughts of Wang Guangyi: A collection of critiques and interviews*. Beijing: China Youth Publishing Group.

Li, X. (2015). "The Artistic Experience of Wang Guangyi." In Wang Junyi (ed.) *The Art and Thoughts of Wang Guangyi: A collection of critiques and interviews*. Beijing: China Youth Publishing Group.

Lü, P. (2015). "A History of Criticism—Wang Guangyi's Artistic Experience." In Wang Junyi (ed.) *The Art and Thoughts of Wang Guangyi: A collection of critiques and interviews*. Beijing: China Youth Publishing Group.

Merewether, C. (2015). "About the Socialist Visual Experience—An Interview with Wang Guangyi." In Wang Junyi (ed.) *The Art and Thoughts of Wang Guangyi: A collection of critiques and interviews*. Beijing: China Youth Publishing Group.

Morawski, S. (1970). "The Basic Functions of Quotation." In A. J. Greimas (ed.) *Sign, Language, Culture*. The Hague: Mouton.

Paparoni, D. (2015). "Wang Guangyi and the Empty Complexity." In Wang Junyi (ed.) *The Art and Thoughts of Wang Guangyi: A collection of critiques and Interviews*. Beijing: China Youth Publishing Group.

Pearsal, J. (ed.) (1998). *The Oxford Dictionary of English*. Oxford: Clarendon.

Shakespeare, W. (1947). "The Tragedy of Romeo and Juliet." In *The Riverside Shakespeare*. Boston: Houghton Mifflin.

Wiseman, M. B. (2007). "Subversive Strategies in Chinese Avant-Garde Art." *Journal of Aesthetics and Art Criticism,* 65(1).

Yan S. (2015). "Wang Guangyi in the Tide of Contemporary Art." In Wang Junyi (ed.) *The Art and Thoughts of Wang Guangyi: A collection of critiques and interviews*. Beijing: China Youth Publishing Group.

# Part IV

# Words and Images: Two Instruments to Describe the World

# Wang Guangyi: On Contemporary Pop Art, "Covers," Remix, and Political Theology

Babette Babich 巴比特. 芭比希

## Overview

In what follows I discuss the art and thought of Wang Guangyi with an orienting overview of the notion of the contemporary and the post-contemporary as well as the broader context of Pop Art, including the culture of the "cover" and "remix" and "mash-up," latterly borrowed from the music industry. In particular, I focus on the changeable coincidence of contemporary art with the contemporary moment, pop, and commercial art (and capital speculation) with reference to Andy Warhol, Jean Baudrillard, and Arthur Danto, and thus Duchamp along the way. I additionally discuss the Kantian aesthetics of disinterested distraction, via Paul Virilio, and on the level of the political, shock and performance art, including Marina Abramović/Ulay, as well as Christo and Jean Claude, the Fluxus group, and German agit prop (Joseph Beuys and Bazon Brock), with a brief allusion to the political sociology of Okakura's "teaism"— between Japan and China. I conclude with a reading of Wang Guangyi's "New Religion" in the context of the cultural spiritual imperialism that has always disturbed us less than the scandals of today's global Church centering on financial abuses and sexual harassment.

## Contemporizing the Contemporary: Pop Art, Covers, and Remix Culture

What counts as contemporary art? What is pop art? Is contemporary art what contemporary art museums currently exhibit? Is contemporary art whatever was once called contemporary art? Or—on the model of the modern and the postmodern[1]—is past contemporary art the referent for post-contemporary art? What about pop art? Is there contemporary pop art? What, given the connection between found art and Duchamp's ready-mades, is the relation of the copy or the "cover" to remix?[2] How do such iconographic questions relate to the political and the theological?

All these terms have different meanings, all these questions, different answers, in different contexts, for different claimants. The contemporary is arguably the most elusive of all because it is a sliding term: the referent shifts: time changes. Hence, the question of the contemporary charges philosophical reflection and theorizing about art and what we regard as contemporary by contrast with what previous generations called contemporary. At issue is also the changing contemporaneousness of an imperative, social and cultural, that also witnesses to passing fads, i.e., what once had counted as contemporary and is now no longer regarded as contemporary. The problem is all the more patent in the case of pop art as the very post-datedness, the pop aspect of pop art per se, maintains its then-contemporary aura.[3] At the same time, little seems to have a more precarious claim, qua art, than pop art.

If contemporary art can seem in need of a secure definition, reference to the post in post-contemporary highlights the move to what one may call, perhaps most of all in a digital context, *remix thinking*: adaptation, cooption, appropriation, and so on. By way of a reflection on covers (musical and otherwise) and on the culture of the copy (both art works and human beings, as Nietzsche tells us), Wang Guangyi is an exemplar of contemporary pop art as artist. Here, I explore his work via Jean Baudrillard as well as Arthur Danto and Andy Warhol.

Philosophic authors have themselves thematized, if not always thematically or explicitly so, the question of covers or remix, the question of the contemporary, but particularly of interest for philosophers has been the theme of pop art. Such authors include Giorgio Agamben, who also writes on kitsch,[4] Jean-Luc Nancy,[5] the late Paul Virilio, and his writing on "shock art,"[6] in addition to Danto,[7] and, by way of negative provocation, Baudrillard who, like Danto, wrote on Andy Warhol's pop art,[8] and Peter Osborne[9] and Michael Newman (on conceptual art),[10] or via a kind of object illustration of pop theoretical exposition (a graphic novel on Walter Benjamin) but also thematic reflections, Howard Caygill,[11] in addition to the Australian art historian, Terry Smith,[12] the anthropologist Paul Rabinow,[13] and others in addition to artists like Liam Gillick[14] and Wang Guangyi, himself,[15] articulating theoretical reflections on the contemporary. I will return to these authors below. Here, I begin with the culture of the (musical) cover and remix and mash-up culture.

## Remix and the Culture of the Cover

Like Thierry Bardini's discussion in his assessment of "junkware,"[16] the notion of remix is marked today as contemporary. In music, remixing includes sampling from extant recordings, re-recording, recombining, mixing up. The same holds in film, the same (but here it gets complicated) in the graphic arts. Like the remix, the musical *cover* is always already more than a copy or reappropriation (there are, as we shall see, legal elements) and what is key in both cases is the quintessentially Benjaminian means of technological—and, in the case of music and film, acoustic, performative—reproduction. As Eduardo Navas observes, entire musical genres are shaped by the practice (the literal culture or application) of remix, thus, taking off from Benjamin but even more from other reflections—particularly Adorno—which other reflections, fitting for remix, do not come to mention in his work, "The relation of music and culture is defined on material terms by the rise of mechanical reproduction, which evolved into electronic reproduction."[17] Today we typically hasten to add "digital," just in case the Philip K. Dick allusion to "electronic reproduction" somehow had not covered this.

For David J. Gunkel, the Deleuzian schema articulates the fate of the (post-Heideggerian) ontological difference as a question for which Benjamin already offered an answer. By contrast with the *Phaedrus* (alluded to but in this locus unread),[18] Plato's reference to textual repetition as printed (and hence liable to be read), and repeated (all without any guarantee of enlightenment as the "author" intended, whatever that is henceforth to be taken to mean), that is, *ad infinitum*, Gunkel explains that "remix does not consist in the technological preservation and reproduction of some original and prior live performance. It instead manufactures new originals from copies."[19]

The reference is to Baudrillard and the simulacrum, and below I will bring in Baudrillard and the question of the copy or the cover. Yet, like Lawrence Lessig who has been helpfully writing about this for years, Gunkel also foregrounds as key to any discussion of aesthetics and ethics (and law) the matter of money: who is paid, via whom, and how, foregrounding what is today increasingly unquestioned (putting this in question was key to Nietzsche's critique of Christianity), that what is "good" is to be paid for what one does.

In his own unsung reflection on the culture of the copy, that is humanity: the remix, the "antiquatedness" of the same in what he called the third technological revolution, Günther Anders, writing from the point of view of the musician and phenomenologist of psychological acoustics on layered radio broadcast echoes in the 1930s and image culture (print, film, TV) in the 1950s and 1960s could serve as counterpoint.[20] While refusing (as Platonic) in good Derridean/Deleuzian form, the privileging of the original, the *original* original (now to be seen as a fiction) is replaced by a "new original" for which, back to the issue of licensing fees, as all of this is about copyright culture, the originator has every expectation (if not now, then later) to be paid. And yet, and this is the point that Anders will insist upon, this same remunerative expectation accelerates remix culture: give us this day, as Anders ironically prays, "our eaters,"[21] or to translate for our terms today: our followers or subscribers, *likes* and *retweets*, with an ultimate monthly fee option for Patreon, a boon for musicians and ASMR artists, more elusive for academics who are not Jordan Peterson, and the like. And so the cycle that is the culture industry, emphasis on industry—*content is king*—continues.

As William J. Levay writes with respect to mash-up culture, less than the question of esteeming as better or worse than the original, "the aesthetic value of the mash-up; rather, its authorship is the more interesting issue."[22] Things are still more complicated in the graphic arts: if Warhol reproduces a print, it is still he who does the pull, likewise Wang Guangyi. Robert Rauschenberg's "combines," which can seem to be visual versions of a remix, whatever Michael Fried's critical reservations,[23] are his alone, even where one has to emphasize, as the sociologist Howard Becker rightly emphasizes for his own part, as Gunkel is also careful to observe, the *communal* character of music, the *communal* character of the art world as such: art schools, art galleries, museums, and thence indeed to critics and theory and philosophy. In the case of music, that community is blurred by the ambiguity of the reference. In addition to the questions Anders and Adorno (and Kittler et al.) pose to the mechanical/technological/electronic (and digital) means of reproduction (the record player, the radio, down to the speakers themselves),[24] considered at a phenomenologically crucial level of reproducibility as such, who is it who can be said to author and thus to fabricate or "make" the music? This requires a reference more to the demiurge of the *Timaeus* than the erotic theology of the *Phaedrus*. In the case of the music industry, the writer is credited along with the record producer, rather exactly on the model of the text, where sometimes—foreign as this notion may be to academic authors—authors are paid, and where the publisher's share of the profit to perpetuity is always the lion's share (sometimes the only share). For example, although it was the singer Leslie Gore who made *You Don't Own Me* a hit, it was the two (male) authors who were paid residuals, in addition to the fees paid not to the singer but the corporate record label, in this case, the producer, Quincy Jones.

As Gunkel explains (referring in the process to the remix as to the cover): "The mash-up, therefore, does not so much violate authorship as it exploits and demonstrates that the concept of authorship has always been a construct that has its own history, assumptions, and political interests."[25] Thus, typically, how-to-books on remix culture include chapters on property and copyright law. Copies of copies of copies—more than a matter of staying on the right side of the law, at issue is a material question. Thus, Gunkel quotes Jacques Attali's emphasis on the fundamental dependence of music today on the paraphernalia of electronic reproduction, not as an accident or a glitch but purposefully, deliberately (this is not Attali's emphasis): "concerts of popular music, tours by artists, are now all too often nothing more than copies of the records."[26]

## Pop Art and Big Business: Commercial Art as the Art of Copying the Copy

Christina Chang emphasizes the search for a definition of Pop Art with an almost Certeaulian metaphor, alluding to the plastic hyperreal (itself a reference to Baudrillard) in her essay, "Beyond Pop's Images: The Immateriality of Everyday Life."[27] Chang quotes the artist-poet, Richard Hamilton:

*Pop Art is:*
Popular (designed for a mass audience)
Transient (short-term solution)
Expendable (easily-forgotten)
Low Cost
Mass produced
Young (aimed at youth)
Witty
Sexy
Gimmicky
Glamorous
Big Business.
This is just a beginning.

(Richard Hamilton, 1957)[28]

Hamilton influenced Andy Warhol (and vice versa, as Chang contends that Warhol himself makes the claim) and to this Warholian extent there is an inevitable alliance between Pop Art and "Big Business."

Pop Art's industrial enthusiasm for profitability coordinates with applied design to this day, both corporate and municipal. Fine art meshes with (if it was not always thus, one should consider Richard Brilliant's discussion in his *My Laocoon* and, even more, Thierry Lenain's and my own discussions of Michelangelo in the context of the Laocoon)[29] *applied art*: the "commercial artist" makes good.[30] As Warhol is frequently cited as saying: "being good in business is the most fascinating kind of art."[31] To be good in business as to be good in art, qua artist, is successfully to market or commodify one's brand[32] (Figure 7.1).

But where Wang Guangyi has been called "the Chinese Warhol," not only writing on Warhol but in the wake of some of Warhol's own more iconic images, including Warhol's own portrait(s) of Mao, Wang Guangyi takes the parallel further, including the religious element.[33]

More than many mainstream approaches to the philosophy of art, but also more than Marshall McLuhan and even more than Guy Debord, Jean Baudrillard, given his focus on the market "system" of marketable "objects" and his attention to what he calls the "political economy of the sign," and the simulacrum may help us

**Figure 7.1** Andy Warhol, *Mao* (1974).

understand the pop effect of distribution or dissemination, as Wayne Koestenbaum personalizes this with respect to Andy Warhol as "twinship."³⁴ This allure, this "twinning," yields glamor by proximate association, rubbing shoulders with celebrity.³⁵ Hal Foster echoes the point to highlight the fascination Warhol held for academics, patent in the case of the analytic philosopher of art, Arthur Danto, himself, like Warhol, an artist in the 1950s but which fascination is illuminated by the hyperreal in its French continental articulation. As Foster writes,

> doubling was the primary Warholian device. (For me it became delirious one night in the early 1980s at a club called Area, as I watched Jean Baudrillard, the theorist of the simulacrum, watching Warhol posing as "Warhol" in a bare diorama of his own making, as if he were the wax model of his own dead specimen. I thought one of them would have to explode.)³⁶

Foster goes on to develop this point as doubling-unto-death.³⁷ Yet the double-death reference is already well developed by Becky Cowser who earlier invoked Warhol's use of replication, multiplication, via fetish and the neon/black velvet simulacrum that is Baudrillard's *America*.³⁸ For Cowser, who names Warhol "The Celebrity Death Machine," the pre-occupation that is quintessentially American matches the changelessness that is death, and in particular the perfectly preserved, dead celebrity, the dead actress: that is the simulacrum³⁹ (Figure 7.2).

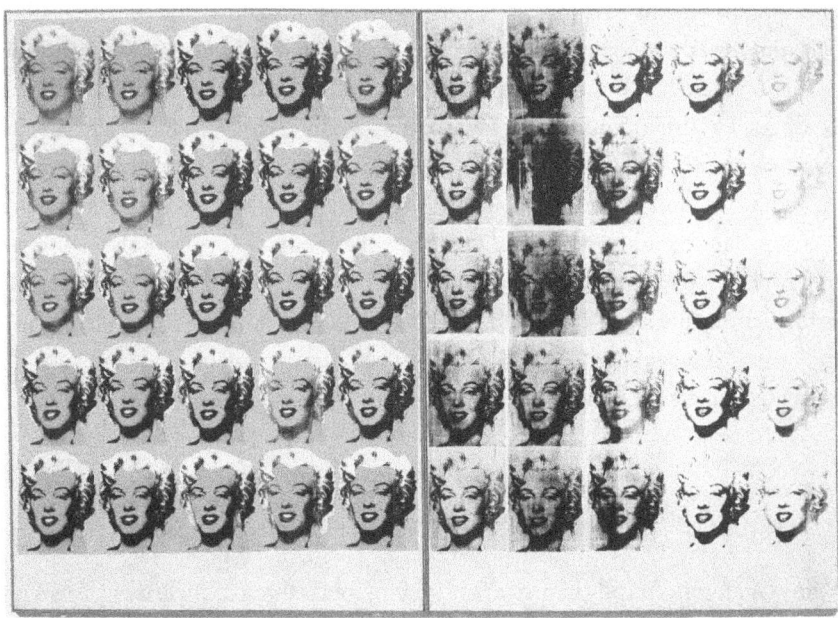

**Figure 7.2** Andy Warhol, *Marilyn Diptych* (1962).

Baudrillard invokes the simulacrum and takes it home, to where we continue to live our lives. In today's transhumanist era, as we await our "upgrades," we live in the culture of copy and remix, which seemingly embraces every metonymic expansion. Thus, Baudrillard can seem to have never been more timely:

> Everything can have a second birth, the eternal birth of the simulacrum [Americans] dream of baptizing everything a second time and only accord value to this later sacrament which is, as we know, a repeat performance of the first, but its repetition as something more real.[40]

For Baudrillard, the earmark of American culture (and we should never forget that Baudrillard is as much a thinker in a sociological and anthropological mode as in a philosophical mode) is a matter of faith. More generally as the culture of America is "the world," to quote a Coke commercial from years ago, we *believe* in the culture of the cover, the culture of the copy, mash-up, remix, and we are blithely unconcerned with the fades or losses due to replication: the copy, so we suppose, is quite as good as the original, hey, maybe better. No data creep in the machine, of that we are sure. We take this beyond internet downloads, and so goes the remix segue, corporate culture and, in some cases, the law of the land contends, stipulates, decrees that GMO crops are the same as non-GMO.[41]

In this way and without a hint of irony, philosophers debate the ethical future of robots (when we get them),[42] as indeed of algorithms as shifting and making entire governments (Trump), whole body/head transplants, and solving global warming by transposing (this is another kind of upload/download) human life to the surface of the moon or Mars or Venus, and so forth. As Cowser presciently observes, Baudrillard misses the force of his own insight just to the extent that he fails to see how "far ensconced Americans were in the reality of the simulacrum."[43]

Setting Warhol as the null-point of modernity,[44] Warhol becomes the moving locus for Baudrillard: pop simulacrum of the contemporary. If Warhol also managed to morph his Marilyn series into a Mao series, it may be argued that Wang Guangyi is the heir. In the sense that Baudrillard foregrounds above, as Hal Foster argues this, Wang Guangyi has the twinship. Thus, with his own Mao series, and beyond, Wang Guangyi exemplifies contemporary pop, inevitably as we shall see: political.

## Wang Guangyi: Chinese Political Pop

Wang Guangyi, typically named in the metonymic fashion of advertising agencies and promotional literature, as a representative of Chinese Political Pop, when not declared a "titan" among contemporary artists,[45] instantiates contemporary art and yet his work exemplifies the political iconic reflections, including the parodistic and ironic or distancing elements of Baudrillard, as suggested above well beyond Danto's more American, philosophically analytic take on art as art,[46] a central theme in Danto's work.

The notion of the "cover"—thus the replay, reprise, taking over of an existing work as one's very own—has its elusive cultural history and is, as we saw above, typically invoked, like mash-up and remix, with reference to music.[47] In a monograph dedicated to the culture of the cover, *The Hallelujah Effect*,[48] I backtrack from pop music (Cohen's *Hallelujah* et al.)[49] to Adorno's reflections on radio broadcast and repetition, that is, commercial pop music, just because only repeated plays make a cover worth covering or prove its priming efficacy (this broadcast programming Adorno named *The Current of Music*),[50] read back into a thematization of Beethoven (and the Greeks) in Nietzsche's *The Birth of Tragedy out of the Spirit of Music*. Repetition, usually discussed with respect to Nietzsche's eternal return, here concerns the copy as copy. As Nietzsche reminds us in an aphorism dedicated to "Copies" in the section of *Human, All too Human* on the human being in interaction with others, "Not rarely, one encounters copies of significant people; and for most people, as with paintings, the copy is more pleasing than the original."[51] Nietzsche's point is meant as provocation. It is not clear that the provocation would work today as we not only prefer the cover to the original but quibble over which covers exceed the others and how.

If Wang Guangyi "covers" or echoes Warhol,[52] his "cover" of Warhol's Mao Zedong foregrounds political poster art, as in the case of Wang Guangyi's 1988 reduplication, *Mao Zedong: Red Grid No. 2* (Figure 7.3). For his own part, Warhol "covers" or reproduces Campbell's soup cans, *Brillo Boxes*, *Marilyn Monroe* (1962), the original being a victim herself of the culture industry, like Elizabeth Taylor. Danto analyses Warhol's portrait, *Liz* (1963), in perfect Warholian fashion, by highlighting, to clinch his argument, the speculative value added. Robyn Meredith, in her *Forbes* article on the speculative futures of Chinese art, as it were, regarded as an index of the value of American high-end brands, makes a similar argument simply by using the sale prices of Wang Guangyi's paintings.[53] But, as in the case of Danto's estimations, and in accord with the challenge of keeping things contemporary or up to date, the conclusions themselves are subject to revaluation, appreciation—or loss.

The *Forbes* article meant to make a wry point, or two, not including Meredith's titular filmic allusion to Peter Greenaway's 1988 *Drowning by Numbers*. In his homage to Warhol, Wang Guangyi "covers" Coke and Pepsi and thus, arguably, the

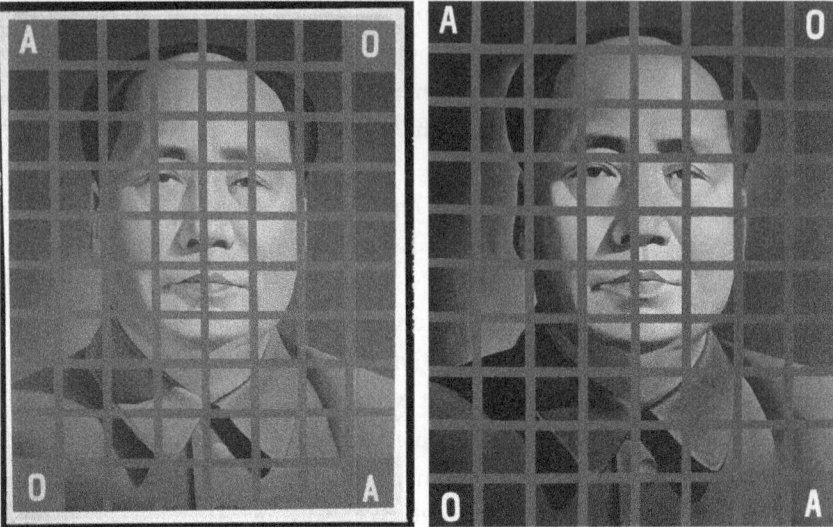

**Figure 7.3** Wang Guangyi, on the right, *Mao Zedong: Red Grid No. 2* (1988), oil on canvas, 150 × 130 cm; on the left, *Mao Zedong: Red Grid No. 1* (1988), oil on canvas, 150 × 130 cm.

icon(s) of American capitalism, as collages, as pastiche. Here (and it can be useful to read Howard Caygill on Benjamin, less for color, despite the title and beauty of Caygill's sustained reflection on Benjamin's own word painting, describing the city Moscow, foregrounding a traffic light, a "red signal," than for what may be the most perspicuous discussion of aura in Benjamin's iconic study to date),[54] it is almost impossible, such is the contemporary force of the pop image that is Coca-Cola, to bracket our responses to that same image. Thus, Wang Guangyi brings cliché images of Coca-Cola, the "real thing," complete with accidentally Lacanian overtones, together with Chinese political iconography: the result layers icon on icon.

The power of the imagery of *Great/Mass Criticism* underscores the ease with which the capitalist red of Coca-Cola, the branded soft drink, can be brought into coincidence with the cultural images of Communist Chinese revolution.[55] The commentary remains in the juxtaposition as achieved. And not less in the difference between the scattered serial numbers, asserting individual distinctions between products in the age of technological reproduction, as these can often look the same, no change in design, and yet distinguishable thereby. The 1.2 in the *Mass Criticism* Series echoes various instaurations of popular products, the iPhone being iconic among these, but so, too, to quote the title of Steve Fuller's plea for the desirability of human upgradability, we may now say "remixability," *Humanity 2.0.*[56]

I have been using the term "cover" on metonymic loan from the music industry, and it is important to foreground that, like a monetized YouTube video, the term cover, its application and reference, its origin and definition is an industry affair. Thus, any artist who undertakes to perform, that is, to put out their own version or re-recording of another artist's work "covers" the original version, which may itself be a cover of a still more original version, in re-releasing the same song. In painting, Wang Guangyi "covers" Warhol. In the case of *Great Criticism*, Wang Guangyi "covers" the iconography of commercials for Coca-Cola (echoing Warhol to be sure) together with the graphic iconology of the Chinese Cultural Revolution.

In every case, a financial, commercial dimension is key to the cover, as is the issue of replication, which may include revisitation, like Warhol's *Marilyn Monroe Diptych* or Wang Guangyi's *Mao Zedong: Red Grid No. 2* (or even that same artist's own work, frozen in time as the work of art in the age of mechanical reproduction freezes the work of art; this is what is meant by the loss of aura). Here, where there can be a cult of "first editions," the "original" exists no more than does Leonard Cohen's original *Hallelujah* or Warhol's "first" print of *Marilyn Monroe* or, indeed, inasmuch as this remains the iconic simulacrum of contemporary art, Duchamp's *Fountain*, which is, as Danto and others remind us, only preserved as a Stieglitz photograph, the physical "original," seemingly a one-off, plumbing design, having vanished, only to be fabricated in post-facto versions (by the artist to be sure) to meet museum demand.[57]

Duchamp, Warhol, Cohen's song, other songs, other works, think of Rauschenberg or Lichtenstein, think of Ai Weiwei, or, qua performative self-installation, *Marina Abramović: The Artist Is Present* (MOMA, March 14–May 31, 2010), especially in her encounter with her former collaborator, Ulay, itself reprising, as the event also varied their (disparately located) collaborative performance event *Nightsea Crossing* (1981–87), or sitting across from the actors James Franco and Alan Rickman, such echoes and remakes characterize contemporary remix, cover culture. Indeed, literal coverings are sometimes, "literally," a part of this, like Christo's 1985 Paris installation, *The Pont Neuf Wrapped*, or in Berlin (itself a project that took decades to organize, for obvious architectural and for perhaps less-obvious but equally patent political reasons), from 1971–95, *Wrapped Reichstag*.[58]

Inverting the order of Leonard Cohen's 1988, *First We Take Manhattan*, with the *Gates* as installation (Figure 7.4), by "covering" New York's Central Park with "saffron" swags hung from periodic stanchions, Christo and Jean Claude could compel visitors to the park to become, willy nilly, visitors to and through the

**Figure 7.4** Babette Babich, *People Wash*. February 22, 2000.

*Gates* by having to pass by, pass under, pass through, a kind of "people wash," a title I assigned to a photograph of the installation.[59] The "found work of art" here was the park itself, including its nineteenth-century design, but not less, in a deliberate or incidental echo of Donovan's allusion in his *Mellow Yellow* to a color (or a girl)—*I'm just wild about Saffron, and Saffron's wild about me*—the February blue skies of the installation.

Historically, the origin of the term "cover" is obscure and routine: every YouTube version of Psy's *Gangnam Style* is a "cover" of the original. To this extent, precisely as Adorno's "currency," cover culture tests the elusive question of taste, less good or bad, high or low, but personal fancy as the key to pop and to art history as this favor makes the pop star a star, Beyoncé, kd lang and so, too, by analogy, Andy Warhol, Wang Guangyi.

## "Perhaps Simplicity Outshines Complexity."[60] Coca-Cola and Political Pop

Mixing, as gallery info materials will tell us about Wang Guangyi, agitprop with kitsch, post poster art, as it were, and thus patently post pop, the contemporary aspect is the most telling as it determines whether an artist remains on the cutting edge or post cut. If the contemporary is a moving target, it is also the negative image of Benjamin's angel of history: blown forward by the sheer accumulation of the past, detritus, ancient references, forgotten images, holy writ and the ever-demanding allure of the newest, latest name, which just to matter also has to be a known name, so one may compare Wang Guangyi and Ai Weiwei and still hearken back, even after all these years as Wang Guangyi does, to Andy Warhol just as we saw at the start (Figure 7.5).

It is the issue of the found, the object made art by the eye of the artist, the artist's whim, in its inception by decree as this constitutes what becomes Avant Garde with Duchamp and the same might seem to hold for Wang Guangyi with his object images, political posters and the juxtaposition of Mao and the ubiquitous Coca-Cola that is for some, most particularly advertising gurus, synonymous with positive globalization.

The reference to Andy Warhol is patent but the allusion is difficult to the extent that although himself a former artist of the same generation, ergo a contemporary, and from this vantage point, an art critic, long-term, for the *Nation*, Arthur Danto was never the most politically sensitive of critics, not even in the sphere of art. Hence, quite apart from issues of capitalist production, Danto never grasped the reasons why there might be an animal rights movement. This theoretical gap even more than the analytic–continental divide, separates Danto's *What Art Is*[61] from Paul Virilio's *Art & Fear*.[62] Virilio goes a step further than Baudrillard, indicting contemporary art, artist and audience included, gallery and museum curator alike, of a by no means coincidental trade in pain together with insensitivity (think Kant as Virilio invokes the claim, essential to the

**Figure 7.5** Wang Guangyi, *Great Criticism: Andy Warhol* (2002), oil on canvas, 300 × 200 cm.

aesthetic contemplation of disinterested interest), and not less of contemporary boredom (Virilio like Bourdieu, like Baudrillard, is a sociologist by formation) matched to contemporary distractedness. For Virilio what is at stake is less the attention-seeking that is Shock Art, or political art performance demonstration, think of Pjotr Andrejewitsch Pawlenski's 10 November 2013 auto-performance, *Red Square* in Moscow, or again, the varied tours, naked and not, silent and not, of self-exposition as recalled above in the case of Ulay and Marina Ambramović. At a certain Kantian extreme, Virilio traces the disinterest of disinterested interest to a clinically scientific limit: less Nietzsche's "cold angel"[63] than the cool distraction of the art lover: surrendered, collectively, to the attention deficit disorder induced by gallery audio guides and/or Android/iPhone, swipe to meet up, or to tour the Tate Gallery.

In an insightful reflection, Wang Guangyi tells us, "As for Warhol, he makes the ordinary even more ordinary—he lives in the light of day."[64] Wang Guangyi's point concerns the artist's greatest challenge in the age of popular pop artists, the spotlight, the interviewers, the museum opening, the gallery event: How can one deal with questioners who come to ask one just what would baffle even a Socrates at the beginning of philosophy in the West, challenge Kant, the reading of whose books, Wang tells us, often left him "perplexed."[65] It is not for nothing that a 2012 retrospective of his work in Beijing was titled: *Thing-in-Itself: Utopia, Pop and Personal Theology*.[66]

For Wang Guangyi, Warhol cuts to the ordinary level of life as we live it and that is on terms of corporate manufacture:

> the elimination of "individuality or personality" is key to the essence of Warhol's works ... You see them as by-products of industrialization, of mass production, and so on. This is exactly where his greatest contribution lies—in industrializing artworks. He chooses meaningless images, transmits these meaningless images in meaningless fashion, and convinces everyone that they are actually meaningful.[67]

If Wang Guangyi simply reflected on Warhol we would already have a great deal, but he offers us more by noting, drawing on Klaus Honnef to do so, pairing Josef Beuys with Warhol, "that contemporary art has its true aura." As Wang Guangyi explains, "What Beuys does is to use politics as a means of doing. From the same viewpoint, Warhol's art is a means of removing the so-called aura of art."[68]

To this extent, the claim is made, and here there is an echo with the work of Bazon Brock, one of the original fluxus group and originator in 1959 of what

**Figure 7.6** Babette Babich, *Denkerei*. Berlin, Kreuzberg, May 14, 2012.

Brock then called, in a display of zen or better said, yogic muscular fitness, echoing others, like Leonard Cohen, who did the same, referring to lectures given in a headstand position, "action teaching."

Brock's agit prop still "serves," not only with variously staged "pleasure marches"—art is fun, sheer delight and artworks, as Heidegger noted, are sent here and there across the land, so Brock reasons, why not tour the artist himself, the happening itself, including, coopting the art-public as well?

And the thinking is contagious, agit prop meets remix: thus, at a conference on Marx and Nietzsche in Weimar, January 2018, his assistants, Stefan Wilke and Marina Sawall, invoked Brock's example (and deployed his images) during their own lectures.[69] Above all, perhaps most of all, Brock's project is archaeo-institutional, that is, exemplified in the architectural commercial design of an institution dedicated to himself and his own work,[70] to the amusing frustration of local thinkers who had hoped to come along for the ride and were dismayed to find that that was not and would not be so (this, too, is action teaching), all exemplified in his Berlin *Denkerei* that shares with Warhol and Wang Guangyi an affinity with the Coca-Cola font (Figure 7.6).

The pink D of Brock's *Denkerei*, alliterated in his self-groomed slogan, *Denker im Dienst—Thinker at Work, Thinker at Your Service*—takes for granted the kind of lettering that Brock would have recalled from his own youth in the 1950s. Bazon Brock's *Denkerei* thus comes across—and the effect in Kreuzberg is quite dissonant, architecturally, aesthetically—as nothing so much as a Philadelphia soda fountain transplant: an old-fashioned, trans-drugstore fountain in Berlin.

The effect is effected, in part, by curved glass, linking what the Germans call *Jugendstil* with 1930s streamlining, Flash Gordon style, not postmodernism but future-modernism: glass and chrome, stylized Bauhaus, but it is also effected by nothing more graphic artist *artistic* than the font. This is the kind of thing one can do with words typeset in print on page or glass. This is what commercial artists (we call them designers) are paid to do. The design, down to the font choice as well as the pink color, does the work. The cognitive shock comes in with Brock's unsaying sayings. *Thinker for sale*. And in an age of pop philosophy, Stoics to win friends and influence the self, invocations of the "existentialist café" appropriated by analytic philosophers after decades of disdain, in an era where university philosophers are rated for "impact," nothing perhaps, and if only it sells, could be more timely.

For his own part, Wang Guangyi, who thematizes some of the contradictions of capitalism *in situ*, claims a clear influence, split between the fluxus artist Joseph Beuys (who was to be sure again, one of Brock's associates), Wang also underscores the force of priming, advertisement, and thus the value of the kind of services Brock claims (*pro forma*, thus Brock writes aphorisms that work the way Joseph Beuys marveled at Warhol's discourse for its astonishing ability to keep silent even while speaking—the irony is pure German. Warhol's words, as Beuys observed, unsaid themselves, functioning as their own antidote).

Wang Guangyi's argument underlines the working force of the culture of the "cover." Giving a certain reading to Warhol, attending to him, featuring him, the philosopher critic Danto "covered" Warhol on the art scene, channeling Warhol as he did (and of course, as already noted, Danto was himself an artist before he turned to philosophy), thus in the more conventionally journalistic or literary sense, *covering* Warhol for the art public, and thereby "making" Warhol *Warhol*:

> In April 1964 Warhol exhibited Brillo boxes in the Stable Gallery on East 74th Street in Manhattan. Danto went and saw those works, and he was the one who gave Warhol's art its transcendental value.[71]

As in the case of the culture of the cover, where what is important is radio airtime, Danto gives Warhol *exposure*: as a critic, Danto writes about Warhol and thus celebrates him as an artist and does so for another audience as a philosopher of art. Note that this exposure is far from an ordinary or routine affair of scholarship, for philosophers are notoriously abstemious in their writing about one another (hence not only do philosophers often fail to note contemporary artists, but they omit mention of their own contemporaries, perhaps especially those with cognate or affine interests or areas of specialization).[72] In this way, the Hungarian philosopher of art, Béla Bacsó and the Italian philosopher of cognitive perception and art, Tiziana Andina would be exceptions writing on Danto as they do, yet it remains instructive that even though Danto himself is famous enough, and even though he has politely perished (sometimes perishing helps colleagues to read a philosopher's work and sometimes perishing can end a citation cartel: it is hard to say), Danto is relatively sparely noted.[73]

Elsewhere I explore the sociological salience of the habit of non-citation endemic among philosophers[74] where the operating principle would seem to be that if one does not cite others one has a greater claim, at least on the surface of it, to be doing original work oneself.

## Covers and "Covers": Tea and Sympathy

The artist needs technique, the pop artist, mystique. A pop meditation that can seem to transcend this distinction towards the Heideggerian letting be of both art and aesthetics echoes in the remix original that is Kakuzō Okakura's *Book of Tea*.[75] Originally written in English and first published in 1906, Okakura, according to contemporary scholars of Japanese culture, "made" tea and flower ceremonies a central feature of Japanese culture,[76] which last tea-culture scholars argue to have been a "cover" of Chinese tea culture.

With respect to the current theme, such reflections are important owing not merely to our tendency to favor the remix version, to prefer the copy, as Nietzsche says, that is the contemporary reinterpretation. We prefer the newly "updated" or "modernized" translation, whether on the model of Ezra Pound's "translations" of Chinese poetry[77] or Emily Martin's new version of Homer's *Odyssey* or analytic philosophy's rediscovery of Stoicism, or existentialism (after years of disdaining continental colleagues who wrote on Sartre and de Beauvoir and Camus), and so forth. In general, pop versions of philosophy are remixes. The same reception is liable to fade over time (thus Pound's renderings have fallen into opprobrium in recent years). But remix (not remake) is characteristically celebrated over earlier efforts as an "advance," like the broad claims made for new versions of old translations (technically, on the remix, remake, model, these are re-translations, which are then claimed to be preferable to earlier versions: thus Robin Waterfield's or Allan Bloom's retranslations of Plato's *Republic* are preferred by certain cadres to Cornford and others). If one can corner the coin of philosophic citation, think of the new translations of Nietzsche, one hopes thereby, this was also done for Hegel, to corner the market of ideas.

In the case of music, it is easy to think that there is some mechanism by which a popular taste ("popular demand") emerges by democratic assessment, which is then the source or basis for the kind of music current on the radio (and this "currency" significantly still matters despite the hackability of all digital counts, from presidential votes to YouTube views). Hence Adorno, who dedicated much of his life to refuting this assumption, foregrounds the advertising culture that constitutes the cultural industry.[78] Similarly, one assumes there is a tradition of tea-and-flower ceremonies, and thus the relevance for artists (and as one enthusiastic book presents the technique, likewise designers, likewise philosophers) of a book recounting that same tradition: *The Book of Tea*.

In art, as this is emphatically associated with ambiguity and the contrasts of contradiction in Okakura, the discussion brings in the art of the "incomplete," expressed as the art of "*wabi sabi*" in a handbook specifically directed to artists of the "impermanent, imperfect,"[79] artists of—and, in the spirit of Okakura's "teaism," all artists, most explicitly remix artists, seem to be artists of—things unfinished.

Okakura emphasizes the narrowness of Western sensibility and if, notoriously, the "Christian missionary goes to impart, but not to receive,"[80] significant as we recall his reflection on Westerners regarded from an Eastern point of view, "we used to think you the most impracticable people on the earth, for you were said to preach what you never practised."[81]

In an era preoccupied with sources—a dissonant preoccupation given the disinclination of philosophers today to cite or "do" history in favor of what is by default assumed to be the "original" work, as analytic philosophy imagines itself to be doing this—it has been claimed that Martin Heidegger took his ideas from the German translation of *The Book of Tea*, which would make *Being and Time* perhaps the most famous "cover" of an ancient tradition that may be traced back to China.[82] Indeed, Okakura includes cover elements even as he explains that greatness consists in non-imitation: "It has been said that the Greeks were great because they never drew from the antique."[83]

To be sure, it is unwise to claim Greek originality. The Greeks were remix masters: excelling, in Nietzsche's words, at the very "fruitful borrowing" that is the culture of the cover.

Wang Guangyi emphasizes the beauty that characterizes the productive qualities, qua industrial, of Warhol's work by contrast with Beuys's aesthetic complexity. Some part of this art is beyond the art of arranging evident in

Wang's Political Pop art. The point is illuminated by Heideggerian letting fall, as I elsewhere analyse *Gelassenheit*[84] and as Okakura relates the challenge of arrangement, order, and cleanliness:

> Rikiu was watching his son Shoan as he swept and watered the garden path. "Not clean enough," said Rikiu, when Shoan had finished his task, and bade him try again. After a weary hour the son turned to Rikiu: "Father, there is nothing more to be done. The steps have been washed for the third time, the stone lanterns and the trees are well sprinkled with water, moss and lichens are shining with a fresh verdure; not a twig, not a leaf have I left on the ground." "Young fool," chided the tea-master, "that is not the way a garden path should be swept." Saying this, Rikiu stepped into the garden, shook a tree and scattered over the garden gold and crimson leaves, scraps of the brocade of autumn! What Rikiu demanded was not cleanliness alone, but the beautiful and the natural also.[85]

Carefully chosen, the random is deliberate: "scattered over the garden," leaves of "gold and crimson," the "brocade of autumn"—do mark Okakura's English— the arrangement pushes beyond order, "the natural also," and we are unnerved. Cue Beuys. Where Duchamp's urinal was a plumbing fixture, isolated from any plumbing functionality (as Danto discreetly emphasizes), Wang Guangyi's "cover" of Duchamp picks up the same reference and takes it further—like the Greeks who knew "how to pick up the spear and throw it onward from the point where others had left it."[86]

In Wang Guangyi's *New Religion—Prophecy* (2010) we read a religious inscription (Mathew 10:36: "A man's enemies will be the members of his household")[87] completely covering in Greek uncial characters (note the font) a photograph of a urinal, as Duchamp's *Fountain* was a photograph. But where the ready-made lies on its back (as Danto tells us) this urinal is right side up, visible behind the inscription, a real one, used, or worse yet, in use.

We may also discern the practice of decomposition in Michel de Certeau's attention to the art of what passes qua non-retainable, apart from habit, the practice that leaves no trace beyond memory *and* art.[88] The everyday as Wang Guangyi emphasizes, fades from notice in its disintegration.

On the level of art and practical, tactical know-how, this is the art of finding beauty not in the "ready-made" styles of found art, designated via the name of the artist in the fashion of analytic philosophy of art (*What is art? When is art? Art is whatever we*—artists, museum curators, we, the experts, we, the aestheticians— say it is),[89] but and just the disintegration of the gesture, the action of revelation (or occlusion) that is error, what Heidegger named *errancy*. The city dweller—we recall that de Certeau's phenomenological and hermeneutic examples are explicitly, evocatively Parisian and, similarly, Giorgio Agamben invokes the fashion industry of his own Milan, and the agitprop philosopher and theological activist, Ivan Illich, writing his last book about a book, *In the Vineyard of the Text*, a book about design and typescript (fonts again, in this case, as copies of handwriting), drew his illustrations from the mountains around Vienna as from his youthful travels in Japan, and in his reflections at the end of his life, he shares the same *genius loci* by telling us of what had been his dream of Mediterranean seas for his old age by contrast with the twice daily flooding of the flat lowlands around Bremen.[90] The same, *ceteris paribus*, for any city dweller, who observes as de Certeau writes, tracing a path among favored spots, in the ambit of buses, metro stations, markets, and kiosks, the art of wandering is the art of getting lost in an ordered fashion, the artist who fashions, the eye that sees a fallen petal not in its Keatsian moment: *forever wilt thou love*, but shading grades of disarray to nothingness.

The "released" art of *Verfallenheit* allows what is fallen to fall, frames or brackets enframing, allows what is apart from the frame to intrude, a shaken tree, scattered leaves. This is Rikiu's story, but it can also be the art of a Joseph Beuys or the art of photography or of film, which is perhaps more of this kind than other art genres, consider Hertzog, or Greenaway's 1985 *Zed and Two Noughts*, the kitsch-artfilm of *Verfallenheit*, with its by-the-numbers ugliness.[91] Or Wang Guangyi's bleeding neon *Last Supper* (see Figure 3.1).

## In the Money: Taking Coca-Cola Back to the Fountain or Theological Aesthetics

Jan Jagodzinski identifies "Guangyi Wang's critical commentary on communist capitalism (or is it capitalist communism)."[92] A clear cover of the portrait of Mao hanging in Tiananmen Square, Gate of Heavenly Peace, Beijing, China, Wang himself compares his own *Mao Zedong AO* to its mass-made origins. But in just this way, qua cover, as we have seen above, *Mao Zedong AO*, the first work in Wang's newer Mao series departs from a store-bought, "embroidered portrait,"

> as Wang says, "Posters are paper, and fragile. Embroidery is on cloth, a textile. It'll survive long term." Wang likens this prefabricated portrait of Mao to Marcel Duchamp's infamous use of a readymade urinal; and in a gesture similar to the dada artist inking a mustache and "L.H.O.O.Q." on a postcard of the Mona Lisa,

**Figure 7.7** Shi Xinning, *Duchamp Retrospective Exhibition in China* (2000–1).

Wang applied his hallmark grid and the letters "AO" in black paint onto what was, after all, just another image of Mao.[93]

If *Mao Zedong AO* (see Figure 4.2) echoes Warhol's *Marilyn Monroe*, in its poster print origins and its variants on iterability, Wang's *New Religion—Prophecy* (2010) retains a reference to Duchamp, as the same reference is significant throughout Danto's reflective life.

The focus that Wang has on conceptual art echoes Ai Weiwei, who emphasizes that

> the entire value of any work of art is only ever conceptual. After Duchamp, the existence of any art, its value, is entirely conceptual. Duchamp brought a new concept to modern art.[94]

If the reference is not as patent as Shi Xinning, *Duchamp Retrospective Exhibition in China* (2000–2001) and the long-standing interest in and influence of Duchamp's *Fountain* on Chinese artists, the cover force is clear with respect to the ready-made (see Figure 7.7).

Karen Smith argues that, for Wang Guangyi, the "inimical benchmarks to surpass"[95] are Duchamp and Beuys and, patently, Warhol. The challenge is to understand the role of the ready-made, especially for an artist who takes Warhol as exemplifying the beautiful. What is the industrial work? What is the *work* of art? How conceive the notion of art in the era of mechanical, technological, fetishized (as we have been calling attention to this) as *digital*, reproduction?

It is no accident that Benjamin raises this question after the avant-garde, in the specific wake of futurism (Italian), all in all "new" art, conscious of itself as new. With the birth of political pop, the artist lives with the contradiction of the notion. The reference above to the "cover" makes it plain that what is at issue is a system of credits and licensing fees. When political propaganda is brought together with advertising icons like Coke (but also Canon and Louis Vitton and Porsche, all high-end retail names to be sure), there is and cannot but be a question of censorship in the name of protecting creative rights, claimed in the case of the artist but which typically amount to producer's and distributor's rights. This is why Horkheimer and Adorno speak of the culture *industry*. This is also the driving force behind the privacy laws in the European Union and the legislation contra net neutrality in the United States.[96] Privacy is less a concern than the need to be sure that a quote can be traced back to an original. *Content is king*.

In the case of *New Religion—Pieta*, 2011 (see Figure 13.2) we have the almost mechanically cartoon sketch, dark image, linear neon outline of the foreshortened Christ (in the image and likeness of Wang Guangyi himself), and this is among the works included in a 2014 solo show entitled "Negatives of Idols."[97]

If the idols of religion—and not less of communist icons like Mao—have lost their salience, the power of the same idols remains in recognizability. Nietzsche could conclude his aphorism *Der tolle Mensch*, the "mad man," in *The Gay Science*, by having the same prophet failed after his efforts to speak to the people, the same "people" Wang is careful to distinguish from the masses, gathered as they were to hear him announce his search for God in the market place (and thus bent on making themselves into the mass human being), declaring the churches nothing other than the tombs and sepulchres of god.

If Danto is right when he argues that museums today have taken over the place of religion in popular culture, then Wang echoes the same point using the same images, both for their recognizability as for their iconic force. The concept behind the ideal of Mao, the concept behind the *Pieta*, stands despite the ablating wind of the market that blows such angels backwards with a force Benjamin's angel could never have imagined.

**Figure 7.8** Jeff Koons, *Made in Heaven* (1989).

This is the literal detritus of everyday history, the immense accumulation of plastic in our oceans, poisons in our air, the wasting force of weather and its geoengineered control, which we academics hasten to deny. We cannot imagine the needful ceremonies we will have to invent, as Nietzsche says, to recall some of the reflections of Okakura (and Koren), to be equal to the deed we have done. Retelling ourselves our lives, rebranding the artist, one can argue that Wang Guangyi is not an artist of political pop but attuned to theological aesthetics, an artist of the transcendent. The iconography of this interpretation works as well as the iconographic account of political pop art.

I began with, I return to Baudrillard. We have the same lines, the same upward aspiration: the velvet Jesus is on the same plain, aesthetically speaking, in terms of pure kitsch, as the Las Vegas Elvis and his imitators. The difference is that this transcendence is, like Jeff Koons's *Made in Heaven*, utterly branded and thus secure (Figure 7.8).[98]

Advertising, as Baudrillard and Adorno do not fail to remind us, sells the system itself as much as it sells the advertised product in question. Religion does the same, a point that Marx and Nietzsche had already made, and we are reminded by Ivan Illich that even school, and by extension, the museum, *pace* Danto, does the same. What Wang Guangyi can teach us is to pay attention to the functional "simulacrum of divinity."

The phrase I take from Baudrillard:

> Outside of medicine and the army, favored terrains of simulation, the affair goes back to religion and the simulacrum of divinity: "I forbade any simulacrum in the temples because the divinity that breathes life into nature cannot be represented." Indeed it can. But what becomes of the divinity when it reveals

itself in icons, when it is multiplied in simulacra? Does it remain the supreme authority, simply incarnated in images as a visible theology? Or is it volatilized into simulacra which alone deploy their pomp and power of fascination—the visible machinery of icons being substituted for the pure and intelligible Idea of God?[99]

Baudrillard extends Nietzsche's insight. In the same light, we approach one of Wang Guangyi's more complicated, politically charged, theological echoes, via the title of his series *New Religion, Mourning Christ*, "covering," so we might say at this point, Mantegna's *The Dead Christ*, rinsed with blue, itself an echo of Mantegna's Louvre *St. Sebastian*.

God is dead: our Hegel tells us so. And Nietzsche repeats this in *The Gay Science*, again we recall that churches today are sepulchers. Like Hans Holbein's entombed Christ, Wang Guangyi gives us a vision into and beyond what is unseen.

Dissonance remains and claims us and Wang Guangyi's *New Religion— Concern* shows a prelate, embodiment of theological colonialism, as if to illustrate the contours of today's religious crisis, sex abuse, financial scandals, the refusal of women as priests, and a church that coopts cultures, as capitalism consumes everything. This is political theology, here, to conclude, with Baudrillard's convergent account:

> Underneath the idea of the apparition of God in the mirror of images, they already enacted his death and his disappearance in the epiphany of his representations (which they perhaps knew no longer represented anything, and that they were purely a game, but that this was precisely the greatest game—knowing also that it is dangerous to unmask images, since they dissimulate the fact that there is nothing behind them).[100]

## Notes

1 A review of a then-debate is in this sense instructive. See the contributions to Ingeborg Hoesterey, 1991.
2 See Wallis et al., 2002 museum catalogue and, recently, in addition to Lessig, 2008, Gunkel, 2016. Largely, thematizing film and the clash between "our system of law" and what the producer/creator calls the "derivative nature of creativity" (reading a bit of Marx might help here), but distinguishing covers (subject to licensing and fees) and knock-offs, see Kirby Ferguson's *Everything is a Remix* on YouTube (and Vimeo, owing to copyright troubles): www.everythingisaremix.

info/watch-the-series/. See, too: Andersen, Kozul-Wright & Kozul-Wright, 2007, and focusing on changing technological means while still focusing on music, Hesmondhalgh & Meier, 2018.
3 See for comparison, Reynolds, 2011.
4 See for comparison, Agamben, 2009: 40 et seq.
5 Nancy, 2010.
6 Virilio, 2003/2000.
7 Most obviously, for example Danto & Goher, 1997, although the question of the contemporary is also a theme in Danto, 2013, as well as Danto's reflections on Duchamp: "Marcel Duchamp and the End of Taste." See, of course, classically, Rosalind Krauss, 1985. Danto's reading of Duchamp can be productively augmented with Jean Clair's more nuanced exposition (Clair, 2000).
8 Baudrillard, 2005. See for comparison, Baudrillard, 1981.
9 Osborne, 2013.
10 See Newton, 1999.
11 Caygill, Coles, and Klimowski, 2015.
12 Smith, 2010: 366–83.
13 Rabinow, 2011.
14 Gillick, 2010.
15 Wang Guangyi, "On Andy Warhol: Perhaps Simplicity Outshines Complexity." For the original Chinese text, see *The Beijing News*, October 9, 2013. Translated by Lina Dann and annotated by Yu-Chieh Li and Lina Dann. http://post.at.moma.org/sources/12/publications/243. Accessed December 21, 2017.
16 Bardini, 2011. Bardini's book is to be sure rather more about DNA, but the parallel is part of his point of departure.
17 Eduardo Navas, "Remix" in: Navas, Gallagher, 2018.
18 Gunkel may be leery of repeating himself here. See Gunkel, 2008. To be sure, Gunkel is not utterly opposed to repetition and his comments here on Baudrillard and music echo his earlier online essay: Gunkel, 2007.
19 Gunkel, 2016: 61.
20 I discuss this as the "Prometheus effect" in the uncut version of Babich, "Radio Ghosts: Günther Anders, Phenomenology's Phantoms, and Digital Autism," *Thesis Eleven*. Forthcoming.
21 Anders, 1980: 15.
22 Levay, 2005: 23. See too Babich 2016 where I emphasize Howard Becker's focus on the communal nature of the thing that it is to "make" music, socially, performatively, and with reference to the industry. Here, what is at stake is nothing so direct as a cover, although just as ephemeral as the "song" sung, what works in mash-up is versioning, literally mashing up, as Levay cites Richard Hebdige:

> The hip hoppers "stole" music off the air and cut it up. Then they broke it down into its component parts and remixed it on tape. By doing this they

were breaking the law of copyright. But the cut 'n' mix attitude was that no one owns a rhythm or sound. You just borrow it, use it and give it back to the people in a slightly different form. To use the language of Jamaican reggae and dub, you just version it. And anyone can do a "version." Hebdige, 1987: 14.

23  Michael Fried, "Art and Objecthood," *Artforum* 5 (June 1967): 12-23. Reprinted in Fried, 1998: 148–72.
24  For a discussion of the speakers in particular, see Babich, 2014.
25  Gunkel, 2008: 501.
26  Attali, 2003: 118.
27  Chang, 2005: 6–24.
28  Chang, "Beyond Pop's Image," 6. 5.
29  Richard Brilliant, 2002. See also, beyond Hatfeld, 2002 for a discussion of Michelangelo, Lynn Catterson, 2005, Lenain, 2012, Charney, 2015, and, again on the Laocoön, Babich, 2017a.
30  As Linda Bolton's overview makes plainer perhaps than some other accounts, Warhol begins and never quite departs from his origins as a "commercial artist." Bolton, 2002: 10 et seq..
31  Ibid.: 36.
32  See, for a reading drawing on Bourdieu (rather than Baudrillard), Cook, 2003: 66–76.
33  Huang, 2014.
34  Koestenbaum, 2001.
35  This too is not limited to the pop per se, if it is relevant to popular artists as such. See Heinich, 1996.
36  Foster, 2002. See for comparison, Heartney 1999: 35–36.
37  Ibid.
38  See Cowser, 1998: 7–12.
39  "In this painting, a simulacrum masterpiece, numerous images of Celebrity Marilyn (simulacrum Marilyn) and Death Marilyn (real life Marilyn) are side by side. Celebrity Marilyn is excessively, garishly painted, but her image, literally, and figuratively, is intact in all twenty-five portrayals. But in Death Marilyn, there is hardly a clean replication of her image to be found. If she is not severely eradicated from the picture via black ink, she is non-existent and slipping off the page. It is in Celebrity silkscreens such as this that Warhol succeeds in capturing Death and Celebrity in culture 'America' via the simulacrum—for it is Monroe's superstar Celebrity image, superficial and beautifully vacant, that can remain unscathed after her Death." Cowser, 1998: 9. Cf. Pollock, 2017, Churchwell, 2004, Baty, 1995.
40  Baudrillard, 1988: 41.

41 In this spirit, a recent protechnology conference fed its attendees—no scientific studies needed, please—from a conference banquet celebrating what it called "Frankenstein" food as a point of honor.
42 See, taking our own cyborg extendedness as point of departure, Bateman, 2018 in addition to, among many other authors, Gertz, 2018, Devlin, 2018, and Gunkel, 2018.
43 Cowser, 1998: 8.
44 Baudrillard, "Starting from Andy Warhol (1990)" in *Baudrillard,* 2005: 43 et seq.
45 Lee, 2016.
46 See for references on Danto and Warhol, Andina, 2000, as well as Danto himself, most recently in Danto, 2013.
47 See for a discussion, Babich, 2018.
48 See Babich, 2017a.
49 *The Hallelujah Effect* thus reviews the pop music of Leonard Cohen (1934–2016) filtered through various "covers" of his *Hallelujah*—specifically k.d. lang but also the more universally preferred male artists associated with that work, like Bob Dylan or Jeff Buckley or Rufus Wainwright. Andy Green of the *Rolling Stone* features the 1988 audio version in his article "Flashback: Bob Dylan Covers Leonard Cohen's 'Hallelujah': Long Before the 'Hallelujah' Craze, Dylan Covered the Tune during a 1988 Never Ending Tour stop in Montreal," *Rolling Stone,* 13 October 2016. See for the audio link: https://www.rollingstone.com/music/videos/flashback-bob-dylan-covers-leonard-cohens-hallelujah-w444773.
50 Adorno, 2006. See for further discussion, Babich, 2014: 957–96.
51 Nietzsche, *Human, All too Human,* §294.
52 See Baudrillard, 1968, and 1970.
53 Robyn Meredith, "Numbers by Painting," *Forbes* (January 10, 2007).
54 Caygill, 1998.
55 See for one discussion, Tang, 2016.
56 Fuller, 2011.
57 See for an overview, Judovitz, 1995: 124 et seq.
58 This same challenge would inspire Christo and Jean Claude to market their project, *The Gates* by issuing effectively canonized "first" editions in the form of signed project drafts or sketches. The event as event captured public imagination: a cover of Christo's former covering actions.
59 Babette Babich, *People Wash (Menschenwaschanlage oder Schlendern durch Christo und Jeanne-Claude, The Gates).* Central Park, New York City, February 22, 2005. In Babich, 2009: 113, a copy of the 2006 illustration, appears—precisely thanks to the design exigence of the Bauhaus University Press—in full color.
60 Wang, 2013.
61 Danto, 2013.
62 See again, Virilio, 2003.

63  I discuss some of this in Babich 2019.
64  Wang, 2013.
65  Ibid.
66  *Thing-in-Itself: Utopia, Pop and Personal Theology—Wang Guangyi Retrospective Exhibition* (2012.10.14—2012.11.27), Today Art Museum, Beijing.
67  Wang, 2013.
68  Ibid.
69  See Brock, 1977: 561 et seq. and 764 et seq.
70  To this extent, *ceteris paribus* (i.e., with addition of a certain intensity, Brock is not named "Bazon" for nothing), Brock exemplifies Baudrillard's good humored description of Warhol: "Everything that characterizes his work—the advent of banality, the mechanized gestures and images, and especially his iconolatry—he turned all of that into an event of platitude. It is him and nobody else!" Baudrillard, 1990: 43.
71  See for comparison, Danto and DeSalvo, 2003.
72  I discuss the culture of non-citation explicitly in Babich, 2017c: 259–90.
73  See, in addition to the Italian cited above, the English version of Tiziana Andina, 2011, as well as Béla Bacsó's discussion of Danto in connection with his catalog essay (Bacsó, 2012). Note that my point is not gainsaid by honorific collective studies (i.e., Rollins, 2012) nor indeed typical festschrifty collections as these are often more diffuse than their ostensive focus on Danto. See, too, in German and in addition to Michael Lüthy's occasional reflections, Katharina Bahlmann's and Daniel Martin Feige's necrologue, via Nelson Goodman who has long continued to be influential in Germany (Bahlmann and Feige, 2014).
74  See Babich, 2017c.
75  See Kakuzo, 1906. This is a work in English as Okakura received his first education in English (a typical consequence or result of Western imperialist educational conventionalism, which is also evident in Okakura's own reflections) before studying Japanese and Chinese. Okakura's book was written specifically for English readers and has been subsequently re-rendered, more than once, back into Japanese and into thirty languages. See on this, the Romanian scholar's discussion of the working (forward and backwards) of this translation of (and on) Japanese culture, Holca, 2013: 85–103 and see, too, Fuwa, 2005: 13–19. See for comparison, on *wabi sabi*, Koren, 1994 and Liu Carriger, 2009: 140–57, who, in turn, draws for her performance analysis on Hirota, 1995 and Soshitsu Sen, 1979.
76  See, again for discussion, Holca, 2013.
77  See Pound, 1950 and 1963. And for one discussion, see Williams, 2009: 145–65.
78  Adorno, 2015 and see too Horkheimer & Adorno, 1972, as Adorno and Eisler, 2005.
79  Koren, 1994: 7. See for a very indirect but philosophical discussion, Babich, 2015: 1–10.

80  Okakura, 1906: 10.
81  Ibid.: 9.
82  See here a note in Reinhard May, *Heidegger's Hidden Sources: East Asian Influences on his Work* (London: Routledge, 1996), 118. May refers to the claim that »*In-der-Welt-sein*« appears in the German translation of Okakura's 1906 book, which as May reports here, was said to have been presented to Heidegger in 1919. May does not cite the German text which is itself translated from English: "Die chinesischen Historiker haben vom Taoismus stets als von der »Kunst des In-der-Welt-Seins« geredet, denn er handelt von der Gegenwart, von uns selbst. In uns begegnet Gott der Natur, scheidet das Gestern sich vom Morgen. Die Gegenwart ist die sich bewegende Unendlichkeit, die legitime Sphäre des Relativen. Die Relativität sucht die Anpassung; Anpassung aber ist Kunst. Die Kunst des Lebens beruht in der konstanten Anpassung an unsere Umgebung. Der Taoismus nimmt das Weltliche hin, wie es ist, und sucht, im Gegensatz zu Konfuzius und den Buddhisten, nach Schönheit in unserer Welt der Pein und Klagen." Okakura 1919 [Orig.: *Chinese historians have always spoken of Taoism as the "art of being in the world," for it deals with the present—ourselves. It is in us that God meets with Nature, and yesterday parts from to-morrow. The Present is the moving Infinity, the legitimate sphere of the Relative. Relativity seeks Adjustment; Adjustment is Art. The art of life lies in a constant readjustment to our surroundings. Taoism accepts the mundane as it is and, unlike the Confucians or the Buddhists, tries to find beauty in our world of woe and worry*. Okakura, *Book of Tea*, 58] To be sure, had one wished to show Okakura's influence on Heidegger, one might have begun a little earlier in the same chapter, where Okakura writes, self-referentially: "Translation is always a treason, and as a Ming author observes, can at its best be only the reverse side of a brocade,—all the threads are there, but not the subtlety of colour or design. But, after all, what great doctrine is there which is easy to expound?" Okakura, 1906: 48.
83  Okakura, 1906: 92.
84  See, cited above, Babich, 2017c.
85  Okarura, 1906: 87–8.
86  Cowan and Cowan, 1962: 30.
87  Reference is drawn here from Huang and Wang, 2013.
88  See Certeau, 1980.
89  Danto, 2013 and Danto, 1997. See for comparison, as Danto titles his own book forty years later in response to George Dickie's influential, "What Is Art? An Institutional Analysis" in: Dickie, 1974.
90  Illich, 1996.
91  Note that one might find the same sensibility in Eisenstein or Bergmann's 1957 *The Seventh Seal* or Gabriel Axel's 1987 *Babette's Feast*, Orson Welles' 1942 *Citizen Kane*, or Alain Corneau's 1991 film: *Tous les Matins du Monde*.

92  Jagodzinski, 2010: 46.
93  Cohen, 2012.
94  Online: 26 Apr 2013—16 Jun 2013, DUCHAMP and/or/in CHINA, Ullens Center for Contemporary Art. www.google.com/culturalinstitute/beta/exhibit/wRR7AVkv. Accessed December 26, 2017.
95  Smith, 2006: 85.
96  See Guertin, 2012.
97  Wang Guangyi Solo Exhibition, "Negatives of Idols," November 16, 2014. Springs Center of Art, Beijing.
98  I discuss Jeff Koons in Babich, 2012: 50, 58–69.
99  Baudrillard, "Simulacra and Simulations," Poster and Mourrain, 2002, 169. Originally published as *Simulacra and Simulations*, in Baudrillard and Foss, 1983.
100 Ibid.: 170.

# References

Adorno, T. W. (2015). *Culture Industry: Selected essays on mass culture*. Abingdon: Routledge.

Adorno, T. W., and Eisler, H. (2005). *Composing for the Films*. London: A&C Black.

Adorno, T. W., and Hullot-Kentor, R. (2006). *Current of Music: Elements of a radio theory*. Cambridge: Polity.

Agamben, G. (2009). *"What is an Apparatus?" and Other Essays*. Palo Alto: Stanford University Press.

Agamben, G. (2009). "What Is the Contemporary?" In Agamben, G. *"What Is an Apparatus?" and Other Essays*. Palo Alto: Stanford University Press.

Anders, G. (1980). *Die Antiquertheit des Mensch. Zweiter Band. Über die Zerstörung des Lebens im Zeitalter der dritten industriellen Revolution*. Munich: Beck.

Andersen, B., Kozul-Wright, R., and Kozul-Wright, Z. (2007). Rents, Rights N'Rhythm: Cooperation, conflict and capabilities in the music industry. *Industry and Innovation*, 14(5): 513–40.

Andina, T. (2010). *Arthur Danto: un filosofo pop*. Roma: Carocci; Engl. trans. *Arthur Danto: Philosopher of Pop*. Cambridge: Cambridge Scholars Publishing.

Attali, J. (2003). *Noise: The Political Economy of Music*. Trans. Brian Massumi Minneapolis: University of Minnesota Press.

Bahlmann, K., and Feige, D. M. (2014). "Arthur C. Dantos Kunstphilosophie. Eine kritische Bestandsaufnahme." *Zeitschrift für Kulturphilosophe*, 8(2): 323–41.

Babich, B. (2007). Greek Bronze: Holding a Mirror to Life. *Yearbook of the Irish Philosophical Society 2006*, 7: 1–30.

Babich, B. (2009). "Une promesse de bonheur"—Von Plastik zu Poesie. In: Wilke, S. (ed.) *Die Glücklichen sind neugierig* (7–43). Weimar: Verlag der Bauhaus Universität.

Babich, B. (2012). The Aesthetics of the Between: Space and Beauty. In Brinkmann, V., Ulrich, M., and Pissarro, J. (eds.) *Jeff Koons. The Sculptor* (58–69). Frankfurt: Schirn Kunsthalle Frankfurt.

Babich, B. (2014). Adorno's Radio Phenomenology: Technical Reproduction, Physiognomy and Music. *Philosophy and Social Criticism*, 40(10): 957–96.

Babich, B. (2015). Heidegger on Technology and Gelassenheit: Wabi-sabi and the Art of Verfallenheit. *AI and society, Journal of Knowledge, Culture and Communication*, 32(2): 1–10.

Babich, B. (2017a). *The Hallelujah Effect: Philosophical Reflections on Music, Performance Practice, and Technology*. Abingdon: Routledge.

Babich, B. (2017b). From Winkelmann's Apollo to Nietzsche's Dionysus. In Reschke, R. (ed.), *Nietzsche Forschung. »…An Winkelmann anzuknüpfen …«? Winckelmanns Antike, Nietzsches Klassizismuskritik und ihre Blicke in die Zukunft* (167–92). Berlin: de Gruyter.

Babich, B. (2017c). Are They Good? Are They Bad? Double Hermeneutics and Citation in Philosophy, Asphodel and Alan Rickman Bruno Latour and the "Science Wars." In Angelova, P. et al. (eds.) *Das Interpretative Universum* (239–70). Würzburg: Königshausen & Neumann.

Babich, B. (2018). Musical "Covers" and the Culture Industry. *Research in Phenomenology*, 48(3): 385–407.

Babich, B. (2019) "The Question of the Contemporary in Agamben, Virilio, Danto: Nietzsche's Artist — Nietzsche's Spectator." In Assis, P. de and M. Schwab (eds.) *Futures of the Contemporary*. Leiden: University of Leiden Press.

Bacsó, B. (2012). Reductive Art. The Work of János Megyik. In *János Megyik. The Space of the Image* (268–73). Budapest: Ludwig Múzeum/Museum of Contemporary Art.

Bardini, T. (2011). *Junkware (Posthumanities)*. Minneapolis: University of Minnesota Press.

Bateman, C. (2018). *The Virtuous Cyborg*. London: Eyewear Publishing.

Baty, S. P. (1995). *American Monroe: The Making of a Body Politic*. Berkeley: University of California Press.

Baudrillard, J. (1968). *Le système des objets*, vol. 33. Paris: Gallimard.

Baudrillard, J. (1970). *The Consumer Society: Myths and structures*. Paris: Gallimard.

Baudrillard, J. (1988). *America*. New York: Verso.

Baudrillard, J. (1990). Starting from Andy Warhol. In Baudrillard, J. (2005). *The Conspiracy of Art*. New York: Semiotext (e): 115.

Baudrillard, J. (2005). *The Conspiracy of Art*, New York: Semiotext (e).

Baudrillard, J., and Foss, P. (1983). *Simulations*. New York: Semiotext (e).

Baudrillard, J., and Levin, C. (1981). *For a Critique of the Political Economy of the Sign*, vol. 262. St. Louis: Telos Press.

Bolton, L. (2002). *Andy Warhol*. London: Franklin Watts.

Brilliant, R. (2000). *My Laocoön: Alternative claims in the interpretation of artworks*, vol. 8. Berkeley: University of California Press.
Brock, B. (1977). *Ästhetik als Vermittlung. Arbeitsbiographien eines Generalisten*. Köln: DuMont.
Catterson, L. (2005). Michelangelo's "Laocoön?" *Artibus et historiae*, 52: 29–56.
Caygill, H. (1998). *Walter Benjamin: The colour of experience*. London: Routledge.
Caygill, H., Coles, A., and Klimowski, A. (2015). *Introducing Walter Benjamin: A graphic guide*. London: Icon Books.
Charney, N. (2015). *The Art of Forgery: The minds, motives and methods of master forgers*. London: Phaidon Press.
Chang, C. (2003). Beyond Pop's Image: The Immateriality of Everyday Life. *Bulletin*, 15: 5–24.
Churchwell, S. (2004). *The Many Lives of Marilyn Monroe*. London: Granta Books.
Clair, J., and Duchamp, M. (2000). *Sur Marcel Duchamp et la fin de l'art*. Paris: Gallimard.
Cohen, A. (2012). "Reasoning with Idols: Wang Guangyi," *ArtAsiaPacific*. Mar/Apr http://artasiapacific.com/Magazine/77/ReasoningWithIdolsWangGuangyi. Accessed December 21, 2017.
Cook, R. (2003). Andy Warhol, Capitalism, Culture, and Camp. *Space and Culture*, 6(1): 66–76.
Cowan, M., and Cowan, M. (1962). *Friedrich Nietzsche: Philosophy in the tragic age of the Greeks*. Chicago: Regnery.
Cowser, B. (1998). The Culture "America": Warhol, Celebrity, Death and the Simulacrum. *The Sloping Halls Review*. 5: 7–12.
Danto A. C. (2013). *What Art Is*. New Haven: Yale University Press.
Danto A. and DeSalvo, D. (2003). *Andy Warhol Prints: A Catalogue Raisonné 1962–1987*. New York: D.A.P/Ronald Feldman Fine Arts/Andy Warhol Foundation for the Visual Arts.
Danto, A. C., and Goehr, L. (1997). *After the End of Art: Contemporary art and the pale of history*, vol. 197. Princeton: Princeton University Press.
De Certeau, M. (1980). *The Practice of Everyday Life*. Berkeley: University of California Press.
Devlin, K. (2018). *Turned On: Science, Sex and Robots*. London: Bloomsbury.
Dickie, G. (1974). *Art and the Aesthetic: An institutional analysis*. Ithaca, NY: Cornell University Press.
Feldman, F., Schellmann, J., and Defendi, C. (2003). *Andy Warhol Prints: A Catalogue Raisonné 1962–1987*. New York: DAP.
Fisher III, W. W. (2004). *Promises to Keep: Technology, law, and the future of entertainment*. Palo Alto: Stanford University Press.
Foster, H. (2002). The Deathly Double. *London Review of Books*. https://www.theguardian.com/books/2002/mar/18/warhol.
Fried, M. (1998). *Art and Objecthood: Essays and reviews*. Chicago: University of Chicago Press.

Fuller, S. (2011). *Humanity 2.0: What it Means to be Human Past, Present and Future.* London: Palgrave.

Fuwa, N. T. (2004). Translation as a Counter-Colonial Tool: Okakura Kakuzo's The Book of Tea. *Studies in English and American Literature*, 40: 13–19.

Gertz, N. (2018). *Nihilism and Technology.* Lanham: Rowman & Littlefield.

Gillick, L. (2010). Contemporary Art Does Not Account for that Which is Taking Place. *e-flux Journal*, 21. https://www.e-flux.com/journal/21/67664/contemporary-art-does-not-account-for-that-which-is-taking-place/

Goldstein, R. (1967). Pop Eye. *Village Voice*, 19.

Guertin, C. (2012). *Digital Prohibition: Piracy and authorship in new media art.* New York: Bloomsbury Publishing USA.

Gunkel, D. J. (2007). Blind Faith: Baudrillard, Fidelity, and Recorded Sound. *International Journal of Baudrillard Studies*, 4(2): 1–13.

Gunkel, D. J. (2008). Rethinking the Digital Remix: Mash-ups and the Metaphysics of Sound Recording. *Popular Music and Society*, 31(4), 489–510.

Gunkel, D. J. (2016). *Of Remixology: Ethics and Aesthetics after Remix.* Cambridge: MIT Press.

Gunkel, D. J. (2018). *Robot Rights.* Cambridge: MIT Press.

Hatfield, R. (2002). *The Wealth of Michelangelo.* Rome: Edizioni di storia e letteratura.

Heartney, E. (1999). Andy's icons. *Art in America*, 87(6): 35–7.

Hebdige, D. (2003). *Cutn'Mix: Culture, identity and Caribbean music.* London: Routledge.

Heinich, N. (1996). *The Glory of van Gogh: An anthropology of admiration.* Princeton: Princeton University Press.

Hesmondhalgh, D., and Meier, L. M. (2018). What the Digitalisation of Music Tells Us about Capitalism, Culture and the Power of the Information Technology Sector. *Information, Communication and Society*, 21(11): 1555–70.

Hirota, D. (1995). *Wind in the Pines: Classic writings of the Way of Tea as a Buddhist Path.* Fremont, CA: Asian Humanities Press.

Holca, I. (2013). Around the World with a Book: Okakura Kakuzo's *The Book of Tea* and its Transformations. *Analele Universitatii Crestine Dimitrie Cantemir, Seria Stiintele Limbii, Literaturii si Didactica predarii*, 1: 85–103.

Hoesterey, I. (ed.). (1991). *Zeitgeist in Babel: The Post-Modernist Controversy.* Bloomington: Indiana University Press.

Horkheimer, M., and Adorno, T. W. (1972). *Dialectic of Enlightenment.* New York: Herder and Herder.

Huang, Z. (2014). *Politics and Theology in Chinese Contemporary Art: Reflections on the work of Wang Guangyi.* Paris: Skira.

Huang, Z., and Wang, G. (2013). *Politics and Theology in Chinese Contemporary Art: Reflections on the work of Wang Guangyi.* Milan: Skira.

Hull, G. P. (2004). The Music Business and Recording Industry. New York: Psychology Press.

Illich, I. (1996). *In the Vineyard of the Text: A commentary to Hugh's Didascalicon.* Chicago: University of Chicago Press.

Jagodzinski, J. (2010). *Visual Art and Education in an Era of Designer Capitalism: Deconstructing the oral eye.* Frankfurt am Main: Springer.

Judovitz, D. (1998). *Unpacking Duchamp: Art in transit.* Palo Alto: University of California Press.

Koestenbaum, W. (2005). *Andy Warhol.* London: Weidenfeld.

Kohn, A., and Kohn, B. (2002). *Kohn on Music Licensing.* Bob Kohn.

Krauss, R. E. (1986). *The Originality of the Avant-Garde and Other Modernist Myths.* Cambridge, MA: MIT Press.

Lenain, T. (2012). *Art Forgery: The history of a modern obsession.* London: Reaktion Books.

Leonard, K. (1994). *Wabi-Sabi for Artists, Designers, Poets and Philosophers.* Berkeley: Stone Bridge Press.

Leonard, W. (1952). Tower Ticker. *Chicago Daily Tribune.*

Lessig, L. (2008). *Remix: Making art and commerce thrive in the hybrid economy.* London: Penguin.

Levay, W. J. (2005). The Art of Making Music in the Age of Mechanical Reproduction: The Culture Industry Remixed. *Anamesa: An Interdisciplinary Journal*, 2(1): 21–38.

Liu Carriger, M. (2009). Consuming Culture: The Japanese Way of Tea in Performance. In Counsell, C. and Mock, R. (eds.) *Performance, Embodiment, and Cultural Memory* (140–57). Cambridge: Cambridge Scholars.

May, R. (2005). *Heidegger's Hidden Sources: East-Asian influences on his work.* London: Routledge.

McLean, Don (2004) "On the Incorrect Use of the Term 'Cover.'" https://don-mclean.com/2004/08/26/cover-versions/. Accessed 21 January 2018.

Nancy, J. L. (2010). Art Today. *Journal of Visual Culture*, 9(1), 91–99.

Navas, E., and Gallagher, O. (eds.). (2017). *Keywords in Remix Studies.* New York: Routledge.

Newman, M. (1999). After Conceptual Art: Joe Scanlan's Nesting Bookcases, Duchamp, Design and the Impossibility of Disappearing. In Newman, M. and Bird, J. (eds.). (1999). *Rewriting Conceptual Art (Critical Views)* (206–11). London: Reaktion.

Nietzsche, F. W. (2012). *Philosophy in the Tragic Age of the Greeks.* Regnery Publishing.

Okakura, K. (2012). *The Book of Tea.* New York: Duffield and Company.

Osborne, P. (2013). *Anywhere or Not at All: Philosophy of contemporary art.* London: Verso.

Padgett, R. (2017). *Cover Me: The stories behind the greatest cover songs of all time.* New York: Sterling.

Griselda Pollock, P. (2017). The Missing Wit(h)ness: Monroe, Fascinance and the Unguarded Intimacy of Being Dead. *Journal of Visual Art Practice*, 16(3), 265–96.

Poster, M., and Mourrain, J. (2002). *Jean Baudrillard: Selected writings*. Stanford: Stanford University Press.

Pound, E. (1950). *The Cantos of Ezra Pound*. New York: New Directions.

Pound, E. (1950). *Translations*. New York: New Directions.

Rabinow, P. (2011). *The Accompaniment: Assembling the contemporary*. Chicago: University of Chicago Press.

Reynolds, S. (2011). *Retromania: Pop culture's addiction to its own past*. New York: Farrar, Straus and Giroux.

Rollins, M. (ed.). (2012). *Danto and His Critics*, vol. 11. John Wiley & Sons.

Sen, S., and Sen, S. (1979). *Tea Life, Tea Mind*. Boston: Weatherhill.

Shemel, S., and Krassilowsky, M. W. (2007). *This Business of Music*. New York: Watson-Guptill Publications.

Smith, K. (2008). *Nine Lives: The birth of avant-garde art in new China*. Timezone 8 Limited.

Smith, T. (2010). The State of Art History: Contemporary art. *The Art Bulletin*, 92(4), 366–83.

Tang, X. (2016). Socialist Visual Experience as Cultural Identity: On Wang Guangyi and contemporary art. In Li, J. and Zhang, E (eds.), *Red Legacies in China: Cultural Afterlives of the Communist Revolution*. Cambridge, MA: Harvard University Press.

Virilio, P. (2003). *Art & Fear*. London: Continuum.

Wang, G. (2013). On Andy Warhol: Perhaps Simplicity Outshines Complexity. In post.moma.org. Original Chinese version: *The Beijing News*, October 9, 2013.

Wallis, Si et al. (eds.) (2002). *Remix: Contemporary Art & Pop*. London: Tate Publishing.

Williams, R. J. (2009). Modernist Scandals: Ezra Pound's Translations of 'the' Chinese Poem. In: Sielke, S. and Kloeckner, C. (eds.), *Orient and Orientalism in US American Poetry and Poetics*. Bern: Peter Lang.

Xuan, L. J. (2016). Art Titans: Wang Guangyi. *The Straits Times*, January 19.

# 8

# The Globalist Dimension of Art: Wang Guangyi and Transculturalism

Davide Dal Sasso 沙毅奇

## Introduction

The development of technology, along with communication and transportation systems, has been decisive for the conformation of the current globalist context, characterized by an intensification of the exchange between models and references of different cultural origins. This process inevitably involves artistic production. What exactly are the outcomes that have been achieved in this respect? And, in light of this productive cultural exchange, what is the current condition of art?

To answer these questions, I will first consider the perspective of a "transnational hybridization"[1] between different cultures, through which art can be understood as a social phenomenon following the rules and relations between institutional structures that work in a fragmentary rather than uniform way, as we are often mistakenly inclined to believe.[2] Then I will address this perspective by evaluating the globalist dimension of art in relation to both transculturalism—understood as a reciprocal exchange between cultures that has been implemented in the last thirty years—and the coexistence of traditionalist and conceptualist creative-procedural models, which (individually or combined) contribute to define the current condition of art. Here is my proposal. The following factors define the globalist dimension of today's art: on the one hand, transnational hybridizations and transculturalism, that is, the reciprocal influence between different cultural models; on the other hand, the artists' adoption or rejection of traditional or conceptual operational rules and their choice to achieve innovative syntheses through their potential combination.

In order to evaluate whether this theoretical perspective is sustainable, after presenting this framework, I will take oriental artistic production as a reference model, investigating in particular the works of the Chinese artist Wang Guangyi. The reasons for this choice are the following: his production exemplifies the current globalist dimension of art, understood as the outcome of both the influence of Western culture on the Eastern one, and the impact of the latter on the former. Wang Guangyi adopts a dual operative methodology, so his works allow me to evaluate the innovations and specificities deriving from the affirmation of conceptualism in the context of Chinese artistic production. Moreover, much of his work manifests continuity between traditional and contemporary art. Therefore, it also shows the persistence of certain processes typical of traditional art that still remain on the agenda in today's art.

## The Regions of the Global Village and the Transnational Hybridization

The present condition of culture and art—and, inevitably, their relationship—in the light of the considerable changes due to globalization can be investigated from a different perspective than the one usually adopted: the perspective of fragmentation rather than uniformity. From this standpoint, one should also consider the forms assumed by relations and institutions in place because of the various cultural structures whose mixture is neither global nor local. Instead of thinking of the world in the metaphorical terms of a "global village," that is, according to a standardization of cultural models as if they coagulated into a uniform whole, we should consider the fragmentations, regional diversities, and relational processes that favor transitions and exchanges. This is the perspective advocated by Noël Carroll.[3]

There are several reasons to support this view, according to Carroll. First of all, it is necessary to consider that not all the geographical areas of the planet are integrated so as to share the same commercial, economic, monetary, communicative conditions, and so forth that we are used to today, so we cannot state that there is a global interconnection network that is now valid for the whole world. Second, globalization can be understood as an advanced stage of capitalism that, on the one hand, amplifies the new possibilities of exchange and commercial interaction but, on the other, also increases fractures and gaps between the various economic actors involved in commercial and cultural exchanges—which, on closer inspection, existed before capitalism and its modern social affirmation.

In this regard, Carroll notes that current globalization has an "immemorial lineage,"[4] and he mentions Alexander the Great (who as we know contributed to the spread of Greek culture in the Ancient World), trade between Europe and Asia, the Silk Road, and the Mongol and Muslim conquests that helped to put in contact most of the world. Therefore, the idea that globalization corresponds to a specific phase of our recent history is a bit thin, because when it comes to commercial development there is a long historical tradition prior to capitalism and its current logic. Therefore, globalization seems rather like the repetition of a model of exchanges and relationships that has already occurred in the past and is being implemented again today. Third, the impact of the media and the fast and extensive transformations of communication, rather than contributing to standardization of the continuous acceleration of information exchanges, shows an evident diversification of the types and degrees of communication itself.

Perhaps, regardless of the label used, the historical phase we are referring to is nothing more than the recent recovery of a process that has been going on for centuries, Carroll notes. However, the world today appears as "one world,"[5] and this is largely due to the convergence of different cultures that allows people to experiment with, and share, dishes, customs, and practices that occur in geographical areas different from those of their origin. Much of this process is supported by media communication, decisive for what Carroll calls "transnational hybridization."[6] The media are everywhere; they are based on a massive use of images—and this confirms the central role of icons in our societies—and they are decisive to bridging gaps and facilitating exchanges of information. However, as already mentioned, the latter does not happen uniformly on a planetary scale.

At the same time, art manifests its transnational condition through the succession of multiple hybridizations that determine its continuous mutation. What does this mean exactly? First, that art is far more regional than global— "if by 'global' we mean to refer to something homogeneous in every corner of the world."[7] Second, that the globalist dimension of art is due in large part to the appropriation of models and references coming from artistic and cultural expressions of various origins. Let me try to look closer at these first points.

"On the one hand we want to say that it is undeniable that we have entered a new era of globalization both in general and with respect to art. But, on the other hand, with just a little pressure, the notion of globalization in both respects appears to come apart."[8]

The involvement of national actors in the process of globalization takes place in a heterogeneous way. As Carroll notes, this happens on a regional rather than a global scale. The very pervasiveness of the global connection system is questionable. So much so that hybridization, a mark of the current artistic expressions, is not exclusively due to the spread of the Internet. Hybridization is not, in fact, a recent phenomenon. However, these observations do not amount to claiming that there have been no changes compared to the past. On the contrary, they support the need to understand the concept of "globalization," not in terms of a totality, or of a Hegelian *Zeitgeist*, but in those of a non-cohesive network of "transnational relations" that are developing on different levels and following different rules and norms.[9]

Considering the possible forms that these relationships can take, the examination of globalization requires an understanding of the modes of transnational organization. That is, the new types of cultural structures that characterize our world locally. An example of this relational condition is the art world, a "transnational and integrated" institution.[10] If we think of it in global terms, as happens in the majority of cases, we encounter several difficulties: many artists do not belong to this global institution because they do not participate in big international exhibitions or are known only at a regional (if not provincial) level. According to the alternative conception, namely, considering the art world as a "single, integrated, cosmopolitan institution ... organized transnationally,"[11] it is possible to understand the participation of several artists in the overlap of traditions and practices, converging in the international presentation and distribution network of their art. This also makes it possible to explain why numerous artists active on the international scene are manifesting this transnational hybridization through their research (think, for example, of artists Candice Breitz and Fiona Tan, Gabriel Orozco, Rirkrit Tiravanija, or director Tsai Ming-liang).

The methods of exchange are what make the difference between the current transnational system of art and that of the past. Since the fifteenth century there have always been considerable exchanges between the East and the West. There are numerous works that prove this, attesting to the hybridization between different cultural models—Carroll cites a detail of Hans Holbein's painting, *The Ambassadors* (1533): the carpet depicted is of Ottoman origin. This hybridization confirms a historical precedent of exchanges and influences between Oriental and Western models. However, even if Oriental artifacts, decorative motifs, and craftsmanship were appreciated by Westerners, no Eastern artwork or author appears in the historical narrative of European art.

The history of art has developed following a regional linearity. "A European might collect Chinese porcelain or drawings, or, for that matter, later, pre-Columbian art, but these collectibles and the artists who created them did not enter the 'big story' of art as it was told in the West."[12] Despite the influence of Oriental art on the Western one, the two narratives and canons remained distinct. In the past, Oriental art has been conceived as foreign to the Western one, although it has had a considerable impact on the evolution of the latter. This distinction has been so incisive that it has led to the assumption that there are two different worlds of art.

The various regional and national poles converge in the current transnational art world, based on methods of exchange and hybridization that contribute to a cultural reciprocity that holds together a large number of artists, works, curators, and artistic projects from different geographical areas. Transnational hybridization stands out even more in the large international exhibition systems: festivals, biennials, quadrennials, and so forth. In Carroll's words:

> The base of the emerging transnational institution of art includes its network of coordinated venues, its "always-on-the-go" curatorial-managerial class, and its preferred productive idioms. But it is also held together by means of a number of shared discourses, both artistic and critical. Artists, presenters, critics and just plain art devotees share a number of conceptual frameworks and hermeneutical strategies that facilitate understanding transnationally.[13]

On the one hand, the large exhibition systems attest to the continuous rebalancing of the art world on the basis of transnational rules and regulations as well as institutional figures, especially critics and curators. On the other hand, they manifest the current expressive combination that characterizes today's art in close relation to its globalist dimension. With regard to this second point, Carroll notes that art forms such as painting and sculpture are less privileged today, especially when compared to the adoption of other expressive means such as photography, video, and installations. These are new forms of expression that, also by incorporating the critical component that characterizes the new art, from within such a system of transnational relations re-hybridize with social and political contestation, directly criticizing museums, art institutions, and the international exhibition system—that is to say: the art world. According to Carroll, in accordance with the current art world, a new model of conversation has also been imposed, one that involves all its actors: "transnational conversations" involving those who produce and those who receive art by virtue of various idioms, language games, themes and "sense-making strategies."[14]

The globalist dimension of art is therefore compatible with hybridization, with transnational relations, and with a meaningful production system that attest to the continuous consolidation between different art and cultures. These are the signs of an art world that should not be understood in the sense proposed by the philosopher George Dickie, but in that of a "cultural escape" characterized by its language games and its communication, distribution, and reception networks.[15]

## Directions of Modern Art

A significant passage in Carroll's analysis—largely shareable, especially in relation to his attempt to understand the current condition of art, bringing transnational relations and hybridizations to the fore—is the one concerning the shared strategies for the production of meaning and for associative courses that characterize contemporary art. In order for this exchange and sharing to be possible, there has to be a discursive structure shared transnationally by artists, the public, and other actors of the art world. The strategies for the production of meaning are in fact based on mutual knowledge on the part of the artist, users, and other actors of the art world. The artist uses these strategies, being aware both that the public and the other actors know them, and that they are "formal devices" frequently adopted in contemporary art. Shared language games are thus formulated on the basis of methods such as: radical juxtaposition, estrangement, or ways to decontextualize objects and images from their usual settings.[16]

In my view, this sharing is made possible also by virtue of what we can consider as the traditional creative model that still holds in contemporary art, despite the numerous innovations introduced throughout the last century. Parallel to the introduction of conceptualist practices, painting and sculpture have retained their centrality. Given the innovative communication possibilities offered by tools such as photography and video, as Carroll remarks, these practices are less privileged but have not completely disappeared.[17] And this is very important. If we consider the artistic production of the twentieth century, we cannot help recognizing that painting and sculpture have remained part of the different artistic experimentations that have gone on until today. From the avant-garde to abstract expressionism, op art, pop, and hyperrealism, up to transavantgarde, graffiti art, and the most recent multimedia and photographic combinations—again focusing on iconic manipulation and dissemination—art is still based on the operational rules, conventions and procedures of the past. These are certainly modified depending on the context, but they retain their traditional normative core. Therefore, contemporary artworks are still largely paintings and sculptures. Of course, this does not mean that art today is the same as in the past. Rather, its evolution is due both to the affirmation of conceptualism and to the preservation of a traditionalist creative and procedural model; these two models—conceptualist and traditionalist—can potentially combine in view of a pluralist synthesis, as shown by the artistic production of the last thirty years.

This evolutionary structure—decisive for art to be either conceptual or traditional, or else a pluralist synthesis of the two—can be recognized by examining the various artistic productions of our time. Both in Western and in Eastern societies, it is possible to see both the outcomes of conceptualism and those of traditional conventions and procedures, decisive for current artistic practices to be (also) a continuation of those of the past. Two main factors mark the traditionalist model: (1) according to it, the development of art takes place mainly within the pictorial and sculptural production; (2) it aims at maintaining the visual salience of the works, largely through the use of iconic appropriation and dissemination practices, decisive for the purposes of their social valorization.

Therefore, several different factors define the current condition of art. First, its globalist dimension, based on transnational relations and institutions that emphasize local and regional contexts. Second, the pluralist synthesis obtained by combining the rules for artistic creation of the traditionalist and the conceptualist models. Finally, the mutual cultural influences between East and West that have mostly intensified during the last thirty years.

## The Twentieth Century in China

In the 1980s there was a general resumption of conventional artistic procedures in reaction to conceptualism. This return to pictorial and sculptural productions in defense of craftsmanship and of iconic dissemination spread in the United States, in Europe, and soon also in China. Chinese contemporary art can be considered both the result of the adoption of stylistic and representational models typical of modern European art, taken up by numerous artists during the first half of the twentieth century, and the affirmation of a reflection on subjectivity elaborated in the 1990s through the work of numerous artists active since the late 1970s.

The revival of modernist experimentation took place in the early 1980s, when China was home to numerous artistic groups that converged in the '85 New Wave Movement.[18] It was a heterogeneous movement that was diversified on a geographical scale. The artists of the North promoted works characterized by symbolism understood as a variant of the European modernist models, trying to express their interest in theology and in the philosophical speculations inspired by Hegel and Nietzsche. The works of artists active in central China expressed interest in mysticism and the religious experience. The artists of the South-West created works that evoked Expressionist and Surrealist art production, giving great importance to existentialist philosophical speculations. Philosophy of language, science, and hermeneutics were, instead, the objects of the artists of the South-East, who created works of conceptual art.

In the 1990s, Chinese art also engaged in a shared reflection on subjectivity, but was affected by the advance of the economic and systemic model of Western art. According to historian Huang Zhuan, it is possible to discern contemporary Chinese art from the modern one by considering the two main themes addressed by the artists active in the period after 1990: the relationship between conceptual art and linguistics, and the internationalization of Chinese art. Both should be understood as reactions to "the colonial hegemony of Western contemporary art"[19] in the early 1990s. This is the historical and cultural context in which Wang Guangyi began his artistic research.

In the early 1980s, during his academic training, Wang Guangyi concentrated his research on classical art and modern philosophy. The first outcomes of this period are the two pictorial cycles *Frozen North Pole* (see Figure 1.2) and *Post Classical* (see Figure 4.1): both series show the repetition of iconic models belonging to the pictorial production of the past, but also the synthesis of the model of traditionalist production that prevailed in China in those years. This was one of the two reference models of the '85 New Wave Movement. In its heterogeneity, it testifies exactly to the evolutionary order that, in my view, characterizes today's art in its globalist dimension. Both cycles are in fact in full harmony with the return to classicism and conventional practices that characterized the Western artistic productions of the past, making them evolve. Since the second half of the twentieth century the evolution of art has been made possible both by maintaining the traditionalist model, based on conventions and procedures that attest to the continuity between contemporary and past art, and by adopting the conceptual model decisive for the renewal of practices and the subsequent extension of the domain of art to new material entities.

A first remark that can be made here concerns the influence between Eastern and Western cultures. According to historian Huang Zhuan, modern Chinese art "came to accept" the classical artistic tradition from the West and later also the modern and contemporary ones. In this regard, he writes: "modernity and modern art are, after all, Western cultural phenomena, and contemporary Chinese art is the product of the direct influence of contemporary Western art. Only by understanding its conceptual and artistic sources can we engage in an academic evaluation of contemporary Chinese art's unique traits and potential development."[20] With these words Huang Zhuan introduces only the first of the reasons that led him to investigate contemporary Chinese art using theoretical and philosophical models elaborated in Western cultures. The other two reasons are the rejection of impartiality and the denial of a historical interpretation based on the clash with the West, from which Chinese culture and art would have emerged as a response. Rather, he points out that both the Chinese cultural and artistic context and Wang Guangyi's research must be considered in relation to the developments and conception of Chinese Pop Art, to the 1990s passage from the Enlightenment culture to that of consumerism in China, and to the consequent appropriationist method that spread in contemporary Chinese art. These aspects inevitably call for a reflection on the relationship between art and politics, which is useful also to analyze the mutual influence between Eastern and Western culture.

## Art and Politics

In 1985 several Chinese artistic groups joined in the New Wave Movement. The latter also included Wang Guangyi, who at the beginning of his career belonged to the Northern Group. The year is the same as the production of the pictorial cycle *Frozen North Pole*, a symbolic expression of the artist's new goals: the defense of a rationalist view of the world,[21] and the use of iconographic themes typical of the Western historical and religious tradition as opposed to a markedly introspective art. The aim of his pictorial research is not to convey political messages or propaganda, but rather to let the spectator ask several questions about his or her artistic experience and what he or she can *do* with these artworks.[22] In fact, as Wang Guangyi noted, the members of the '85 New Wave Movement engaged in a "pragmatic mode of expression," or an "action program."[23]

The idea that artistic practice can be understood as an action with repercussions on society refers to the relationship between art and politics—a recurring theme in philosophical and theoretical debates on which several contemporary artists have often reflected. In 1985, during a conversation about the relationship between art and politics with the writer Michael Ende, German artist Joseph

Beuys clarified his idea of "social art": an extension of art and of the concept of "art," made possible by human action and participation in society. Beuys defended the liberation of creativity by claiming that art has the anthropological task of reconfiguring the "social body." Instead, Ende believed that the artist's task is the production of images in order to introduce new attitudes aimed at a renewed social *habitus*. Those were two different conceptions of art. Ende's was based on inventiveness, representationality, and ambiguity—criteria that underlie a traditional conception of art and which guarantee the continuous production of new visual forms. Beuys's focused instead on human creative freedom and artistic ability and was aimed at the renewal of society. A central point of discord between the two was the possible cognitive function of art. Ende excluded it completely; Beuys instead considered it the main character of social art which, therefore, has value in relation to social and political actions.[24]

The link between politics and art is also a mark of Wang Guangyi's work. Some have identified it above all in his most famous cycle of paintings, *Great Criticism*, but this means misinterpreting the intentions of its author. Instead of a duplicate of American Pop Art or a form of cynical attestation of Chinese Political Pop, the cycle should be understood as a synthesis of the reflection developed by Wang Guangyi with respect to the program of action, and of spiritual emancipation, that can be achieved through art. *Great Criticism* certainly manifests the dual nature of Chinese Pop Art, based on the convergence between images of China's political history and the places of the capitalist commercial system in the contemporary West.[25] At the same time, I think that the cycle can also be read as one of the first examples that attest to the affirmation of the globalist dimension in contemporary art, based on the reaffirmation of the traditional model by virtue of both transnational hybridizations and the mutual influence between Eastern and Western cultures—that is, in a word, *transculturalism*.

The first signs of this evolutionary process of art go back a few years earlier, to a time marked by the widespread artistic adoption of conceptual practices. Wang Guangyi's research came to a turning point precisely during the ideation of *Great Criticism*, between the late 1980s and early 1990s. Several of his works from this period are based on the adoption of innovative methods offered by conceptualism: *Inflammable and Explosive* (1989) (Figure 8.1) and *Comparison between Chinese and American Temperature* (1990). As several critics have noted, these works attest to both the removal of the artist's "humanist passion,"[26] a legacy of the first phase of his poetics, and a transition in his research toward the return to the traditional model that will later mark the *Great Criticism* cycle. As for the first work, Huang Zhuan notes that the artist has no desire to "shape"

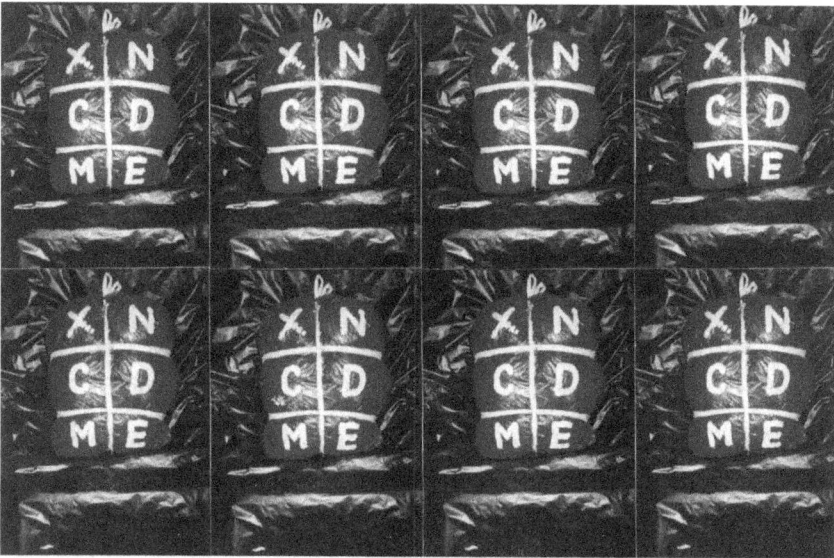

**Figure 8.1** Wang Guangyi, *Inflammable and Explosive* (1989), installation with cotton, plastic bags, etc. 50 × 60 × 35 cm/piece (3 pieces).

the historical instability of that period or to express a political judgment about it. Rather, creating a work close to Arte Povera, Wang Guangyi aimed to translate the crisis by dissolving the problems of reality into reality itself.[27] The work thus anticipates the political approach that will characterize the reflection on different temperatures, entrusted to the use of real thermometers that indicate the climatic and cultural difference between China and United States. These works belong to the first reunification of the world, after the fall of the Berlin Wall. They are affected by the beginning of the cultural "thaw" and the overcoming of the world bipolar system in relation to the changes that occurred in the Soviet Union and the countries connected to it. These signals do not seem to be extraneous to Wang Guangyi's poetics of that period, also conceivable as the substratum on which, soon after, he would build his globalist approach to art.

From this standpoint, perhaps, Wang Guangyi's artistic research then seems even closer to Beuys's. Both are interested in the possibility of suggesting a new freedom of thought and action through creativity and social criticism. Both are attentive to the possible points of contact between art, mythology and spiritual reflection. However, Beuys places activism and relational and participatory practices at the center of his work, aimed at defending his idea of social art by largely adopting the conceptual model. Wang Guangyi, on the other hand, works at the intersection of art and politics, while maintaining a constant interest in tradition and the mutual influence between cultures—as shown by the depictions that make up his monumental cycle, *Great Criticism*.

## Transculturalism

Let us go back for a moment to Huang Zhuan's reflection: modern Chinese art has "come to accept" first the classical artistic tradition and then the modern and contemporary ones from the West. According to the historian, Chinese contemporary art would be "the product of the direct influence of contemporary Western art."[28] Do we have to understand this influence only as unidirectional? As if it were the Eastern adoption of the methods, rules, symbols, and iconic references of the Western art world? In my view, this would be a partial choice. This "adoption" that characterizes Chinese cultural and artistic development could be partly due to the influence exerted by Western culture on the Eastern, and partly due to the opposite cultural impact. In other words, the Chinese artistic context of the last thirty years could be one of the most vivid attestations to the mutual influence between Eastern and Western cultures: that is, what we could call transculturalism: the mutual permeability between different cultures which, by means of transnational relationships and hybridizations, characterizes the current globalist dimension of art. Such a mutual exchange can be expressed in very different ways in relation to the experimentation procedures and the tools chosen to create the artworks. If this path is viable, embracing the transnationalist structure Carroll has identified, contemporary art could then be understood as a manifestation of iconic styles, conventions, procedures, and motifs that, despite belonging to the past, are now taken up again precisely in the light of this cultural reciprocity, which will progressively intensify even more in the future.

In this perspective, one could also explain the common traits shared by numerous works produced in Eastern or Middle East geographic areas and those of Western origin, thus evaluating the extent of the traditional component within much of today's globalist art.

However, in less abstract terms, what does this all mean? First, that the current condition of art is the synthesis of a change certainly due to innovations introduced by conceptualism, but also to the preservation of rules, conventions, and procedural directives of past cultures that cannot be traced back to a given area of the globe: rather, they arose because of transnational relationships.

Second, that today this is possible because, together with the potential pluralist synthesis between creative models, this mutual influence between different cultures has been consolidated over the last thirty years.

The first reason to support these observations is that today's art is still, to a large extent, traditional—also in relation to its globalist dimension, as evidenced by its new flowering, which took place around the 1980s. We can capture this traditional component of art in a notion that is often used to indicate artistic production deriving from the traditionalist model: the notion of "visual arts."

The second reason is that the numerous theoretical issues about art that occupied a prominent place in the past are still there today, confirming the ongoing presence of the traditionalist model of art: for instance, the problem of understanding the content of the artwork in relation to its description and that of the synthesis between vision and knowledge in relation to the conventions underlying the artistic creation.

## The Scope of "Visual Arts"

We are hardly willing to accept that a "modern" or "contemporary" work of art—be it an avant-garde painting or a hyperrealist sculpture—might be essentially traditional: namely that it might be based, in large part, on creative rules and procedural conventions taken from the past. Rather, we are inclined to consider the artwork in the light of the innovations it introduces. Although certainly relevant, these innovations are essentially visual and do not characterize that work—and others that could be of the same kind—to such an extent as to make them different from what they are: paintings and sculptures. It has often happened that the elimination of an icon from a pictorial surface has been understood as a dominant character of the artwork to the point of making us forget that, ultimately, it was still a very traditional artistic object: a painting, that is, a set of pictorial strokes on a surface. Invariably, when the referents changed, the forms were overestimated or underestimated, and the materials chosen contributed to obtaining surprising visual effects, we made the same conjecture with sculpture. In both cases we have grasped innovation by finding it in the appearances, in the external features of the artworks.

Of course, it cannot be denied—and in this is art's power—that an artwork is such not only for the materials that make it up but also by virtue of the imaginative stimulation that it is able to offer in relation to its content, be it more or less decipherable. After all, it is because their contents are not completely decipherable that artworks attract our attention—and this again favors art precisely on the side of traditionalists, that is, visual, production. The less we know about an artwork, the more we are attracted to it. The more ambiguous the artwork—that is, the less its content is completely decipherable—the more we are interested in it by exploring its appearances. Not being able to completely access the content—understood not only as the reference of the representation, the subject of the work, but also as its underlying idea—the attention is therefore captured by the visual representation and by its external form, decisive for it to become an object of interest for the viewer and for the success of the imaginative and interpretative response that completes the subjective experience of the work.

Today, art manifests its most typically classicist traits. Ambiguity, technical-manual skills, inventiveness and visual salience of images are some of the criteria that we usually refer to when using the notion of "art" that we have conventionally learned to share throughout history. These criteria are the same we use for numerous contemporary works, precisely because the latter manifest the traits of tradition and classicism. In other words, today's art invites us to reflect on the possibility of identifying a line of continuity from Giotto and Mantegna to Henri Matisse, Andy Warhol, up to Gerhard Richter and Takashi Murakami. Being all authors of pictorial or sculptural works, these artists operate within the traditional model of artistic production. Their works certainly contribute to the introduction of new experimentation, which can be explored in different ways compared to the past. However, belonging to the same creative model of artistic production, they are considered variations of pictorial and sculptural production. Each of these works is therefore characterized by specificities concerning the representation and its referents as well as the techniques of execution, while still belonging to tradition.

With his research, Wang Guangyi confirms the perspective I have outlined so far. His artistic production refers to the Renaissance and the avant-garde of the early twentieth century. As clarified during a conversation with the art critic Demetrio Paparoni, part of Wang's work was guided by the possibility of identifying the common features between Giotto's frescoes and Picasso's paintings.[29] What does this mean? Perhaps, it is true that they are not as different as they are often believed to be, since both fall within the same sphere of production and evolution of visual arts.

The notion of "visual arts" summarizes the formal and visual primacy of art in relation to the introduction of internal elements of innovation within the pictorial and sculptural production. With respect to the latter, considering specifically the combinatorial possibilities and the changes of three-dimensional structures and materials, the notion of "plastic arts" is also used. Both are, however, inadequate to capture innovations due to practices related to conceptualism, which contribute to the evolution of art in a completely different way.

Different reflections are aroused by works based on the use of objects, materials, human bodies involved in performances, written texts, and video or photographic recordings of actions and events. That is, works that derive from a new creative model of artistic production, which emerged in the 1960s. It is possible to identify its origin in Marcel Duchamp's use of ready-mades: in place of an appearance, he offered an apparition. The snow shovel, the bottle rack, the urinal—all objects that Duchamp considers "manifestations." Those, indeed, are simple objects that are defective compared to traditional artistic objects precisely for a debasement of their formal salience, thus aiming at getting "a reaction of visual indifference, united to a total absence of good or bad taste."[30]

Duchamp shows the possibility of creating works of art that aim at a depletion of aesthetics on the level of subjective appreciation and taste in relation to the external appearance and form of the artworks. In this way he anticipates the reductionist approach that will characterize numerous artistic practices from the 1960s onwards. Parallel to the introduction of ready-mades, however, there was also a creative renewal process that would lead to the subsequent affirmation of conceptual art. Through conceptualism are introduced new rules for artistic creation—rules that affected the evolution of art for over a decade. This evolution happened over two essential phases. At first, artists aimed to bring *ideas* to the fore as opposed to the artistic object. Later, in the 1970s, they consciously returned to using new material entities in order to express ideas.

In particular, in its first phase, conceptual art could also be conceived in relation to the introduction of new forms of art, which are hardly explained by the notion of "visual arts," but do not fall under the traditional notion of "plastic arts" either.[31] Far from being not aesthetic or immaterial, rather conceptual art has transformed the works into "material conductors of ideas":[32] objects, materials, human bodies, textual, video and photographic recordings that guarantee the conveyance of artworks' contents or part of them. In order for this to be possible, the artists intentionally provide information and clues concerning the project of their work in order to share their ideas publicly. This process of clarification was consolidated in the 1970s, when the problem of the value of art became obviously central. On the one hand, conceptual works of art expressed the social and political value that art claimed in those years, imposing a necessary revision of the critical discourse concerning it.[33] On the other hand, these works also revealed the continuous and insistent pursuit of poiesis through a substantial reductionist approach that brings to the fore the problem of the evaluation of art.³⁴

The works produced during the following period, from the 1980s to the present day, should therefore be considered in the light of the affirmation of both conceptualism and transculturalism. Perhaps they could be understood as possible hybridizations between conceptual and plastic arts.³⁵ Or rather, looking at the pluralist synthesis that characterizes the artistic production of the last thirty years, they could also be thought of as variants of the conceptual model.

I believe that several conceptual works by Wang Guangyi could also be considered from this perspective: for instance, the already-mentioned *Inflammable and Explosive* and *Comparison between Chinese and American Temperature*, produced prior to *Great Criticism*, but also some of the later ones. I am also thinking of much more recent works like *Temperature* and *Things-In-Themselves* (Figure 8.2), made between 2010 and 2012. The first work consists of about two thousand thermometers installed on the wall. Even accepting a deeper teleological meaning, as explained by the artist, we can nevertheless assume that the thermometers immediately transmit the ideas of "temperature variation" and "climate change of an environment," ideas related to the theme that the artist intends to deal with in his work: global warming. The accessibility of the project component of the content is one of the main characteristics of conceptual works of art. The description of the thermometers makes it possible to go back to the idea that the artist expresses and to grasp his reflection, which is certainly much more elaborate than the clues offered by the work. The next step made possible by this kind of work, engaging the spectator in an appropriate interpretative process, is thus to grasp a reflection on the influence of temperature on the environment and ask questions on ecological, cultural, social, political, relational changes, and so on. In this way, Wang Guangyi is able to show his ability to make useful indications explicit and, at the same time, to increase the "enigma of the perceptual instability of temperature changes."³⁶ One of the artist's objectives, in fact, is that of being able to interpret through his own works the Kantian notion of "thing in itself" in terms of a power that escapes our knowledge and is beyond the presence of the perceivable material object.³⁷

Composed of about five thousand jute sacks containing rice and bran, *Things-In-Themselves* is a work that develops this last reflection. The 2012 installation is based once again on the accessibility of the content. The environment of the room is entirely covered by bags, and the user who enters it has, first of all, an olfactory experience of the scent given off by the cereal contained in the sacks. The olfactory experience allows her to associate the work's modified

**Figure 8.2** Wang Guangyi, *Things-in-Themselves* (2012), installation with sacks of rice and rice bran, etc. Variable dimensions.

environment to that of a granary. In other words, it allows her to get as close as possible to Wang Guangyi's idea. The stacked bags, instead, favor a reflection on the relationship between content and container. The artist clarifies that those materials "do not have a particular meaning," "do not symbolize anything" and, in a sense, "resemble the influence" that the term "thing in itself" has had on him.[38] Also, in this case it is a question of being able to translate Wang Guangyi's (certainly much more articulated) reflection on the phenomenon and the thing in itself. The core of these works—and of all the works that, for the same reason, can be deemed conceptual—is that they give the spectator a set of indications and clues that do not exhaust the overall meaning of the work but facilitate its understanding at a first basic level. That is, they allow us to go from the material residue back to the idea, or ideas, that the artist wants to convey through his work.

## The Tradition in Novelty

Let us now try to examine Wang Guangyi's works that attest the continuity between today's art and that of the past. They include *Materialists*, a group of sculptures in glass fiber and millet, made in 2002; *Pietà* and *The Last Supper* (both painted in 2011) or else the most recent triptych, *How to Define Sindone to Human Beings?* (2013). As Paparoni noted, a work keeps its aura because not all of its meanings are comprehensible. However, this is also a characteristic of the artwork in the traditional sense, which, we might say, is such precisely because it conceals a large part of its meanings. What makes these works attestations of the traditionalist creative model is not only the practice dedicated to the iconic appropriation—in the two paintings of 2011 we find Mantegna's dead Christ and Leonardo's celebrated painting depicting the Last Supper. Rather, it is Wang Guangyi's will, also shared by many other contemporary artists, to return to seeing the artwork in terms of visual inventiveness based on the production of images or, as in these cases, iconic variants that—both on the representational level and on that of content—can be said to be *opaque*. In other words, it is difficult to recognize the references of the representation, and the works conceal the ideas that originated them.

What does *How to Define Sindone to Human Beings* represent? What is its ideational content? What ideas do the *Materialists* sculptures convey? If we tried to answer by affirming that today's art is characterized by a high degree of ambiguity and therefore of interpretive freedom, both because of the impossibility of (fully or partially) grasping the referents of the depictions and the contents of the works, we would be wrong. If this is the case today, it is because contemporary art retains a creative model that, we might say, has remained "genetically" the same throughout history, based on rules for artistic creation and conventions that can certainly undergo variations, but are the same as in the past. And this is also shown by the fact that today's art, like that of the past, is still based on the possibility of concealing a large part of the contents behind icons. Some theoretical reflections developed during the twentieth century reveal this approach.

The problem of understanding paintings and sculptures is related to their description and to the historical and cultural contexts of the artwork and the user alike. Today, as in the past, not everyone is able to understand the meaning of a visual work of art, since one often fails to grasp even the depiction itself, lacking the necessary historical and cultural references that have been lost over time. This explains why not everyone today is able to recognize Pope Innocent X in the first canvas of the triptych, *How to Define Shroud to Human Beings?* (a figure inspired by Velazquez's portrait of 1650), and the German artist Joseph Beuys in the last.

As to the content of a work of art and its description, art historian Erwin Panofsky[39] defends the following thesis: an adequate description of an artwork is possible by knowing its style and reliability depends on a necessary historical study. Without going into detail, in a nutshell his argument is as follows. Describing a work by focusing on the perceived material object means formulating a simple "formal description," which is insufficient because, at most, it provides details concerning the colors, their nuances and the relationships that make them compositional elements of the work. What is decisive is, instead, "a knowledge of general principles of depiction," that is, a "stylistic knowledge" corroborated by a historical reflection. In the light of this knowledge it is possible to access a "secondary level of meaning," thus transforming purely formal elements into symbols.[40] To explain how this transformation takes place, Panofsky considers what he calls a "sphere of phenomenal meaning" and a "sphere of meaning dependent on content." The latter sphere refers to the knowledge of sources that may be familiar or foreign to those who seek to understand the work.

Lacking this knowledge, one will probably not understand what the artist wants to portray. In order to provide an adequate description of the work it is necessary that the latter is placed "within the history of style"[41] in order to go beyond a formal description, which is rather basic. The discovery of the "sphere of meaning" is possible according to higher-level knowledge: the theory of types. With the notion of "type," Panofsky refers to the result of a fusion between phenomenal meaning and content-based meaning. This fusion would guarantee that the former is the vehicle of the second. In this way, the content-based meaning would depend on the type developed by an artist in relation to the cultural heritage and the history of tradition that allows both the artist and the user to grasp the meaning of the work and, above all, to interpret it correctly. In this perspective, the content of the work would also correspond to what Panofsky regards as "a fundamental attitude towards the world which is characteristic in equal measure of the individual producer, the individual period, the individual people, and the individual cultural community."[42]

We could consider Panofsky's argument as a confirmation of the thesis laid out in these pages: traditional creative rules, procedures, and conventions are still present in today's art, raising once again the questions of the adequacy of the descriptions and interpretations of the works in relation to historical continuity and shared knowledge. These questions primarily concern the traditionalist creative model—that is, the visual arts—which cannot be tackled neglecting the conventions that, decisive for the artistic production of the past, also characterize part of the current one. In the early 1950s, art historian Bernard Berenson[43] confirmed this hypothesis once more. He observed that seeing and knowing become one and the same in the visual arts, understood as the area of artistic production dedicated to achieving a compromise between image and idea. According to Berenson, this compromise is obtained by means of visual representations. The repetition of compromises is decisive for conventions to establish themselves in history. The relevance of conventions is therefore such that "the history of all expression, of all the arts, and of the visual arts in particular, should be, can be, nothing but an account, and perhaps an attempt to interpret its successive conventions".[44]

Based on this observation, we can therefore see that the works resulting from the adoption of the traditionalist creative model allow us to go back to the conventions established throughout history that characterize art as we traditionally know it. As for the present analysis of Wang Guangyi's works, this means that *Materialists*, *Pietà*, *The Last Supper*, and the triptych *How to Define Sindone to Human Beings?*, are all works that reveal these conventional foundations, in the light of which we can recognize paintings and sculptures representing certain subjects and expressing certain contents that we can only partly grasp. Ideas remain partially or completely hidden behind the images. Thus, on the one hand, in terms of Berenson's reflection this means accepting that the artistic tradition was developed mainly through the compromise between vision and knowledge obtained in the field of visual arts. On the other hand, we might also suppose that the introduction of new conventions that radically renewed the tradition is mainly due to conceptualism. Berenson offered theoretical support for this thesis when he wrote, "a tradition, a convention, needs constant manipulation to vivify it, to enlarge it, to keep it fresh and supple, and capable of generating problems and producing their solution".[45]

An initial explanation about the current condition of art could therefore be given by recognizing that the acceptance, rejection, and possible synthesis of the creative models underlying the artist's work correspond both to the maintenance and the renewal of conventions. Furthermore, in order to clarify the globalist dimension of art, one cannot overlook transnational relations, hybridizations, and transculturalism: that is to say, the factors that are characterizing the creative scenario of the contemporary world in the direction of a cultural reciprocity between East and West. Something that, as we have seen in these pages, is also attested by the artistic production of Wang Guangyi.

# Notes

1. Carroll, 2007: 134.
2. See for comparison, Carroll, 2007.
3. See Carroll, 2007.

4   Carroll, 2007: 131.
5   Ibid.: 132.
6   Ibid.: 134.
7   Ibid.
8   Ibid.: 135.
9   See Carroll, 2007: 135-6.
10  See for comparison, Carroll, 2007: 132.
11  Ibid.: 136.
12  Ibid.: 137.
13  Ibid.: 140.
14  See Carroll 2007: 140; for more details see in particular ibid.: 136-42.
15  See for comparison, Carroll, 2007: 140-2.
16  Ibid.: 140-1.
17  Ibid.: 140.
18  See Huang, 2013.
19  Huang, 2013: 28
20  Ibid.: 33.
21  See for comparison, Lu, 2013.
22  See Paparoni, 2013.
23  See for comparison, Wang, 1986.
24  See Beuys and Ende, 1989.
25  See for comparison, Huang, 2013.
26  See for comparison, Lu, 2013.
27  To learn more see Huang, 2013: 44-5.
28  Huang, 2013: 33.
29  See Paparoni 2013: 13-14.
30  Duchamp, 1994: 191.
31  See Lopes, 2007.
32  See Dal Sasso, 2014.
33  See for comparison, Dorfles, 1982.
34  See for comparison, Migliorini, 2014.
35  See for comparison, Lopes, 2007.
36  See for comparison, Yan, 2012.
37  See for comparison, Wang, 2012.
38  Ibid.: 388.
39  See Panofsky, 1932.
40  Ibid.: 469-70.
41  Ibid.: 471.
42  Ibid.: 479.
43  See Berenson, 1953.

44  Berenson, 1953: 35.
45  Ibid.

# References

Berenson, B. (1953). *Seeing and Knowing*. London: Chapman & Hall.
Beuys, J., Ende, M. (1989). *Kunst und Politik,* Wangen/Allgau: FIU-Verlag.
Carroll, N. (2007). Art and Globalization: Then and Now, *The Journal of Aesthetics and Art Criticism*, 65(1) (Special Issue: Global Theories of Arts and Aesthetics): 131–43.
Dal Sasso, D. (2014) Exploring Conceptual Art, *Philosophical Readings*, 6(2) (Special Issue Realism and Anti-Realism: New Perspectives): 101–114.
Dorfles, G. (1982). *Il divenire della critica,* Torino: Einaudi.
Duchamp, M. (1994). *Duchamp du signe. Ecrits*, M. Sanouillet éd. Paris: Flammarion.
Huang, Zhang (2013). *Politics and Theology in Chinese Contemporary Art. Reflections on the work of Wang Guangyi*. Milano: Skira.
Lopes, D. M. (2007). Conceptual Art Is Not What It Seems, in P. Goldie and E. Schellekens (eds.), *Philosophy and Conceptual Art*. Oxford: Oxford University Press, 238–56.
Lu Mingjun (2013). *Inflammable and Explosive Objects* (1988); *Inflammable and Explosive* (1989); *Comparison between Chinese and American Temperature* (1990); *China Thermometer* (1990), in D. Paparoni (ed.), *Wang Guangyi: Works and thoughts 1985-2012,* Milano: Skira: 88–91.
Lu Peng (2013), *The Back of Humanity* (1985); *Frozen North Pole* (1984–85), in D. Paparoni (ed.), *Wang Guangyi: Works and thoughts 1985-2012,* Milano: Skira: 38–43.
Migliorini, E. (2014). *Conceptual Art,* nuova edizione, a. c., ed. by D. Dal Sasso, Milano-Udine: Mimesis.
Panofsky, E. (1932). *Zum Problem der Beschreibung und Inhaltsdeutung von Werken der Bildenden Kunst,* "Logos," 21: 103–19; Engl. trans., On the Problem of Describing and Interpreting Works of the Visual Arts, *Critical Inquiry*, 38(3) (Spring 2012): 467–82.
Paparoni, D. (2013). *Deifying the Human and Humanizing the Divine. The art of Wang Guangyi*, in D. Paparoni (a c. di), *Wang Guangyi: Works and thoughts 1985-2012,* Milano, Skira: 11–37.
Wang Guangyi (1986). *Us—The Participants of the '85 New Wave Movement*, in D. Paparoni (ed.), *Wang Guangyi: Works and thoughts 1985-2012* (2013). Milano: Skira: 316.
Wang Guangyi (2012). *About Things-In-Themselves,* in D. Paparoni (ed.), *Wang Guangyi: Works and Thoughts 1985-2012* (2013). Milano: Skira: 387–9.
Yan Shanchun (2012). *Temperature 2010-2011*, in D. Paparoni (ed.), *Wang Guangyi Works and thoughts 1985-2012,* Torino-Milano: Skira: 284–7.

# Part V

# Erasing the Emotions

9

# Grief and the Power of the Mind

Carola Barbero 宝凯乐

> *Le bonheur est salutaire pour le corps,*
> *mais c'est le chagrin*
> *qui développe les forces de l'esprit*
> M. Proust, *Le temps retrouvé*

## Introduction

At the Spanish Pavilion of the *Exposition Internationale des Arts et Techniques dans la Vie Moderne* in Paris in July 1937, the mural-sized oil painting on canvas, *Guernica* by Pablo Picasso, was exhibited for the first time. *Guernica* is considered one of the most moving paintings in art's history. It was created by Picasso after the Nazi bombing earlier that year of the Basque village of Guernica, in the northern part of Spain. The emotions it evokes are universal and timeless, hence not necessarily connected to that specific event. In the painting there is a bull with eyes opened in astonishment, a woman grieving the death of a child lying in her arms, a horse falling in agony under which there is a dead man grasping a broken sword from which buds a flower, a woman seemingly scared and carrying a lamp witnesses the scene, while another with arms raised in terror is entrapped by fire.

It is a painting with strong symbolism, and many interpretations have been offered by critics in order to explain it. Undoubtedly it is, as intended by its author, a work reminding humanity how much suffering and devastation war can bring. Hence, it is also a universal symbol of human suffering, fear and astonishment caused by evil and injustice.

Let us start by asking a simple question: If we observe *Guernica* without knowing anything about the Nazis' bombing on April 26, 1937, what do we see?

We see a strong scene emotionally charged with a bull, a horse, some desperate women, a man and so on. We see those emotions represented with force in the painting: they are there, on the canvas, in front of us. They hit us, call us into question, and make us feel uneasy. We catch all the desperation when looking at the eyes, at the tense expression of the faces, at the opened mouths, at those raised arms. We see (and maybe also feel) the emotions there represented.

Needless to say, if we also knew in response to what particular event the painting was created, we would undoubtedly comprehend something more by contextualizing those emotions to the shocking event that took place when the Nazi German and the Fascist Italian warplanes bombed Guernica, the village giving the title to the painting.

According to some, *Guernica* is not only one of the strongest anti-war paintings, but it is also a canvas depicting ancient tragedy and reminding us that "all that we love is going to be lost."[1] Its being universal explains also why, even if we do not know anything about it, what we grasp by simply looking at it is its powerful emotional force.

There is a famous anecdote belonging to the myth connected to this painting: it seems that, looking at a reproduction of *Guernica*, a German official asked Picasso, "Did you do this?" and the artist's reply was, "No, you did." In its simplicity this answer underlines that the tragedy and the suffering there represented are not simply a work of art; they symbolize a universal experience of death and terror derived from a specific historical event. Another anecdote is the one concerning the blood-red tear changing its place on the canvas during the creation but not making the final cut. Why did the blood-red tear continuously change its place? Maybe because a blood-red tear could be everywhere. And why is it not there in the final version? Because *Guernica* is not our past: that tear still bleeds and will bleed forever. When looking at the collapsing Twin Towers in New York on September 11, 2001, a witness of Guernica told that the event was shockingly similar to the one he experienced that April in 1937. *Guernica* is still actual and, unfortunately, our tears will go on bleeding.

Here, what is interesting is that *Guernica* does not aim at speaking about emotions, but at representing them. The same happens with Michelangelo's *Pietà*, the marble sculpture, the only one ever signed by Michelangelo Buonarroti, and representing the body of Jesus in the Virgin's arms after the Crucifixion. It is an impressive statue showing the forsakenness of the son on the lap of his mother, his being in the meantime God and man, while Mary is represented as being very young, maybe for her incorruptible purity. This sculpture symbolizes the purest form of love, the one between mother and son, and what is represented is

Mary's acceptance of God's will, together with Jesus's serenity and forsakenness. This work represents strong and deep emotions and, in its calm magnificence, is characterized as a warning against those who, blinded by fury, point at God, questioning him for our tragedies and pains. How can we react in this way in front of the suffering acceptance of the Virgin holding her dead son in her arms? We simply cannot. The body of Jesus is in his mother's arms, and our questions, even if felt as urgent and important, are not legitimate any more. Exactly as in *Guernica*'s case, also in this case we see the power and universality of emotions transmitted through art.

As is well known, and as the history of philosophy extensively shows, art and emotion[2] have had a long, rich, and often complex—when not even difficult—relationship, since it was not easy to see if the one had a role in favor or against the other. For instance, should we maintain that one of art's duties is that of communicating emotions? Should we consider it good to approach art from an emotional viewpoint, or should we see art conveying emotions as being somehow ambiguous or even blackmailing? Chinese artist Wang Guangyi defends a strong and sharp position in the debate concerning art and emotions, maintaining powerfully that emotions should be removed from works of art in order to allow for rational analysis of the themes/subjects represented by the artist. According to Wang, emotions are dangerous, therefore they should be removed by art. His position is based both on the old dichotomy between reason and passion, and on the idea that abstract and amorphous figures should be more rational and appreciable than fully blooded and emotional ones. But is he right? Should we really extirpate emotions in order to understand and rationally appreciate art?

## Art and Emotion

A philosophical tradition dating back to Plato and Aristotle has profoundly reflected on these questions and, as is well known, different (and often opposite) answers have been suggested.

Plato, in Book X of his *Republic*, strongly criticized art,[3] first from an *epistemological* point of view—insisting that the artist does not really know what he is creating, and that his knowledge is a third-order one (at the first level is the knowledge of forms, typical of the philosopher; at the second level is the craftsman, who gets inspiration from the form to build the physical object; and at the third level is the artist's knowledge, which is a mere imitation of the physical realization of the form). Second, from an *emotional* point of view, by stressing the fact that we, as rational beings, should be able to control passions and desires with our reason, hence we should not stimulate the irrational part of our soul, as for instance dramatic art does (by feeding our irrationality and making us more similar to children who notoriously are unable to distinguish fiction from reality). According to Plato, therefore, art should be treated with suspicion both for what has to do with the kind of knowledge we can derive from it and for the emotions it evokes in us. The emotional side of Plato's critique is precisely the one maintained by Wang Guangyi in favor of emotion's extirpation from art.

But would that be the right move? Should we see rationality and emotion as one against the other? Should we really favor abstraction and lack of any feeling and emotion? Aristotle thinks we should not. In the *Poetics*, he does important work with art, knowledge, and emotions, achieving results quite distant from Plato's. The only point in common between the two is that art is seen by both as *imitation*; but, whereas for Plato its being so underlines a strong and puzzling epistemological weakness (since art is imitation of an imitation), for Aristotle art's imitative nature emphasizes a distinctive feature of mankind, the one thanks to which we begin learning and enjoying knowledge. Furthermore, the kind of knowledge art does impart to us is a special and highly philosophical one, since differently from history "poetry is more concerned with the universal, and history more with the individual,"[4] that is why art actually discloses the domain of possibilities. Art does not concern reality, actualities, but things that "might happen," and this tells us something absolutely important, not only as far as knowledge is concerned, but also for what has to do with emotions since, as a matter of fact, it is because we know that art represents real-world possibilities and therefore is not actual, that we can truly enjoy and contemplate artworks, thinking and feeling accordingly.

Actually, *pace* Colin Radford,[5] we appreciate artworks precisely because we know that what they are representing is merely possible and not actual. This distinction between the artistic and the real domains allows us to contemplate and really appreciate what is represented in the work without having to think about consequences, as happens, instead, when we relate to reality. Art appreciation, hence, is an opportunity to reflect on what is in front of us, to enrich our experience, and to learn from it. We do not behave irrationally in responding to art, but as Aristotle exhaustively explains, in responding emotionally to art we somehow experience (thanks to the *catharsis* of the emotions there represented) those emotional states and learn something important. From here directly comes the central role played by emotions in art appreciation and in art definition as well.

Nevertheless, art is an emotional experience, not only for consumers, but also for art producers, as Romanticism[6] has taught us by defining works of art as the expression of their creators' emotions. Provided it is all but easy to say what an *expression* is,[7] we can assume that works of art express, besides ideas and convictions, emotions, too. Actually, there is a strong sense according to which what the artist does is *expressing himself* in his works.

R. G. Collingwood, in his *The Principles of Art*,[8] presents his expression theory and argues that art should be seen as the expression of the artist's emotions: art is for her/him a medium for communicating her/his feelings. According to this theory, the artist shapes his emotions in the artwork, and people understand it as far as they understand and recognize the very same emotions of the artist's, or rather as far as their imaginative experience is identical with the one the artist had when creating it. Therefore, experiencing works of art means experiencing the very same emotions expressed by the artist in the work itself. A quite strong critique to Collingwood's position comes from those arguing that, whatever expression is, we should not confuse a genetical with a structural approach—that is, we should judge the work of art as such and therefore not consider the process thanks to which the artist has created it.[9]

As a matter of fact, what, for instance, a painting expresses, is given by what is represented, by the colors used and by the style, and not, instead, by the artist's state of mind or intentions. Nonetheless, even if what the work of art is, is independent of the artist's state of mind, in order to properly understand what artworks do express we need know something about the period when the work was created.[10] As Jenefer Robinson explains,

> The artist who made it, the individual style of that artist or the general style within which he worked, as well as facts about the artist's class, race, gender, and individual psychology may all be relevant to determining what is expressed by the work. So it's hardly surprising that we cannot tell a work is an expression of bitterness, disappointment, and exasperation in its author just by paying close attention to "the work itself" independently of its wider context.[11]

## Art without Emotion

Explicitly against any form of expression theory of a romantic sort, Wang Guangyi's strong idea is that the artist, far from expressing his emotions in his works, should be deliberately and explicitly unemotional. Therefore, art is not the expression of the artist's emotions: as a matter of fact, emotions are erased from the artwork by explicit intention.

Nonetheless, leaving aside what the artist does, and what he means by what he does, let us concentrate on the work of art. The work, once created, might be seen as expressing something quite independent from the artist's intentions (think about those artists who cannot be properly said of having intentions, for example, insane artists like Vincent Van Gogh, Edvard Munch, and Louis Wain): actually, the artist could have had no intention of expressing any emotion by his work (because he had no true intentions or because he had in mind something different from what he was actually doing), nonetheless the work of art might express something anyway. Artworks, once created, can be seen as autonomous objects with their form and their content and, consequently, they can, as a matter of principle, express emotions their authors were unaware of, and they can convey emotions even if their authors had no intention of expressing anything at all by means of them.

This intrinsic expressive character of artworks is the attribute thanks to which we are authorized to make inferences about the work articulating emotions, since what it is individuates what it says. Its content corresponds to what the work transmits; and it can communicate emotions also in its saying there is nothing to express emotionally, or that the emotions have been deleted from faces and bodies but, nonetheless, sadness remains, and nothing else matters.

This is exactly what happens in Wang Guangyi's *Red Rationality: Revision of the Idols* (1987), wherein he does reinterpret Michelangelo's *Pietà*, by intentionally removing, erasing, deleting any sort of emotion (see Figure 1.1). The marble statue representing the Virgin hugging her dead son and expressing in the meantime sorrow, desperation, and resignation is transformed into an oil on canvas of 160cm. x 200cm., where some amorphous figures stand (in the back of a red grid).

According to Wang's intentions, in that transformation emotions have been erased. In order to remove any temptation, even the faces, traditionally considered the mirror of our emotional situation,[12] have been deleted, and what we see are these soft blue/grey bodies bent over and stooped. Nevertheless, the colors used and the form given to the bodies could be identified, without any forcing, with the trace of that erasure. As a matter of fact, even if there are no suffering, resigned, or calm faces anymore, what we see in this abstract scene inherits something under the emotional point of view from its original model. Despite Wang Guangyi wanting to represent people (originally having emotions but) without emotions, his painting offers us a clear trace of that erasure, and what we have is still something concerned with emotions that are somehow present, even in their being shown as absent.

## Erasing Emotions/Evoking Emotions

The point is: Does Wang's reinterpretation succeed in replacing the dead Christ and the grieving Mary with soft and faceless figures standing out in a wasteland? In view of his move—based on the conviction that emotions are tendentious and therefore should be taken out of works of art in order to keep a neutral position—of stripping emotions from that classic tragic image by using these strange and featureless figures, are we willing to interpret it as a *true alternative view*? And, if so, which view would be this *alternative view*? It seems that simply erasing people and emotions by transforming them into lumbering puppets meandering in a wasteland does not mean properly to offer an alternative view, this is just an attempt to erase the previous, emotional view. But then are we right in considering Wang Guangyi's *Red Rationality: Revision of the Idols* as articulating the way the scene represented in the *Pietà* appears to someone wanting to eliminate any emotional state?

Wang, believing that emotions are dangerous, wants an art deprived of any emotional dimension, and for this reason he aims at conveying his intention of not expressing any emotion. Nonetheless, the main problem with this painting transforming Michelangelo's masterpiece into a wasteland populated by amorphous figures is that emotions do not seem to be really erased. Do not these figures communicate sadness? Is not the wasteland a strong symbol of grief and desolation? Are not these bodies transmitting dereliction and abandonment? What Wang's painting seems to show is that a work can express emotions even if its author did not want to.

Of course emotions in *Red Rationality: Revision of the Idols* are quite different from, for instance, the ones depicted by Romantic painters (think about Eugène Delacroix's works, created in a realistic style and with characters full of emotions, conveying violence and passion), and they are also different from those typical of the Expressionists who, presenting the world from a totally subjective perspective, distort their characters by accentuating the emotions they are expressing. An interesting characteristic of Expressionism is that it makes clear how something can be represented as abstract and be, in the meantime, full of emotions, and this is important especially if considering that Wang sees the lack of concreteness and of a definite form as a sort of guarantee against a possible emotional impact. Actually, there is no strategy able to keep us safe from emotions and their power. Emotions are always around the corner, quite independently from the author's beliefs.

Let us consider again the intention of erasing emotions. Wang sees emotions as a very difficult business and thinks that maybe erasing them from works could be the right move in order to avoid any danger and be sure that rationality will be safeguarded.

Just erase emotions, and you will be safe. Interesting idea, but maybe not the correct one. Simply *removing* what we think to be the origin of the problem is not always enough to solve the problem. And this for three reasons: (1) maybe what has been removed was not the origin of the problem; (2) maybe there is no problem to be solved at all; (3) maybe we do not really know what needs to be removed.

By recalling the philosophical tradition and the ancient debate between Plato and Aristotle, we have already emphasized how (2), following Aristotle's *Poetics*, could be maintained, specifically insisting on the fact that emotions, far from being identified with a danger, could be seen as a treasure, both for what concerns aesthetic experience and the development of our understanding.

Number (1) focuses instead on what has been removed in order to erase emotions. Wang has deleted human traits and facial expressions from the characters of his painting but, nonetheless, emotions are still present in it: colors, forms, landscape, and structure do transmit emotions as well. Actually, *Red Rationality: Revision of the Idols* is sad, livid, and hopeless even if there are no crying eyes, resigned faces or whatever. This happens because the represented scene may be sad and desperate, despite of its author's will: actually, emotions are still and powerfully in that desolate land where amorphous figures meander.

The last reason, (3), stresses a point that has to do with the relation between art and emotions. Where are emotions in artworks? What is their function? Does the author need emotions in order to create? According to Henry Matisse, emotions are what make possible the act of artistic creation itself: "If one hasn't always emotion, what then? [...] When I came in here to work this morning I had no emotion, so I took a horseback ride. When I returned I felt like painting, and had all the emotion I wanted."[13] Therefore, Matisse believed emotions are necessary in order to create. Maybe this was just *his* need and not a universal one.

Nonetheless, the one concerning art and emotions certainly is an intricate matter, and of course it is not something that can be solved by a simple erasure. Why? Because emotions in art, are in principle everywhere. So, even if the author has no intention to communicate any emotion through and by his art,[14] the artwork itself might still have an emotional impact. This is what happens with *Red Rationality: Revision of the Idols*: actually, even if we have no more emotions concerning Jesus and the Virgin Mary as happens in Michelangelo's masterpiece, we still have a sense of loneliness, sadness, and desperation.

This is an important aspect of the question explaining why, as viewers, we stop in front of this artwork and are gripped by grief even if faces and bodies have been erased. Emotions, exactly like love, are in the air, and there exist no intention or eraser able to remove them once and forever.

# Notes

1 This was M. Leiris' idea according to what Russell writes, 2003: 129.
2 Matravers, 1998: "Great art provides some of the most valuable experiences it is possible for us to have. Such experiences engage many aspects of our mental life simultaneously: filling our senses whilst at the same time making demands on our intelligence, our sympathies, and our emotions," 1.
3 Plato, *Republic*, X, 595a-608b.
4 Aristotle, *Poetics*, IX, 1451b, 11–14.
5 Radford, 1975. In this paper Radford argues that our being moved or, in general, having emotions towards artworks in an evidence of our being incoherent and inconsistent. However, far from being irrational, when we react emotionally to artworks we prove of having understood and appreciated it exactly for what it is, i.e. an artwork, as Weston (1975) underlines.
6 Wordsworth and Coleridge, 2006: "Preface."
7 As J. Robinson (2005: 231–2) underlines: "Some works seem to *express* their author's emotions; others which are not expressions of anyone's emotions nevertheless have *expressive qualities*; some works are simply *expressive* without expressing anything in particular; or perhaps they are played or performed expressively whether or not they are themselves expressions of anything."
8 Collingwood (1963 [1938]).
9 Hospers, 1970: 221–45; Tormey, 1971.
10 As E. H. Gombrich has existensively explained in his *Art and Illusion*, London: Phaidon, 1962.
11 Robinson, 2005: 249.
12 Ekman, 1999: 301–20.
13 H. Matisse, as quoted in an interview with Clara T. MacChesney (1912), in *Matisse on Art* (1995) ed. by Jack D. Flam, 66.
14 Novitz, 1995: 199–203.

# References

Aristotle. *Poetics*, IX, 1451b, 11–14.

Collingwood, R. G. (1963 [1938]). *The Principles of Art*. Oxford: Clarendon Press.

Ekman, P. (1999). Facial Expressions. In Dalgleish, T. and Power, M. (eds.), *Handbook of Cognition and Emotion*. New York: Wiley.

Hospers, J. (1970). The Concept of Artistic Expression. In Weitz, M. (ed.), *Problems in Aesthetics: An Introductory Book of Readings*. New York: Macmillan.

Matravers, D. (1998). *Art and Emotion*. Oxford: Clarendon Press.

Novitz, D. (1995). Messages 'In' and Messages 'Through' Art. *Australasian Journal of Philosophy*, 73(2).

Plato. *Republic*, X, 595a–608b.

Radford, C. (1975). How can we be moved by the fate of Anna Karenina? In *Proceedings of the Aristotelian Society*, supp., 49(6).

Robinson, J. (2005) *Deeper than Reason*. Oxford: Clarendon Press.

Russell, M. (2003). *Picasso's War*. London: Simon & Schuster UK.

Tormey, A. (1971). *The Concept of Expression: A Study in Philosophical Psychology and Aesthetics*. Princeton: Princeton University Press.

Weston, M. (1975). How can we be moved by the fate of Anna Karenina?. In *Proceedings of the Aristotelian Society*, supp., 49(6).

# 10

# Reasoning with Idols: A Conversation with Wang Guangyi

Andrew Cohen

**Wang Guangyi**: In truth, I'm a very contradictory person. As a boy I had a rational approach to things, but over time I discovered other sides of myself. I developed an interest in mysterious things. I grew up in the Northeast of China. Very cold regions tend to create mystical spirits. Being born in Harbin was useful to me: I painted *Frozen Northern Wastelands* in 1985. It is a solemn and minimal work.

**Andrew Cohen**: You tried to stay clear of any emotion in this painting, and yet, when I look at the works of this cycle, the cold plains and the snow, I feel something—a sense of solitude. The figures have no face and there is no communication, they are simply staring into space.

**WG**: Cold, no communication, a sense of silence ... it's true. What I want to express in this painting is the distance between people, the impossibility of understanding inherent in the relationship that people have with the world.

**AC**: As a young man you embraced the theory of removing emotions. Now do you still think it's possible to separate emotions from painting?

**WG**: The older I get, the more I realize that there are things that cannot be explained by reason. All that I can do is investigate the mystery around us. These mysterious things might ignore us, but they can also be the object of our veneration.

**AC**: After *Frozen Wastelands* you moved to the series *Black and Red Rationality*.

**WG**: [Pointing at *Red Rationality: Revision of the Idols*] This is from 1987. It is entitled *Red Rationality: Revision of The Idols*.

**AC:** Interestingly, you have used faceless figures, like those in *Frozen Wastelands*.

**WG:** The paintings of *Frozen Wastelands* are based on ordinary people, devoid of religiosity. Instead, the figures in the *Red Rationality* series come from Christian iconography.

**AC:** In *Red Rationality: Revision of The Idols* you seem to have managed to remove emotions completely. I cannot feel any, even though you refer to Michelangelo's *Pietà*, to Christ and the Virgin.

**WG:** The source is precisely Michelangelo's *Pietà*, which belongs to the Western Christian cultural tradition. However, as a Chinese artist, I am not familiar with this tradition. I have only a vague knowledge of it. This vague knowledge has led me to neglect the details, so as to make it clear how the Christian religion is incomprehensible to us.

**AC:** In the same year, 1986, you painted a picture focused on *Death of Marat* by Jacques-Louis David, from 1793. You chose two figures that were both killed: Jesus and Marat. Why death?

**WG:** When I refer to death, as in *Post-Classic: Death of Marat*, it is because it represents man's destiny.

**AC:** Many art historians have made a comparison between *Death of Marat* and Michelangelo's *Pietà*. Although one is a painting and the other a sculpture, the subject and the formal composition of these two works are similar: the position of the inanimate body, the dangling arm ...

**WG:** Yes, *Death of Marat* is indeed like *Pietà*. This is interesting.

**AC:** One year after *Red Rationality: Revision of Idols* you applied the same grid and the same rational analysis to another iconic figure. This time it was an Eastern figure: Chairman Mao.

**WG:** The Christ of *Pieta* is a Christian idol. Mao is a communist idol. These idols have influenced my life. I learned about the Christian religion in books. Instead, I met Mao Zedong in real life.

**AC:** [Referring to the study for *Mao AO* of 1988]. Is it an embroidery? So are these stitches? Let's turn it over ...

**WG:** Yes, it's an embroidery. At the time, in addition to the posters, there were many embroideries of Mao like this. I wanted to work on a material that could last: a fabric. A poster is made of paper, it is easily damaged. I thought this embroidery would lend itself well. Before deciding to paint Mao, like most artists, I made a study.

**AC:** Is this the first work of the series about Mao?

**WG:** Yes, of course, because it is the first study. Then I elaborated it and made an oil painting on canvas. In China *jiugongge*, the squares used to copy an image, is widely used. It also allows one to make even a gigantic figure "smaller," as it were. The veneration for Mao Zedong can be amplified by people's aspirations for the divine. The subject of this painting is the veneration of the divine as it is amplified by people. If the grid used to reproduce his figure comes to the surface, Mao becomes once again a man.

AC: Seeing Mao through this grid reminds me of the story you told me about when you were a child and your mother used to put paper flowers on the window.

WG: When I was young, I watched my mother do what we call *chuanghua* (window flowers). It is a tradition of the North. Usually, after the new year, we decorate windows with these paper decorations. At sunrise they are very beautiful. This memory is still with me and has influenced me.

AC: When you told me about it, you described the way the objects you saw looked different to you. Is there a relationship between the rational use you make of the grid and the window decorated by your mother?

WG: Yes, I had already thought about that. There is this feeling in my subconscious because the squares on the window provoked an illusion in me. [Wang Guangyi points to the embroidered Mao AO study] This is a ready-made, like Marcel Duchamp's urinal.

AC: So, Duchamp drew whiskers on the image of Mona Lisa, and you painted a grid on that of Mao.

WG: Yes, like Duchamp's mustache on Mona Lisa. This idea is linked to Duchamp. Yes, it's as you say.

AC: Mao therefore becomes like *Mona Lisa*.

WG: Yes, it's a good point.

AC: Have you chosen to put the letters "AO" on the painting because they are the last letters contained in the name of Mao?

WG: Actually, these letters have no meaning. So I chose to add them because they were rather easy to write. Once written the effect was very nice. That's why I added them.

AC: Do you think that it was a subconscious choice to write the letters "AO," because of MAO?

WG: Actually, no. But now that you make me think about it, it could be like that.

AC: Why did you use Latin letters and not Chinese characters for the 1988 *Mao Zedong AO* triptych?

WG: I chose Latin letters because everyone would understand them. I made this for the China Avant-Garde Exhibition, at the National Gallery in Beijing. It was the most important exhibition for Chinese contemporary art. In that year, 1989, the Chinese society was in full reform and was opening up towards a new course. It was a time when people were asking for democracy.

AC: After closing the exhibition, the authorities have made you change the "O" to a "C." Why did they make you do it?

WG: When the authorities came to check, they said that this work was not appropriate. Then they discussed it. To get permission to exhibit the work I had to answer their questions. They said I should change something in the painting. Anything. So in the end I changed something. This "O" ... the background is black, see? All I had to do was draw a line on the right side to turn it into a "C." [He laughs]

AC: Your use of the figure of Mao makes me think of the repetitive pop icons used by Andy Warhol. Has Warhol influenced the triptych *Mao Zedong AO*?

WG: Warhol took common objects and made them noble. This idea influenced me. The fact that my Mao is a triptych could have some link with Warhol, but the main reason why I broke *Mao Zedong AO* into three parts is not related to Warhol but to Eastern philosophy. Laozi says: "The Tao generates One, One generates Two, Two generates Three, Three generates all beings." *Mao Zedong AO* comes from this influence. As time goes by, many more people understand what is behind this work, because the production of idols is a matter of social psychology. In China, this is a period without idols. There are none. People of my age as well as the young people have grown up with the figure of Mao. In this sense, Mao is my idol, the most important memory I have because I have seen his image every day. My first paintings on paper were portraits of Mao. At the time, painting Mao, according to my vision, was like painting a saint. It was something very sacred. Even today, inside me, I still feel that Mao is a sacred figure. I think that the idols and mystical images that a person has seen in childhood leave a profound mark. This impression has its repercussions on me even today. Although today I can see Mao Zedong more rationally, I can not erase the mystical sentiment that he evokes.

AC: A year after painting *Mao Zedong AO* you made a series of works in which Mao is only a *silhouette*. These paintings seem to move the viewer further away from Mao, as they deconstruct his image.

**WG:** My first Mao with the grid was very realistic. In the works you are referring to, I wanted instead to express the idea that, even if Mao had just died, we still had a very vivid memory of him. The later works in which I resumed the figure of Mao have become *empty*. They show an empty greeting. In fact, this sense of emptiness is a shadow. It means that Mao is further and further away from us. He has become a shadow, an illusion. I believe that in creation the artist must maintain a neutral attitude. Perhaps people will interpret the neutral position I take in my work in a different way. As far as I'm concerned, I do not think it's right for an artist to take an explicit position, to declare what he opposes or what he supports.

**AC:** I understand what you mean; your best-known work at the international level, *Great Criticism*, is precisely about neutrality. In these works, the images of communist propaganda and those of Western consumerism balance the scale. When looking at your work one does not sense your judgment on communist propaganda or Western consumerism. We understand that you consider them two coexisting paradoxes.

**WG:** In general, utopian countries use propaganda posters to brainwash people. In Western countries, which have a fetishist tradition, product logos are used to brainwash people. By making these two different forms of brainwashing coexist, I place myself in a position of equidistance from both. I take note of these two different ways of brainwashing. There is not a right one and a wrong one, they are simply two totally different ways of doing it. At first, I did not know what the meaning of the Cultural Revolution was. As a child, I found it very interesting. There were a lot of posters everywhere, showing slogans and illustrations of workers, peasants, and soldiers. These three figures represented the most important categories at the time. When I was in the Red Guard there were many blackboards that were used for propaganda. I also drew figures of workers, peasants, and soldiers on those blackboards.

**AC:** Were you "sent down" during the Cultural Revolution?

**WG:** Yes, I had to go to the country as an educated young man *(xia xiang)*. This was Mao's policy: to send the educated youth to the countryside. I cultivated the land like a farmer. In fact, Mao considered himself the son of a peasant. This was the image that he promoted. For me this was his most fascinating trait. Mao faced a dilemma: on the one hand he wanted the country to be strong, he wanted to build a new modern China capable of entering the industrial and nuclear competition; on the other he wished to be an emperor. The first car made in China illustrates this contradiction. China began producing its own automobiles in 1958. The first model of East Wind (Dong Feng) was not made on the assembly line, but handcrafted, piece by piece. The artists of the Central Academy were asked to add decorative details. The taillights were lantern-shaped and on the bonnet there was a golden dragon [an imperial symbol]. Forty years later I remade that car as an installation (Figure 10.1). My assistants and some workers assembled it by hand. Returning to the first model, I do not know if it was the government that decided to put the dragon on the hood, or if the workers did it to escape their job. This dragon, however, showed the feudal desire to continue to venerate imperial power. Sometimes the spirit goes beyond matter. I think that Mao, when accepting that car, felt like an emperor accepting a tribute.

**WG:** The death of Mao and that of Christ are the deaths of two spiritual leaders. In the Chinese tradition, yellow represents power, so I used yellow to portray Jesus and Mao. I think it is power that controls people's spirit. Controlling the spirit is the greatest and highest

**Figure 10.1** Wang Guangyi, *Water, East Wind, Golden Dragon* (2007–8), installation (cast iron/fiberglass, pictures, etc.), size of the car model: Size: 500 × 190 × 165 cm.

power. People must fight. Fighting you can reach ... success. Now, at the stage of life in which I find myself, I know that success is a very ephemeral opportunity. Perhaps success does not exist. After struggling, you have the impression of having achieved a lot but, after all, perhaps this is not so important. The most important thing is probably to face something, to renew one's state of mind towards things that cannot be known objectively. People should have a feeling of amazement towards things they cannot know. But Mao is a belief. I worship Mao a lot. From my point of view, Mao is like Jesus. I painted the death of two people: that of Mao and that of Jesus. Both of them, however, have the possibility of returning to life. Jesus has already come back to life. As for Mao, I do not know if he'll come back. [The camera shows *The Last Supper* from 2011]

**WG:** *The Last Supper* took six months of work. It's the biggest painting I have made so far.

**AC:** Do the drippings represent blood?

**WG:** It could be interpreted as blood. In my intentions the drippings are an element of oriental mystical philosophy, of Neo-Daoism (*Xuanxue*). This philosophy could also be considered the essence of the East.

**AC:** The details of these abstract shapes and drippings appear to be natural landscapes, classic ink paintings.

**WG:** If you look at the parts separately, each one gives you the impression of a universe in its own right. Christianity asks this question: What was God before creating all beings? This kind of thinking belongs to the West. With this painting I tried to answer this question with my art. I drew on the thought of Laozi, of whom I spoke earlier: Tao generates One, One generates Two, Two generates Three, Three generates all beings, therefore—following this reasoning—what God created is all that comes after Three. Before Three, Tao generates One. This thought belongs to oriental culture, for which the universe has an indeterminate character. I am trying to find a point of contact between the Western Christian tradition and oriental mysticism. I take these two things and put them together.

**AC:** The black is so black in this painting. I think you answered the question about God existence before: blackness. Black void.

**WG:** I think the black is extremely simple. Furthermore, it gives the idea of the impossibility of knowing.

**AC:** And it's three-dimensional. You can get inside. It sucks you in.

**WG:** Yes, it gives a feeling of tremor. I myself, I cannot look at it for too long: it makes my head spin.

*This interview is taken from* Reasoning with Idols, *written and directed by Andrew Cohen in 2012.*

Part VI

# The Circle of Life: Presenting and Representing Food

# 11

# Food Art, a Hymn to Nature

Mary Bittner Wiseman 明玛丽

*Artists are avoiding the pursuit of and concern
with the ultimate ideals of humanity.*

Wang Guangyi

## Prologue

In pursuit of the ideals mentioned in the quotation above, Wang Guangyi has made two paintings and six installations in which food appears in various guises, from the names of fruits written in the series of paintings *Small Criticisms* (1992–3), to the real food that appears in the installations, and on to the words believed to have been spoken by Jesus at *The Last Supper* (2011). These eight works describe a narrative arc that moves from a near-comic take on the *Great Criticism* series to the transformation of bread into the body of Jesus alluded to in *The Last Supper*, a painting in the series *New Religion*. The first and last of the installations, *Flour* (1996) and *Things-in-Themselves* (2000), use flour and rice, respectively, to make metaphysical points about identity and appearance and reality. Only four of the artworks use food as food, and they use it to make the political observation that the state heavily regulates the individual's use of food. Only in the fourth work, *The Similarities and Differences of Food Guarantees under Two Political Systems* (1996), and in the final one, *The Last Supper*, does the relation between China and the West appear as an issue.

Wang addresses the question of the relation between China and the West keenly aware that he himself has been shaped by the recent history of China, whose place and time give him the materials of which he makes his art. These include Mao-era posters, capitalist slogans, staple foods like flour, rice, and millet, state certificates, works in the history of Western art, and news photographs of leaders. Despite the degree to which his culture has marked him—his ninth to his twentieth years were lived under the Cultural Revolution—he read widely in Western philosophy and art history. Kant and Ernst Gombrich influenced him, as did Joseph Beuys and Andy Warhol in contemporary art. His life in China during and after the Mao era and his education in the ideas and art of the West, gave rise to an art whose subjects hide as much as they show. Its challenge is to uncover their secrets,to show how they appear when they are read in a new, another, way.

A stunning example of this is the *Great Criticism* series (1995–2007). These are paintings in which workers appropriated from Mao-era posters are juxtaposed with slogans for Western consumer products. At first blush the paintings seem to be ironic, Chinese works saluting the likes of Coca Cola and Rolex. They are more, however. They show that the images of Eastern workers and Madison Avenue–styled names of Western products exist in order to sell a dream to their targeted audiences, Chinese workers and Western consumers. For the former, it is the Marxist triumph of the proletariat; for the latter, the laissez-faire capitalist dream of a self-regulated market. The Marxist triumph was shattered in 1989 and the capitalist's dream in 1929, but triumphs and dreams do not go gently. The Eastern images and Western words function rhetorically, and Wang refers to them as *propaganda*, which presumes to persuade an audience that what is shown is true, whether or not it is. What is at stake in the propaganda posters and advertising slogans is not truth, however, but faith.

Wang believes that ideologies, of which Maoism and capitalism are two, are like religion in that both have followers whose faith is not threatened by the impossibility of there being an empirical truth about any future event and, therefore, about what is promised. There can be neither empirical nor *a priori* proof that a promised dream will come true or that, if it does, it will be all that was hoped for. Two things remain. One, *faith* in the soundness of the ideas of the kind of person one wants to be and the life one wants to lead, and the idea of how a state wants to organize its political and economic relations and stand in relation to its citizens. Two, a Kantian *transcendental* argument that the choices made by an individual or state are presuppositions and necessary conditions for the fruition of the dream. What is called for is a leap of *faith* that what these choices promise can *transcend* the limits of what now we have and now we know. Faith in the ability of any ideology to transcend these limits is necessary because, although there may be reasons to prefer one system of organization to another, the reasons are rarely compelling.

Wang's art is dedicated to showing its viewers that despite what their culture has conditioned them to believe, they have a choice as to where to put their faith and where to seek transcendence, as he has sought in his work to transcend differences between communism and capitalism, and between Mao's materialism and Western religion. He does not, however, seek to transcend the difference between nature and its myriad others: artifice, culture, or the state with its efforts to control the individual's relation to food by regulation and reward.

Wang's art takes the post-modernist route of inviting viewers to see what lies behind that which is before their eyes so that, alive to there being more than what shows itself and aware that what is there might be like the thing-in-itself, ever a mystery, they will think against the grain of what they see. He does this in an original way with his food art.

What follows is a discussion of the eight works in which food appears. It is in three parts. Only in the second is food dealt with as food; it plays other roles in the first and third sections.

## Part One

*Small Criticisms* (1992–3) (Figure 11.1) is a series of seven paintings in which figures from social realist posters appear, as they do in the *Great Criticism*, but whereas there the figures are alike and posed together, here they are not. A few three-quarter bodies are shown; there are more head-and-shoulders, even more just heads, and then there are hands alone, a foot, and lips. All of the figures are yellow, and most of the canvases are squares of slightly more than three feet. Words appear in all of them, as do the same colors, some paintings have strong blue backgrounds and heavy red lines around each thing, others have pale blue grounds and pink outlines. Food appears in this series in the guise of names: in some of the paintings the words are names of fruits, which are pictured next to their names. In each painting there is a comic-strip-like balloon with words or three-digit numbers in it. The words say where and when the artist was born and say or ask: "Mr. Wang is one of the most important artists in Contemporary art movements in China?"

Differences we take for granted are thrown to the winds, like those between socialist workers in propaganda posters and the individual men and women workers shown in *Small Criticisms*. A question in the form of a declarative sentence is asked in handwritten words with some words crossed out, as in a note scrawled on a scrap of paper. The personal note continues with the artist's

**Figure 11.1** Wang Guangyi, *Small Criticisms—Banana* (1992) oil on canvas, 150 × 120 cm; *Danone* (1993) oil on canvas, 100 × 100 cm; *Mango* (1992) oil on canvas, 100 × 100 cm; *Tooth* (1992) oil on canvas, 100 × 100 cm; *Une Pomme* (1993) oil on canvas, 100 × 100 cm.

not keeping his opinions to himself but expressing them, ironically no doubt, in the scrawl, introducing an autobiographical note into what is not supposed to be about the artist. Further, where images and the words in the *Great Criticism* paintings stand in stark contrast, the close relation between a word and its referent depicted in *Small Criticisms* takes away from that stark contrast. As whimsical as *Great Criticism* is serious, *Small Criticisms* show only fragmented workers' bodies juxtaposed with random words and images of what they stand for. All are separated each from each by broad outlines of color, and all share the picture plane with handwritten words from and about the artist. Color and humor in the seven paintings in the series full of color and humor stand better together than alone because of slight differences among them, for example, some have words in French with no images to interpret them.

*Flour* (1995) is an installation in which flour is not taken to be something milled from grain and baked into bread, but as something that when packaged in a certain way can be mistaken for a drug. The work is two light boxes, approximately two by four by three feet, placed several feet apart and wrapped in artificial fur on four sides with eight bags of flour on the lighted surface of each. The bags of flour look as though they contain drugs. We are told that Wang was thinking of drugs as spiritual grain and flour as material grain: although the flour looked like spiritual grain, it was really material grain.[1] The association of drugs with the spirit and food with the body gives Wang an example not only of something being mistaken for something else, but also of something thought to be spiritual turning out to be material, just as Hegel's world spirit was grounded by Marx's economic forces of production and Western religion's heaven was brought to earth by Mao.

There is, however, another way to read *Flour*. Rather than seeing it as showing how one thing can masquerade as another, look at it as asking what the difference is between things thought to be different, like food and drugs. *Great Criticism* shows communism and capitalism not to be as different as they seem to be insofar as both have to sell their visions to their audience. If conducing to health and altering the mind are supposed to be among the defining traits of flour and drugs, respectively, *Flour* shows the ideas of each to be neither clear (all essential traits are manifest) nor distinct (no essential trait is shared by anything else). Derrida has shown that what is thought to be the difference *between* two things often reappears as a difference *within* each. The difference between helping the body and altering one's mood or mind exists within the class of foods (coffee stimulates), as the difference between helping the body and altering the mind exists within the class of drugs (medicine heals).

In *Small Criticisms,* there are only words for and cartoon images of food. In *Flour* there is real food, but it is contrasted with drugs and used to make points about appearance and identity, asking what, after all, is the difference between the things we think so different. It is not being treated as food *qua* food.

In the four works in Part Two it is. But there, too, the food is compromised by being seen in light of the state's regulation of how one is to deal with the most natural and basic function of providing food for oneself.

## Part Two

In *Quarantine—All Food is Potentially Poisonous* (1996) (see Figure 12.1); food is laid out in the wrong place, as in *Flour* it was packaged in the wrong way, that is, as drugs are. For *Quarantine*, Wang got display shelves from a supermarket whose employees laid out fruits and vegetables as they would have been laid out in the supermarket. The shelves' frame is iron painted green, a color salient in nature, and the boards are unpainted wood. The shelving is along all of one wall and parts of two adjoining walls, the length of the shelves against the full wall twice that of those against the adjoining walls. The frames are four shelves high and placed above them are twenty small-framed posters issued by a quarantine station that promotes food hygiene. Food, if not treated hygienically, can become poisonous, hence, the work's title. A standard reading of the work is that since food is linked with the health of an individual and the state publicizes and requires adherence to measures for individuals to take to maintain their health, the work marks one relation of the state to the individual.

The public display of the hygiene posters is paternalistic at best and repressive at worst, with the title expressing "the insecure and fearful mindset of the public since certainty has disappeared in the post-Cold War era."[2] A Chinese critic, Fang Lihua, wrote this presumably in light of the fact that the end of the Cold War was the end of the hegemony of the one other major communist country, Russia, which would have created greater uncertainty in China than it did in the West. It seems rather that the insecurity and fear were *created* by the insistence of the state's hygiene posters. The work's juxtaposition of the posters and the food is relentless. The dire warning of the posters—if you do not do what they say, your food will become poisonous—not only creates fear, but also intrudes on nature and the independence of the individual. Food is a basic human need, and the earliest peoples spent much of their time working to secure it and discovering by experience what was harmful and what was not.

It is clear that states do and should exercise control over food to the degree in which they support the food industries and regulate the processing and distribution of their products. This, however, is different from what *Quarantine— All Food is Potentially Poisonous* does, which is to present the food on the market shelves as (potentially) poisonous. Food is what can be ingested and transformed into cellular matter, and things that would poison us were we to eat them do not count as food. Food by itself is not poisonous; its exposure to manure, dirty water, chemical spray, and unwashed hands can pollute it with germs or harmful chemicals, making it poisonous. However, to conceive of food as potentially poisonous is to treat what can make a food poisonous as internal to it. In treating the presence of pollutants as the rule rather than the exception, *Quarantine* is polluting the *concept* of food. The intruding presence of the hygiene posters in a beautiful display of foods has the effect of calling into question the purity of the food nature provides for all its inhabitants. The fact that things in nature prey upon and destroy each other is a different matter. That is the battle for survival *within* nature rather than the effect *upon* nature of people who introduce the likes of dirty water and chemical fertilizers and sprays. That nature always wins was shown when *Quarantine* was exhibited in Shenzhen in southern China. The warm humid climate there caused the vegetables to rot and the potatoes, onions, and other tubers to sprout roots that grew by the day. About this, Fang Lihua said: "This spectacle produced another form of beauty, rather than the fear of going rotten."[3]

*The Similarities and Differences of Food Guarantees under Two Political Systems* (1996) consisted of two piles of large rocks from the Alps, one with fruits and vegetables among the rocks, the other with bottles and jars among them. The installation was exhibited in Basel, and the rocks and what was scattered among them were all Swiss. Above each pile were two sets of Chinese food-hygiene posters, fifty in all, some the same as those shown in *Quarantine*. Wang "believes that the system of food management in the West is based on many technical standards and is quite different from that of China."[4] Therefore, the juxtaposition of Western food, bottles and jars, and Alpine rocks with Chinese posters of how to guarantee food hygiene is dissonant. Food and rocks are what they are, both natural, while food-protection policies are whatever the state decrees. They are not natural, but conventional. One note disturbs this nice distinction between what is in the Western and the Chinese elements of the installation. It is the glass jars and bottles that are among the second pile of rocks. They are not natural, but artificial. Moreover, how food is packaged varies with economic considerations just as food-protection strategies do with political ones. Both are conventions. The formation of rocks with bottles and jars seems to be about five times as wide as high and forms a wide-angled triangle. Twenty black-framed posters are in two rows above the rocks, 14 in the top row and 6 in the bottom. The rocks, food, and glass containers are real physical things. The Chinese posters are real, too, but they are representations of people, things, and words.

Difference abounds. First, there is the difference between the manufactured jars and bottles and the natural food and rocks. Then there is the difference between real things, artificial or natural, and representations; and, finally, the one between art and everyday life. The relation of the state to the individual expressed by the state's rules of food hygiene is part of people's everyday lives. Wang's representation of the relation in the installation in Basel, however, is what he has made of it, which is this: its non-representational part, rocks and what is scattered among them, is random and disordered, while the representational posters are lined up in military precision, the wide black frames of each poster dramatically darker than the gray of the rocks. The 14 posters in the top row above the bottles-and-jars pile of rocks are rectangular, and the 6 centered just below them are square. Order and obvious difference govern the poster displays; in the disorder of the pile below neither sameness nor difference can be made out. The idea is that because food production, distribution, and protection depend upon varying things like weather, soil, people's skills and attention, it is

**Figure 11.2** Wang Guangyi, *24-Hour Food Degeneration Process* (1997), installation with Plexiglas, water, fruits, food, and photographs, etc. Variable dimensions.

inevitably done willy-nilly and is in need of the order a state can impose. And since there is no natural or necessary way for a state to do this, it is no surprise that the food guarantees would differ among political systems.

*24-Hour Food Degeneration Process* (1997) (Figure 11.2) speaks to the fact that food will spoil if not treated in certain ways, such as those outlined in the state hygiene posters, for example. Wang's idea was to present the slow rotting process of fruits and vegetables in four sealed 24-inch by 63-inch acrylic cases attached to a gallery wall, together with framed promotional posters about food-hygiene laws. He ended up putting the food in plastic bags, bottles, and jars in unsealed cases. These cases were hung vertically, two on each side of two rows of five posters hung roughly midway between the tops and bottoms of the cases. Again, here are the differences between natural and artificial—food, on the one hand, and acrylic, plaster, and glass on the other—and between real things, fruits and vegetables, and representations, in the posters. There is this difference from *Quarantine*, however: in *Quarantine* there is the ordered placement of the posters and the scramble of food and bottles and jars among the rocks, randomness requiring order, but in *24-Hour Degeneration* there is not order and chaos, but regulation and degeneration. The work demonstrates what would happen were the hygiene laws not obeyed, as though nature herself proves the need for the state to legislate hygiene at the level of the individual. It is not clear, however, that it is necessary to regulate individuals; most states regulate food industries. So far from their degeneration being an essential part of the exhibition as it was supposed to be, the foods were replaced when they became odorous, which is what happens when food goes bad. Wang had set up the installation so that the food's rotting would show nature winning over the state's efforts at regulation, but despite encasing the food in plastic bags, bottles, and jars, he was not able to do this. Nature won over art also.

What was new in *The Era of Materialism* (2000) (see Figure 12.3) is what is hanging on the walls instead of the hygiene posters on the walls of the three installations discussed above. Ten blank white award certificates that were used to reward people for various good behaviors hang in black frames with red mats in rows on the galleries' four walls. In the center of the room stand eight white, rectangular platforms, wider than deep and of different heights. On them are displayed precious things: millet, garlic, flour, green vegetables, and the like. Of the blank award certificates, the critic Yan Sanchun said they were for brainwashing and "were a common sight in China a few decades ago and part of the process of individuals being 'brainwashed' by State ideology."[5] However, we could as well see the function of the certificates to be simply to reward people for doing well and to motivate others to earn one. Giving awards can be, but are not always, or even usually, attempts at brainwashing.

Yan Sanchun further says that the food symbolizes the material dimension and the awards, the spiritual, with the two being inextricable as "carriers for the social system and cultural memory."[6] The certificates can also be read as praising the food itself, presented as it is to the viewers in the way that precious and beautiful objects are displayed. Since food can be said to be the most basic material for human beings, it is a star in the era of materialism. It is what transforms itself into our cellular material and is necessary for life. Marx said that the means through which people are able to ensure their survival determines everything else about their circumstances. Gone is the association of food with poison and degeneration that call for guarantees and quarantines. Now food is a star. In the next two works of art it is represented, not only as precious, but also as having metaphysical primacy and spiritual power.

## Part Three

Of the Kantian notion that gives *Things-in-Themselves* (2000) its title (see Figure 8.2), Wang said that it is

> a concept that is at once extremely ordinary and extremely sacred[7] ... The information I draw from Kant's notion ... is this: behind the object we see there exists an unknown force, which induces it to appear as in a special way, and this force is not something that we can understand through knowledge.[8]

The installation fills a 900-square-meter room with four walls that are stacked to the ceiling, some five meters high, with over five thousand bags of rice and bran. There are seven bright lights overhead that together with the strong odors of rice and burlap "inebriated the senses."[9] The bags had to be stacked so as to slope outward to the ceiling lest their weight cause the floor to collapse, and the effect is that of the walls opening out as though to infinity. "It could be a grain storehouse or it could be a church."[10] An image of the installation appears on the cover of Huang Zhuan's *Politics and Theology in Chinese Contemporary Art: Reflections on the Work of Wang Guangyi*, and on the back of the dust jacket of Demetrio Paparoni's *Wang Guangyi: Works and Thoughts 1985—2012*. Thanks to the splendid monotony and strange beauty of sack upon sack upon sack, *Things-in-Themselves* promises to become an icon of early twenty-first-century Chinese art.

The work could hardly be simpler. Wang stated, "It is a large installation made from burlap sacks [filled with rice]. The material has no particular meaning, though it has a profound impact on all of us. It does not, however, symbolize anything ... If there is too much symbolic significance in the chosen material, then it breaks with the whole concept of the thing-in-itself."[11] The space of the installation, with its mixed odors of burlap and rice reminded him of his days working in a granary when he was twenty, even though a granary would never stack bags higher than three meters. He said that he wanted to combine the sensory perceptions of the granary with "abstract implications" and saw that the gallery's size would let him do that. By enlarging the height of the stacks of grain, the familiar becomes unfamiliar, and "the sense of the unfamiliar leads to spiritual imaginings in people."[12]

These imaginings were for him of a piece with the influence the term "thing-in-itself" had on him. When he described his idea for the installation to others, he saw that "you can't really judge whether something is really good or not through mere description."[13] That is to say, one has to experience what has been described in order to evaluate it. This might not be enough, however, for one cannot always judge what one is experiencing. This is because, Wang implies, there can be something about what one experiences that eludes one's grasp, where to grasp something is to have some sort of conceptual hold on it, to surprise the form, the conceptual shape of it, to separate it out. "The things that we cannot judge ... certainly have something behind them, whether it is what we would call metaphysical or conceptual. It is a kind of transcendent quality, and it is what I want."[14] What it transcends is our ability to capture it in the net of our languages even though we feel its power. It is the thing-in-itself.

We turn finally to a work that is as complex as *Things-in-Themselves* is simple and brings us back to words, but words used in a way other than were the names of fruits in *Small Criticisms*.

*The Last Supper* (2011) (see Figure 3.1) is part of a series of oil paintings, *New Religion*, whose subjects are the spiritual leaders Christ and Pope John Paul XXIII, the political leaders Lenin, Stalin, and Mao, and the philosophers Marx and Engels. The images are appropriated from art history, such as Andrea Mantegna's *Dead Christ* and Leonardo's *Last Supper*, and news photographs. The series includes 13 men in *The Last Supper* (8 sections of 400 X 200 cm) and 5 in *The Guides* (5 sections of 300 X 200 cm). The title of the series refers to Maoism, and the critic Maria Cannarella says of the works in the series: "These paintings suggest that human being's need for transcendence can be seen in the devotion towards those who promote a materialistic vision of history that ... shares a providential view of existence with religion," and she goes on to suggest that the dead Christ in the *Pieta* could be interchanged with Mao in *Death of the Guide*.[15] The implication is that materialistic and religious views of history are inextricable, as Wang claimed the material and the spiritual were in *Flour* (food and drugs) and *The Era of Materialism* (food and award certificates).

The paintings themselves are powerful and beautiful. Photographs of the paintings or news photographs of the famous men appear against a black background, shorn of whatever color the originals had. The faces, arms, and hands of the figures, along with the table of the *Last Supper* and its contents are outlined in pink paint, thin drips of which course down the canvas. One can barely make out the food on the table, but food we know there was. In the *New Testament* it is written: "While they were eating, Jesus took bread, and when he had given thanks, he broke it and gave it to his disciples, saying, 'Take and eat; this is my body.'"[16] The words of Jesus at that supper are supposed to have converted bread into his body, just as the bread anyone eats is converted into the stuff of his body. The differences are clear: the bread that became, upon his uttering the words, his own body was outside his body, as the bread that becomes the body of any one of us does so inside the body. Words transformed bread into the body of Jesus, while digestion transforms the bread that becomes parts of our bodies. And what is the same is clear: a piece of bread has been transformed into the material of a human body.

There are two points to be made, one literal, the other figurative. The first is that we are not able to explain or understand how, finally, digestion works—just as we are not able to understand how Jesus could have transformed bread into his body with words alone. The point about digestion is Hume's. He notes that no matter how fine-grained our analysis of processes like digestion becomes, there is always the further step: How does *this* turn into *that*? The second point is that since the ordinary transformation into our bodies of the melons, oranges, and mangos named in *Small Criticisms* is, at bottom, a mystery, the mystery of the religious transformation can stand as a figure for the material one. This is to suggest that the wonder of nature is on a par with the wonder evoked by the divine. Nature is neither providential nor teleological. It is a system whose galaxies exceed the imagination, and complexities defy understanding.

Wang likens Jesus and Mao in being guides for our lives, and religion and Maoism give us a providential view of history, where guidance and history are both forward looking and presume to transcend the present. They are linear. Nature is not.

The paintings in *Great Criticism* show that communism and capitalism both need to motivate workers and consumers to do and to buy more, and those in *New Religion* show that communism and religion both seek followers whose faith is not daunted by the impossibility of truth for what is promised. Some of the food installations, on the other hand, contrast nature and the state; others comment on the nature of food, showing us something whose borders are permeable (*Flour*) and that is, like a thing-in-itself, something without which human beings could not exist (*Things-in-Themselves*). Food is natural and is, finally, immune to outside control. Its omnipresence and power are movingly captured in Wang's *Things-in-Themselves*.

# Notes

1 Paparoni, 2013: 182.
2 Ibid.: 196.
3 Ibid.

4   Ibid.: 194.
5   Ibid.: 202.
6   Ibid.
7   Huang, 2013: 171.
8   Ibid.
9   Ibid.
10  Ibid.
11  Wang Guangyi in Paparoni, 2013: 388.
12  Ibid.
13  Ibid.
14  Ibid.
15  Paparoni, 2013: 288.
16  The Gospel of St. Matthew, 26:26.

# References

Huang, Z. (2014). *Politics and Theology in Chinese Contemporary Art: Reflections on the work of Wang Guangyi*. Milan: Skira.

Paparoni, D. (2013). *Wang Guangyi: Works and thoughts 1985–2012*. Milan: Skira.

# 12

# Food in Wang Guangyi's Art

Nicola Perullo 裴倪轲

## Introduction: Food in Art

Food and Art: the juxtaposition of these two terms is often vague, leading to confusion in meaning and to superficiality. In fact, this relation has three specific areas that, although they intersect with one another, assume different perspectives with respect to the function of food and the aim of its utilization.[1]

One area is food *as* art that is the status of culinary practice: Can cuisine be art? This is the classic question raised by Simmias and Socrates in *Phedo*—and by cooks and chefs as artists.[2] Today, chefs such as Ferran Adrià are clear examples of this issue. Ferran Adrià of El bulli is a cook who has influenced the language and the code of contemporary cuisine more than anyone else with respect to the theme of art. His work has been compared with that of the avant-garde: first and foremost, with the futurist cuisine of Marinetti, where the meal was thought of as a multisensorial total experience. Adrià was the first and only chef to receive institutional recognition from the "art world," with his participation in the contemporary art exposition *Documenta* 2007. More generally, he started a true revolution that stirred unprecedented interest, not only from the gastronomic community, but also from cultural and artistic institutions.

One can define, then, another field of investigation as art *in* food: the area of combinations and comingling between different artistic media and cooking. This is often made through explicit collaborations among chefs and artists on specific projects, through the creation of edible artifacts that imitate languages and codes of some artworks. This is the case of the staging of the great medieval banquets, in which musicians, actors, and acrobats gave real theatrical performances during their gatherings. Likewise, the marzipan architectures of Carême, the triumphs of sugar, the metamorphoses of Urban Dubois, and the

Escoffier ice sculptures—scenographic setups merged with a dish that they were to integrate—represent some examples of the decorative and mimetic function of the structures built in great cuisine of the nineteenth century. Today, chefs, artists, and designers collaborate during exhibitions on food and art, or in view of the creation of tools or accessories to be included in restaurants. Such as the furniture, the style, the design of the environment, and the background music, everything that flows into the global atmosphere of those restaurants is essential. These places pay great attention to the smallest details, which are sometimes explicitly chosen and designed according to the different culinary expressions.

The third field is food in art. Art has always used food as a subject of representation, from prehistoric graffiti to antiquity banquets and modern still lifes. These representations have covered as many meanings as the field of art itself: religious, ritual, symbolic, expressive, and evocative. The large utilization of food as artistic practice or/and as art material, though, has a more recent history, stemming from the emergence of avant-garde movements of the twentieth century. Futurism and the Eat Art movement are points of reference here: on the one hand, *The Futurist Cookbook* by Marinetti and Fillìa opened up the path for the idea of cooking and eating as a performance art—but it would be better to speak of the *experience of the meal* as a whole. Cuisine could even be, according to some opinions influenced by futurism thought, the real *Gesamtkunstwerk*, the "total work of art," because of its unique capacity of involving all the senses in the aesthetic experience. On the other hand, the Eat Art movement and its founder, Daniel Spoerri, focused on food as material for the creative process and was obviously influenced, like Arte Povera, by the thought of Marcel Duchamp's ready-made. Spoerri created the famous "snare-pictures," made by assembling and fixing objects like food remains of the tables where people really ate, and then displaying them on a wall. Spoerri, and many other artists along the same lines (Allan Kaprow, Dieter Roth, Arman and Joseph Beuys) found in food, as an everyday life "object," a powerful means to express the vital process, the relation between life and death, the contingency of art. Food in art has never been so popular and so extensively discussed as it is today. From Rirkit Tiravanjia to Marina Abramovic, from Vanessa Beecroft to Olafur Eliasson—to recall just a few names among a plethora of artists—the art world of the twenty-first century seems to be more and more involved in food issues, although through many different ways. Food art, as Silvia Bottinelli and Margherita d'Ayala Valva have written, "has been blessed with an impressively positive reception because of its ability to respond to the contemporaneous societal and cultural concerns with food, health, and sustainability."[3]

The position of Wang Guangyi is peculiar within this framework. In fact, though the Chinese artist is not a "food artist" at all, food often has been present in many of his works. Moreover, Joseph Beuys and Andy Warhol, two of his constant artistic references, dealt with food in their art.[4] It seems, then, that a quick review of some topics in Wang Guangyi's works on food may have some interest. However, the general tone and the aims are quite different from the most usual gestures of the food art scene. One can say that the role of food in the works of Wang Guangyi strictly relates to the more general meaning of his art, that is, that food explicitly expresses philosophical meanings. Food has symbolic and metaphysical functions; it is a means to transcend the material culture and allude to a spiritual dimension. From a philosophical perspective, then, one may say that Wang Guangyi's consideration of food originates from a combination of Taoist thought and a position "à la Lévinas." According to the French philosopher, in fact, "metaphysical desire is a hunger that nourishes itself not with bread but with hunger itself;"[5] so, "he undoes the certainty of the discontinuity between hunger for bread and hunger for the other. The objects may be different, but the desire is the same."[6]

## Food in Wang Guangyi's artworks

In the following pages, I will propose some general considerations about the meaning of food in Wang Guangyi's art, following a list of his works related to this topic. As this is something that has never been done, I think it is beneficial to make a list of them. In his works, food occurs in two different ways: one is direct and thematic—often when the term "food" is present in the title of the work—while the other is indirect and implicit.

(A) The thematic area comprises the following works:
1. *Flour* (1995), an installation proposed together with *Drugs* (1995). It is the first work in which Wang utilizes the symbolic element of food in an explicit way. Here, the analogies between flour and drugs are on both a metaphorical, linguistic level as well as material, encompassing the spiritual and the material grain. Here it is clear how the general philosophical position of Wang Guangyi also affects his utilization of food: art should not celebrate everyday life and ordinary gestures; rather, it should trigger reflections on a spiritual level. So material food is material

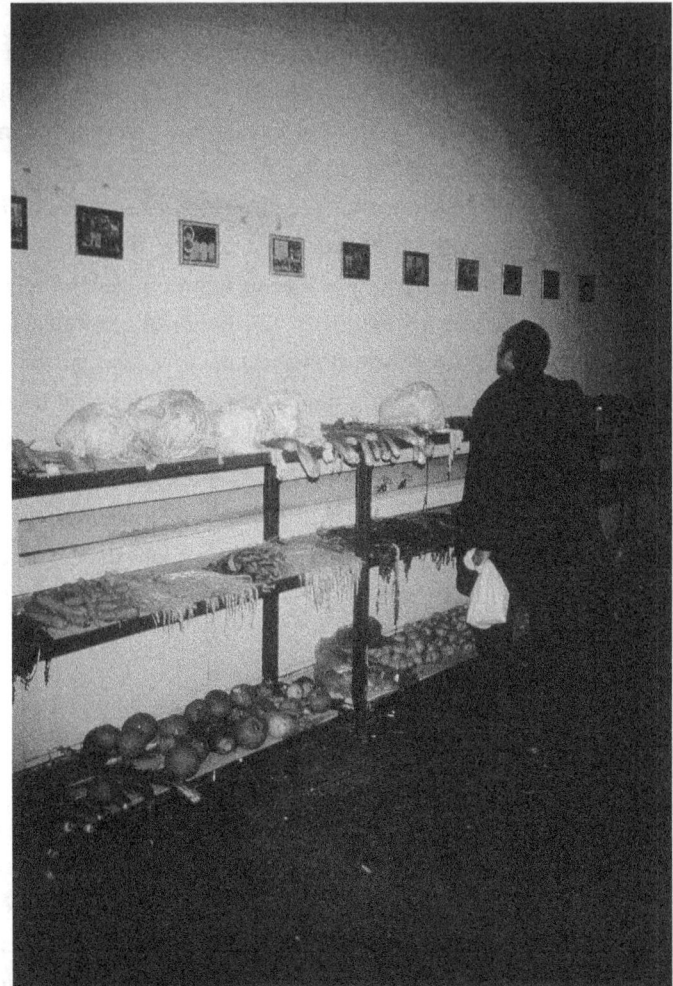

**Figure 12.1** Wang Guangyi, *Quarantine—All Food Is Potentially Poisonous* (1996), installation with official Chinese health quarantine propaganda images, metal racks, wooden shelves, food, etc. Variable dimensions.

and, at the same time, it refers to a metaphysical dimension that can be either spiritual or political.

2. *Quarantine—All Food is Potentially Poisonous* (1996) (Figure 12.1). In this installation, in fact, food assumes a political and social meaning through a philosophical reflection on the problematic relationship between society and the individual. Exhibited for the first time at the Beijing Capital Normal University Art Museum, the work was made with shelves

borrowed from a supermarket, on which fruit and vegetables were placed. Above the shelves hung posters depicting standards and issues related to hygiene and food safety. Here, Wang wants to communicate the individual's mistrust of society. An opposite situation to that is represented by another work of the same period, *Blood Test—Everyone Is a Potential Virus Carrier* (1996), which expresses, instead, the social mistrust of individuals. As Huang Zhuan (Chinese curator, critic, and art historian) stated, it appears that "the paradoxical relationship and psychological reality of controller and controlled mutually govern each other in contemporary civilization."[7] *Quarantine—All Food Is Potentially Poisonous* is a *ready-made* that reflects on political and social manipulation through the issue of food security. The observer is compelled to become aware of the different powers that affect the choices and behaviors of the individual. This installation was revived, albeit slightly changed, in 2008 at the Shenzhen's He Xiangning Art Museum. It is interesting to remember an anecdote: because the climate in southern China is much more humid, much of the fruit and vegetables placed on the shelves has begun to rot, while potatoes, sweet potatoes, onions, and other tubers had started to sprout and grow roots, making the installation "alive" and always changing over the hours. The precariousness of organic matter, the transformation and the transience of bodies is, in this case, a *topos* of food art—especially of contemporary art—and is closely linked to the spirit of the subsequent work examined here.

3. *24-Hour Food Degeneration Process* (1997) (see Figure 11.2). The original design of this installation included different types of vegetables and fruits, and they were supposed to lie in four boxes made of an acrylic material. Six propaganda posters on food hygiene regulations would then accompany the containers. However, Wang Guangyi changed his mind before making this work in Singapore: the number of posters were increased to ten, and the boxes, which were kept open instead, were filled not only with vegetables, but also with plastic bags, bottles, and jars. Soon after, the unpleasant odors released by rotting organic substances occupied all the exhibition space. Because of the complaints of visitors, the museum managers had to replace the

original fruit and vegetables with fresh produce, but this led to a significant misunderstanding: the aim of the installation was ruined, because with it, Wang intended precisely to communicate the degeneration of matter. While in *Quarantine* the inspiration for the Chinese model is preponderant, here in *24-Hour* the Western model holds the centrality in the meaning of the work. Both, however, raise reflections on education and, coherently with Wang's thought, refer to the relationship between the individual and the universal body. Different forms of thought give life to various cognitive attitudes toward the world that reflect its characteristics and significant traits.

4. *The Similarities and Differences of Food Guarantees under Two Political Systems* (1997). Even this work, first exhibited in Basel, expresses the tension between the individual and society; the main idea here is to reflect on the juridical problems concerning food control. The work is made of two piles of stones (picked up from the Swiss Alps), one with fruits and vegetables, and the other with jars and bottles; both the food and packaged food containers come from Switzerland. These piles are dominated by fifty hygiene posters (some of which are also included in *Quarantine—All Food Is Potentially Poisonous*), which are symbols of Chinese culture and its approach to the food system. The stones represent the ways in which the Western states—Switzerland acts as an emblematic case—manage food controls and their safety: the political and health sphere deeply influence the life of the individual, who constitutes the whole of society to which the artist turns his gaze. Through this work, Wang Guangyi compares the two different political and government models and highlights their peculiar problems without expressing an explicit preference between them.

(B) The indirect and implicit works implicating food are the following:

5. *Gentle Black* (1985) (Figure 12.2). It seems to be the first occurrence of a food item in the work of Wang. A girl is shown here, viewed from behind, with an apple placed on the table in front of her. The setting—the food and humanity itself—which turns its back on the observer, appears inorganic. The girl viewed from behind refers to *The Back of Humanity* (1985) series, while the same posture is assumed by the subjects represented in

*Frozen North Pole* (1984–5) and *Post-Classical* (1986–9). Not showing the face of humanity and its features may symbolize the difficulty itself in giving it a form, a form that in the paintings is "embalmed" and petrified to immortalize its existence. There is a freezing of the space–time dimension, and the apple is part of this frozen world as well. It is not a real, physical apple, but rather a metaphysical one. Similarly, in *Big Doll—Madonna and Child* (1988), the Madonna is shown from behind, while the child is in a frontal profile. He seems to look for his mother's breast (nutrition

**Figure 12.2** Wang Guangyi, *Gentle Black* (1985), oil on canvas, 85 × 70 cm.

being hinted at here) but, since she is turning her back to him, he is destined not to find it.

6. *Great Criticism* (1990–2007). This is the most famous and prolific painting cycle of the artist. In this series of oils on canvas, Wang brings together and combines symbolic images of Chinese ideology and graphic elements typical of the Western capitalistic system, including many food-industry logos: McDonald's, Coca-Cola, Pepsi, Carlsberg, Nestlé, and Maxwell House. As has been well argued, this artwork is not part of "Chinese Pop Art," a movement born spontaneously after 1989, and in which many artists took part. Again, the intent of Wang is foreign to the mere political satire, as he strives to show the deep spiritual side of everyday objects. The emblems of the Cultural Revolution embodied by Mao Zedong and the brands that condense the idea of consumerism aim to understand political and philosophical meanings. Political and commercial propaganda become analogous devices that, if stripped of their different purposes, contribute in representing the massification of the individual. Openly foreign to Political Pop, Wang does not address the episodes of a given historical period to comment on them but, through and beyond them, he wants to understand a phenomenon that cannot be explained rationally. What this work proposes is the creation of a "metamythology,"[8] the compendium of images that represent two different and only apparently antithetical ways of life: on the one hand are the Chinese people and, on the other, the individualism of the Western systems. The economic and political structure of capitalism is also depicted through the alimentary imagery that belongs to it, which transcends the very materiality of food, transforming it into a political and social idea of which it becomes the bearer. Coca-Cola and McDonald's are idols, a new religion for the masses. The government holds total domination over the spaces of the individual's life, a space that is largely occupied by the food sphere.

7. *Small Criticism* (1992) (see Figure 11.1). In this cycle, which presents the style adopted in *Great Criticism*, food is depicted through fruit elements (drawings or just words)—bananas, apples, pineapples, watermelons, melons, mangoes, oranges, and

green beans—as well as through roast chicken. Here, there is no apparent logic between non-food and food figures and words, so food seems to have a minor role. However, Wang's art is never decorative or purely ornamental: it seems like these icons suggest a sarcastic and even dramatic contrast with the Chinese workers and characters who populate the cycle.

8. *Studies for International Politics* (1993). This is the title of some works, however incomplete and never realized. Wang was going to use the shape of a sugar container to create a structure that would then have to be recreated in red bricks. As explicit reference to the Berlin Wall, the artist had planned to paint some newspaper pages, following the style of the graffiti present in the original version, in order to make the resemblance even more evident. The idea was to create an installation by dealing with four different themes: politics, war, sex, and drugs. A test was carried out using a container of Chupa Chups in order to reconsider and critically interpret the political dimension following the Cold War.

9. Coca-Cola's logo appears again in *New Media—Beijing Hutong Garbage Cart* (1995)—as a medium of advertising. The call is still aimed at the global and ubiquitous market. The immateriality of the propaganda action put in place by the Western "material cult" and the socialist ideology takes its true form here because the same strategies of communication and manipulation are proposed again, not on a stationary medium like a painting, but on a trolley that can be transported. "Within this virtual setting, [these two brainwashing methods] take on a form of teleological unity."[9]

10. *The Era of Materialism* (2000) (Figure 12.3). The installation consists of ten empty diploma certificates—related to the academic, intellectual, and educational spheres—hanging from the four white walls that surround the room where the work is exhibited. In the same space, eight white cubes are placed—different in size and height—that act as platforms on which various food items are exposed. These food items presented are, for example, millet, bread, garlic, green vegetables, and rice flour, all ingredients that are omnipresent and deeply relevant to the human diet. The emptiness of the certificates is what allows them to assume a broader meaning: they also symbolize

**Figure 12.3** Wang Guangyi, *The Era of Materialism* (2000), installation with printed matter, wooden boxes and food, etc. Dimensions variable.

the brainwashing developed by state ideology and the mental and behavioral leveling of the individual. Furthermore, the food chosen, which represents "food essentiality," is analogous to the material and concrete declination of the same suspended diplomas, metaphors of substantiality in its spiritual meaning. Socialism and the ideology for which it stands are also constituted by the same food that has also nourished the human community, that has contributed to the formation and creation of its members. *The Era of Materialism* can be defined as "a collective social memory";[10] food, in fact, is a device for illustrating this collective memory embedded in the individual choices of everyday life. Here, the material and spiritual spheres are different declinations of the same substance: the cerebral organic matter exists thanks to the introduction of food into the body. As Ludwig Feuerbach states in his review of Jacob Moleschott's *Theory of Nutrition*: "This work, though it deals only with eating and drinking, which are regarded in the eyes of our supernaturalistic mock-culture as the lowest acts, is of the greatest philosophic significance and importance. How former philosophers have broken their heads over the question of the bond between body and soul! Now we know on scientific grounds, what the masses know from long experience, that eating and drinking hold together body and soul, that the searched-for bond is nutrition."[11] Feuerbach proposed a materialistic system on scientific grounds, which is very far from Wang Guangyi's philosophy. However, the idea of transcendence of the mere material aspect of food is evident here: as food involves the whole of the human being, the connection with the metaphysical dimension is assured, once one believes in it; and this is the case for the Chinese artist. Food choices and taste education, therefore, can form and then are, in turn, formed, becoming the emblem of the society that has adopted it as an essential basis for its existence. Compared to *Great Criticism* (1990–2007), in this work the relationship between politics and consumption on one side, and East and West on the other, seems to go deeper and become, at the same time, more clear and tangible. Instead of symbols, images, logos, and emblems, it is an individual, both in the flesh and the eternal, who occupies the center of the stage here.

11. *The Great Scene* (2002). The work is an "archaeological presentation" of the Cold War, made for the first Triennial of Chinese Contemporary Art. The artist has recreated a daily scene that refers to a social dimension of profound poverty, alluding to the condition of migrants working as laborers who carried out particularly wearying tasks in China in the mid-1960s. At that time, Chinese propaganda supported the need to prepare for a possible military conflict, so workers dug bunkers and air-raid shelters, storing food, of which millet is a symbol. This installation consists of wooden and brick beds, on which some blankets are placed, while the floor is covered with millet. Millet represents the mere materiality and the substantial basis on which society

is supported, as well as a symbolic element that recalls the same political orientation.

12. *The Last Supper* (2011) (see Figure 3.1). As the title explains, Wang evokes the work of Leonardo and, in a particularly evident way, that of Warhol—that is, the interpretation of *The Last Supper* of 1986. The personal contribution of the Chinese artist here is to intensify the procedure already put in place by Warhol: to dispel "the details of the work, to leave the observer in front of the weight and the symbolic reach of that event."[12] The use of the negative, then, results in a further elimination of the details of the scene, which is delineated through the rendering of sketched outlines of the protagonists and of the food that stands in front of them. Although food is not well defined, the meaning of the scene persists for the collective imaginary, even though the essential elements do not appear in it.

13. *Things in Themselves* (2012) (see Figure 8.2). In my opinion, it is the most interesting work of Wang Guangyi for an aesthetics of food and taste, so I will delve into the work more deeply. This a majestic installation made up of five thousand burlap sacks containing rice and rice bran, stacked in such a way as to completely cover the walls of the exhibition space. The sacks reach up from the floor to the ceiling, gradually degrading, from a base with a larger perimeter to a smaller, funnel-like top. Because of the weight of the sacks of rice that compose it, it was necessary to use scaffolding that could support the entire work. The original project required the use of two thousand sacks, but then the maximum limit was set to twelve hundred sacks due to logistical issues; in the end, the finished work used up to five thousand sacks. Here the smell of rice serves to go beyond what is visible; the truth is not seen, it is felt. In accordance with the critique of Wang Guangyi of the conception of art as "retina games," here, olfaction is a tool that is used to show the invisible. Olfaction is also a means to react against the dominance of vision in the contemporary food scene and—maybe—against the "gustatory games" of the modern capitalistic system. There is a sort of indifference to vision in the "thing in itself" that is parallel to the deconstruction of the dominance of the visual perception in gustatory taste: "Food does not get used up and

does not disappear, instead it is transformed and it transforms us. To understand cuisine as art, it is necessary to go beyond the equation of "permanent object = visible presence," and the representational perspective that supports it. In an alternative model that is not constrained to the aesthetics of form, and which values instead vital and metabolic aspects, as well as transformation and change, food always leaves a trace even if you cannot see it."[13] "Things-in-Themselves" is a concept taken from Kant, which problematizes the connection between appearance and reality and the sensible world and ideal archetypes.[14]

The material used—jute—has a great impact on the visitor's sensitivity. The sacredness of rice, then, hovers in the air tinged by its emanations, recalling the meaning of life made possible by it, the primary source of sustenance and nourishment of all humanity. The materiality of rice transcends itself: what Wang places in the middle is the aura of phenomena, perceptible in the empty space that surrounds the installation. The "thing in itself" transcends the concreteness of the material used. To recall the terminology employed by the German philosopher Gernot Böhme, the artist here uses a "generator" to *stage* an emotional atmosphere.[15] This consists of the smell of rice and its bran and of the sacks that contain them, in which the memory of the artist is condensed and brings him back to the period of his youth when he had worked in a barn. The past years and their memory have condensed into the olfactory atmosphere set up by Wang. The atmosphere is what escapes from the optically fixed boundaries of the thing-object and permeates all around, a vague entity that "holds in tension affective spacetimes that are both corporeal and incorporeal, *of* and *emergent* from the midst of bodies."[16] When "the thing in itself" is rationalized, it loses all of its "aura," as happens with the sense of smell whose stimuli, if verbalized, seem to lose their function of silent links to emotional situations. This evokes the fundamental Taoist thought that sees in the dialectic of full/empty the same behavior of the universe; the sacks, with their concreteness and their volume, tinge the unoccupied space of itself. The rice is not visible through the sacks: it can only be experienced through the sense of smell. The thing in itself cannot then be understood rationally or intellectually: one can "intuit" it through the aesthetic experience and the total emotional participation. From a visual point of view, the installation gives the observer a sense of "constriction" in space. Knowledge and human work—in this case, the collection of rice bran and rice and their storage—influences the affective sphere of practice of the individual, determining the way in which it is experienced. Smell serves as the perfect tool to go beyond what one sees: because the olfactory stimulus is neither rational nor rationalizable, it bypasses reason, giving a haptic perception immersed in an atmosphere that pushes to go beyond the thing, thus approaching its essence. The sense of smell becomes an instrument to go beyond what is visible; Wang's path "towards the invisible dynamic principle of becoming follows a method in which empirical knowledge and metaphysical tension are integrated."[17] Food is consumption. Food disappears, at least in terms of visual perception. However, it never truly disappears: it is because of this that we can obtain the true meaning of it.

# Notes

1 See Korsmeyer, 2002.
2 See Perullo, 2017.
3 See Bottinelli and D'Ayala Valva, 2017: 3.
4 See Lemke, 2017: 247–61.
5 See Goldstein, 2010: 40.
6 Ibid.
7 See Paparoni, 2013: 350.
8 See Andina and Paparoni, 2016: 10.
9 See Paparoni, 2013: 180.
10 Ibid.: 202.
11 See Feuerbach, 1850: 368.
12 See Andina and Paparoni, 2016: 9 [*my translation*].
13 See Perullo, 2017: 31.
14 See Paparoni, 2013: 387.
15 For an in-depth study of atmospheres, their features and artistic re-creation, see Böhme, 2017a and 2017b.
16 See McCormack, 2018: 31.
17 See Andina and Paparoni, 2016: 23 [*my translation*].

# References

Andina, T. and Paparoni, D. (eds.). (2016). *Wang Guangyi e la filosofia*. Rivista di Estetica, Torino: Rosenberg & Sellier.

Böhme, G. (2017a). *Atmospheric Architectures: The Aesthetics of Felt Spaces*. London: Bloomsbury Academic.

Böhme, G. (2017b). *Critique of Aesthetic Capitalism*. Milan: Mimesis International.

Bottinelli, S. and D'Ayala Valva, M. (eds.). (2017). *The Taste of Art: Cooking, Food and Counterculture in Contemporary Practices*. Fayetteville: University of Arkansas Press.

Feuerbach, L. (1989 [1850]). Review of J. Moleschott, *Theory of Nutrition*, in *Die Naturwissenschaft und die Revolution* [*Über: Lehre der Nahrungsmittel. Für das Volk*. Von J. Moleschott] (Rezension). In: *Gesammelte Werke*. Hrsg. v. Werner Schuffenhauer and Wolfgang Harich. Berlin: AkademieVerlag, Bd. 5, 1989 [1850].

Goldstein, D. (2010). Emmanuel Levinas and the Ontology of Eating. *Gastronomica: The Journal of Critical Food Studies*, 10(3).

Korsmeyer, C. (2002). *Making Sense of Taste: Food and Philosophy*. Ithaca, NY: Cornell University Press.

Lemke, H. (2007). *Die Kunst des Essens: Eine Ästhetik des kulinarischen Geschmacks*. Bielefeld: Edition Moderne Postmoderne.

McCormack, D. (2018). *Atmospheric Things: On the Allure of Elemental Envelopment*. Durham: Duke University Press.

Paparoni, D. (2013). *Wang Guangyi: Works and thoughts 1985–2012*. Milano: Skira.

Perullo, N. (2011). *La scena del senso: A partire da Wittgenstein e Derrida*. Pisa: Edizioni ETS.

Perullo, N. (2013). *La cucina è arte? Filosofia della passione culinaria*. Roma: Carocci.

Perullo, N. (2017). Can Cuisine be Art? A (Heterodoxal) proposal. In Bottinelli, S. and D'Ayala Valva, M. (eds.). *The Taste of Art: Cooking, Food and Counterculture in Contemporary Practices*. (2017). Fayetteville: University of Arkansas Press.

Part VII

# In Dialogue with Wang Guangyi

# 13

# Nothingness, God, the Soul, and the World: A Conversation with Wang Guangyi

Demetrio Paparoni 德沐

**Demetrio Paparoni**: You have just painted self-portraits set in a bathroom (Figure 13.1). I do not remember seeing any self-portraits of you before.

**Wang Guangyi**: I made one when I was a younger I think it was 1996. I sold it a few days after it was finished.

**DP**: I've never seen it published anywhere.

**WG**: I did not have time to photograph it. I have not even kept the preparatory studies. I would not know how to track down the collector who bought that painting.

**DP**: Can you describe it to me?

**WG**: In 1995 and 1996 I worked on the *Passport and Visa* series. At that time, I felt the need to take a break to get away from the complexity of those works. So I painted that self-portrait. I represented myself from the front, in an empty space, placing myself in a position to scrutinize myself.

**DP**: Why did you decide to portray yourself that time?

**WG**: I was going through the works I had already made, and I found an sketch book that I had used back in school, a classic oil painting album. I suddenly felt curious to try to portray myself using a rather traditional technique. I haven't gone back to that topic since. I have been interested in the universal, not the particular—I have no interest in the concrete image. In my works, Mao Zedong or Marx are idols, they are not concrete people.

**DP**: So why did you decide to make your figure part of the picture now? Surely not because you see yourself as an idol.

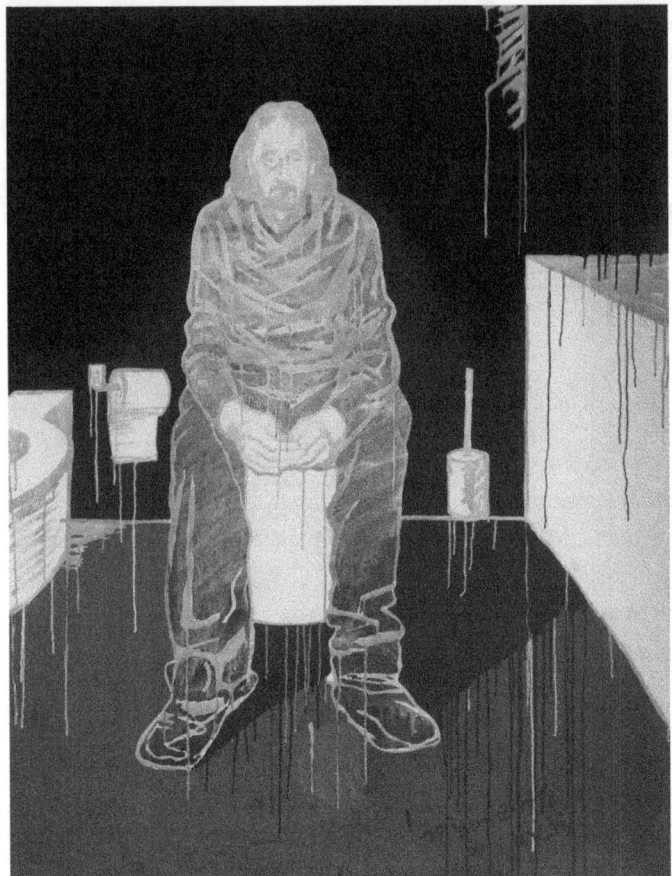

**Figure 13.1** Wang Guangyi, *Daily Life* (2014), oil on canvas, 150 × 120 cm.

WG: Of course not. These new self-portraits express my reflections on the passage from youth to maturity. Somehow, they transcend my person because my art addresses universal issues. Nevertheless, as a human being my age, it is normal for me to feel a sense of loss and estrangement as the years go by. This is probably what led me to portray myself.

DP: I wonder if this self-portrait indicates a change of gear in your work.

WG: It's hard to say. An artist's self-portrait inevitably enters his private universe. Is it possible to give a cultural interpretation of private life? I wonder.

DP: In your work, references to reality, history, and politics are very much in evidence. There is one of your paintings that I like very much, *Study of Popular History*, 2007. In this context the historical reference to the images is given by the writing, placed at the center of each of the three panels.

**WG:** 1948 was the year in which the People's Liberation Army allowed the communists to secure control over Central China. Although the People's Republic of China was declared a year later, it was in 1948 that the Chinese people gave a definitive turn to their fate. But this is not what I wanted to highlight in my painting. The alternation of different forms of power, the imposition of one over the other: this is in the natural order of things in all countries. The inscription "1948" and the history that is behind this date served to introduce the true theme of the work, which did not concern what happened that year, but the role played by necessity and destiny in determining events that affect the lives of people, both concretely and spiritually.

**DP:** In the same way as Marx, Engels, Stalin, Lenin, and Mao, the numerous figures in this painting refer to a precise historical and political moment of Chinese life in the past century. You say you have portrayed them as idols, not as real people, but it is undeniable that the figures and images of your work are anything but foreign to politics.

**WG:** An artist is inevitably a witness of his time. But he can also bring historical figures into his work without any political intent. It is like reading an Italian book on the history of fascism. The author can describe the structure of the totalitarian fascist state regardless of its ethical or political aspects. I mean that you can write or read books about fascism without being a fascist. The message that the historian entrusts to the book, the artist can entrust to the figurative space. In my works, references to a certain historical epoch are the starting point for a conceptual and formal construction that has its ultimate goal in the question of transcendence, which I feel is very present in our society.

**DP:** Do you mean that you are only interested in universal realities, like Plato's ideas?

**WG:** I am attracted to Plato because he addresses what remains and is eternal: ideas. For Plato what is real is the archetype of man, who has an eternal and divine value, while single persons are mortal and therefore their life is about changing opinions, not philosophical truth. Think of the VII book of the Republic, the best known, the one in which the myth of the cave is told. Plato imagines that men, imprisoned in a cave, mistake shadows cast on a wall for reality.

One of them breaks free and notices the deception, but does not want to keep this truth for himself. He decides to go back to free his comrades, who are now used to identifying shadows with reality. For this reason, not only do they not believe him, but they even rebel against him for revealing something true to them. Socrates was also sentenced for trying to awaken the Athenians. When I paint the faces of Marx, Lenin, or Mao I do not represent human faces, but figures that stand beyond the historical evolution and remain as archetypes.

**DP**: In the recent paintings of the *New Religion* cycle you portrayed both the fathers of communism and subjects and themes of Christianity, such as the Last Supper. Within this cycle, the image of the dead Christ, taken from Mantegna, finds its equivalent in the image of a dead Mao taken from a photo.

**WG**: Marxism presupposes a spirit of equality and altruism, which is why I consider it a ramification of Christianity.

**DP**: You put Marx, Stalin, Lenin, Mao, and Christ on the same level, almost as if there were no differences between them.

**WG**: I do not see differences between them. What is the difference for you?

**DP**: Stalin or Lenin imposed their vision of the world by force, while Christ or Confucius only used words to proselytize. It does not seem like a small difference to me. However, … if I think that for centuries the Roman Catholic Church has kept temporal power by repressing all forms of dissent, forcing those who dared to question its dogmas to abjure, preventing the translation of the sacred texts, and condemning heretics to the stake, I can agree with your position.

**WG**: But ideas, religious and ideal drives are not to be confused with temporal power.

**DP**: Of course. Christ's thought should not be confused with the Church's temporal power, like Marx's should not be confused with the social organization implemented by Stalin.

**WG**: These characters have had and continue to have a profound influence on daily life. In representing them I have not been interested in highlighting what differentiates them; if anything I am interested in the correspondences of thought, to understand what the origin of utopias has in common. My aim is to reveal the complexity of life. I do not think that art should exert its influence on society, oppose power, or support it. On the contrary, I consider such a position presumptuous. I am interested in denial and nothingness.

**DP:** But what do you mean by "nothingness"?

**WG:** Nothingness is like air: despite being immaterial, it has its own consistency. Think of the atmosphere. Kant uses the metaphor of the dove: it might feel freer and lighter without air friction; yet, it is precisely air friction that allows it to fly, with the effort of its wings. The immateriality of the atmosphere may make us think of "nothingness," but it is the necessary condition for the dove to fly. The same thing happens to human thought. We may think that we would feel freer by hiding from the weight of reality, but this freedom will produce unverifiable utterances devoid of any scientific value. Therefore, does nothingness coincide with a knowledge emptied of experience? Does nothingness coincide with all that goes beyond finite and measurable phenomena? These are just some of the questions that my work poses, starting from the awareness that even what is considered as "nothingness" has some influence over our lives: life is influenced by nothingness because "nothingness" includes the principles of metaphysical knowledge such as "God," "soul," "world."

**DP:** Shortly before he died in 2013, I met Arthur C. Danto and recorded a conversation with him that was then published in ArtChina. We talked about you, too, but he was only familiar with the paintings of *Great Criticism*. I told Arthur that, referring to Kant, you defined nothingness as "absence from oneself." Arthur replied that he was not interested in the concept of nothingness. "If it's nothing—he replied—it's something. When there is nothing, that's what there is. Wittgenstein wrote that death is not an event of life. But I never gave it much weight." He concluded by saying that he did not know any painter that was really interested in nothingness.

**WG:** There is no doubt that Danto is right. He never talks about things he has not experienced. But for me, "nothingness" is not a concept, it is a sensation.

**DP:** In addition to the brush, do you use anything else to spread the color? A cloth, for example?

**WG:** Never. But I use a particular type of maobi, the brush of the ancient Chinese calligraphy painters. You can understand this by making a comparison between some of my paintings and the works of Bada Shanren made with the technique of ink painting. Bada Shanren influenced me for his ability to get around reality. He thought that reality was foreign to him and that art was autonomous. Like

Bada Shanren and Shitao, I look for answers beyond the physical horizon I see with my eyes: I aim to transcend reality to go towards an unknown that cannot fully take shape. This is why my religious characters from the *Post Classical* and *Red Rationality* cycle have no face (see Figures 1.1 and 4.1).

**DP:** Do you mean that the paintings of the *Post Classical* and *Red Rationality* cycle were influenced by Bada Shanren? I mean on the formal level, in the brushstroke, in the color, and also on the conceptual level?

**WG:** The fact that an artist influenced me does not mean that his influence must necessarily show in my works, even if a latent, subliminal influence can always emerge. This influence should not however be sought on the technical level. With Bada Shanren and Shitao I feel a conceptual consonance, linked to their vision of art and the world. According to their way of seeing things, art expresses a monistic vision, a fusion between the Self and the Things. Bada Shanren and Shitao did not portray nature in a mimetic way, they saw a continuity between the self and the phenomenal beings. This is a recurring motif in my work. These artists made me realize that when I look at a tree, a river or a mountain, I do not do so in the same way as I look at an object. I consider a tree, a river or a mountain as subjects; I put them on the same level as my subjectivity.

**DP:** In the monistic conception you refer to, one can gather a mystical yearning for a fusion with nature. Political Pop, on the other hand, sheds light on an ironic attitude towards the world of goods and consumption.

**WG:** Of course. But do not forget that my art is foreign to Political Pop. I do not think that the monistic vision and Pop politics coincide. I'm not so naive. It must also be considered that the thought of an artist does not evolve in a linear way: it proceeds by intersections and overlaps. When we consider things on an objective level, we judge them, we have an evaluative attitude towards them. If we consider them subjects, we do not judge them, because we place them on our own level. If you look at my paintings of the *Great Criticism* cycle in an objective way you have to consider them on a rational level and, in this light, you can also read them in a political key. If instead you consider them within a monistic conception, this objectivity is lost because the artist identifies with them. This is one of the aspects of the complexity of my work. The works of Bada Shanren made me understand how to look at things. Being an artist, I express myself through images, but I'm not interested in representing people or objects as such. My attention is directed to phenomena, to what they hide, and what escapes rational comprehension. For me the formal question is subdued to the need to anchor the phenomena to what lies behind them, to what Kant calls "thing in itself," which does not have the absolute characteristics of ontology. The goal is to explore the human need to grasp the real without losing sight of spiritual and metaphysical aspirations.

**DP:** This explains your interest in topics such as the "Pieta" or the "Return of the Prodigal Son," which you dealt with in the second half of the 1980s and in particular in the *Revision of Idols* cycle (Figure 2.3).

**WG:** I took Michelangelo's *Pietà* as a model (Figure 13.2) because his representation of the dead Christ in the arms of his mother is one of the most poetic syntheses of human feelings, full of spirituality and metaphysical implications. This representation of death and maternal pain elicits strong feelings, such as compassion. It gives rise to empathy. As an artist I approach this theme through formal analysis, without losing sight of the original metaphysical dimension of the work.

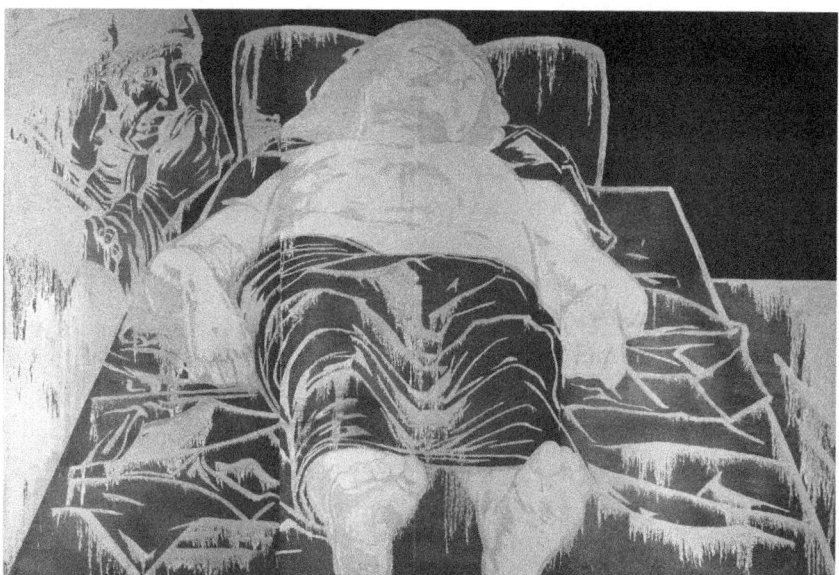

**Figure 13.2** Wang Guangyi, *Pietà* (2011), oil on canvas, 400 × 600 cm.

**DP:** In your version of *Pietà*, as well as in your other paintings dated 1985 to 1987, you have erased the traits of Christ and Mary, which in Michelangelo's sculpture are fundamental in order to involve the beholder. How can one perceive the mother's pain if she has no facial expression?

**WG:** When I made those paintings I had recently read Gombrich, and I was struck by his revisionist approach to history. It was Gombrich who led me to this revision. I thought that if my representation had been excessively faithful, its realism would have taken the religious aspect away from it. Eliminating important details and focusing on the shapes does not make it impossible to recognize the models I was inspired by.

**DP:** Before Michelangelo, Pieta' was represented on a reduced scale in sculpture. Making it in natural scale has transformed an object of worship into a representation of reality, capable of arousing identification.

**WG:** Giving his work the dimension of humanity, Michelangelo managed to express divine greatness. The ingenuity of his choice mirrors the Christian message: God becomes man in Christ and dies on the cross. In Christ lying in the arms of his mother, the divine mission and human piety meet. The natural scale makes us grasp the fragility of the human condition, which we all share.

**DP:** Does this also apply to your work?

**WG:** Certainly. In my work this sense of correspondence is important. When I painted it, in 1986, I was not used to these formats, so much so that I often had to sew different layers of canvas to reach the desired size. Today a two meters by one-and-a-half canvas seems small, but then it was not so. In the paintings of those years I had to keep in mind the distance from which the spectator would look at the work: everything had to contribute to creating a feeling of correspondence.

**DP:** At the same time you have added a red grid, which puts distance between your *Pietà* and those who look at the painting.

**WG:** The red grid allows me to obtain a double effect: it brings the work in contact with the spectator and, at the same time, it is an element of separation. It marks the boundary between what is inside the painting and what is outside of it. On the symbolic level this line of demarcation between inside and outside is a way of clearly showing the separation between the experience of the divine and the ordinary one. In cloistered convents, in which the religious choose to live radically separated from the world, a grid divides the space of the sacred from the area that can be accessed by non-consecrated persons. A parent who goes to visit the son or daughter who has chosen to live in seclusion can speak to them only at certain times and always behind the grating. Adding the red grid while eliminating some elements of the figurative representation for me was a way to accentuate on a formal level the separation between the experience of the divine and that of everyday life.

**DP:** Do you mean that, albeit through the grid, we can still reconstruct the image, which appears transfigured precisely because it is placed in the space of the sacred?

**WG:** If you want to make what you call transfiguration perceptible on a formal level, you cannot help omitting the details.

**DP:** For a Christian, the feeling of piety is part of the essence of belief. In the Christian experience, religiosity and participation in human pain are identified.

**WG:** I am not a Christian and for me pity is more about the sphere of the human, not that of religion. The title of Michelangelo's sculpture, *Pietà*, in Chinese is generally translated as *tongqing*, which literally means "to commiserate," "to feel compassion." If the translation is correct, my religious vision and that of Michelangelo do not coincide because compassion is more than anything else a feeling of the common man, which I feel is extraneous to religion. The fact that I do not take pity as a specifically religious theme, as Michelangelo does, is probably due to my idea of life and death, which in Buddhism are not separable. In China we emphasize how life and death have an indissoluble link. In the West it is not like that. I am affected by this conception, which is expressed in my art.

**DP:** For Christians, the concept of piety does not imply only compassion, but also includes the concept of devotion and veneration of God. It indicates a religious sentiment. In other words, for a Christian, respect for others comes from his relationship with God, whom the Christian calls "father." This makes all men brothers. To explain it better: the adjective "pious" derives from pity. A pious man is a devout, deeply religious man, a man who, even though capable of identifying himself in the earthly suffering of others, is projected towards the transcendent. How does this relate to the concept of "piety" that you want to express in your *Revision of Idols*?

**WG:** I see the artist as a person who has the mission to indicate directions that go beyond finite existence. The artist, like the philosopher or the poet, has his own ideas, which may also be unacceptable and in some way corrosive. Think of Heidegger, his sympathies for Nazism, and his contempt for the Jews. However, if we consider him as a philosopher, we cannot but recognize the unquestionable value of his work. There is a rather famous passage of *Being and Time* in which he affirms that being is always being-in-the-world with our fellowmen. This profoundly human message shows that transcendence is expressed in our relationships with others. It is clear that there is a gap between the Heidegger who adheres to Nazism and the Heidegger who clarifies the meaning of our being in the world.

**DP:** Do you prefer Wang Guangyi the man, Wang Guangyi the artist, or Wang Guangyi the philosopher?

**WG:** For me the figure of the artist and that of the philosopher coincide. The artist, like the philosopher, overcomes every national border to speak to humanity. Although they are people who live in a certain country, artists and philosophers produce images and thoughts that address the world and transcend it at the same time.

**DP:** You're saying that art is able to answer the human need for transcendence.

**WG:** Exactly. The highest purpose of art consists in giving shape to the sense of terror we experience in front of the unknown. This is what I try to express with my art. It is only starting from the sense of fear for what he is unable to control that man has created works of art. The rock paintings of Lascaux, Altamira or Serra da Capivara already reveal this sense of terror in the face of what one cannot understand about the world.

**DP:** The thing that terrifies man most of all is death. Georges Bataille wrote that one can only experience death by dying. It is a good summary of the impossibility of knowing phenomena that have always been a mystery.

**WG:** Every religious or philosophical reflection rests on a way of seeing death, which influences one's conception of existence. Death is a mystery that generates mysteries.

**DP:** When we talk about the representation of death, I cannot help thinking about Francis Bacon: he said that his pictorial reflection arose from seeing meat on the butcher's counter in the Harrods department store in London. Whenever he went to the butcher, he was amazed that he was not in the place of those pieces of meat. He was obsessed with a verse from Aeschylus: "the reek of human blood smiles out at me."

**WG:** His vision was both tragic and realistic. His creations, as much as they were inspired by suggestions, drew on concrete existence.

**DP:** It is curious that, despite expressing this concreteness, Bacon never knew where he was going to go when he started working a painting. He made no preparatory drawings or studies: he gave the first stroke and waited for chance to suggest how to proceed. He said he learned how to organize chance. Obviously, he looked at the world around him, tore up pages from books, and studied newspaper stories, he even had a book on diseases of the mouth, but the way in which his paintings reached the concreteness you speak of is linked to the power of suggestion. His existential vision was so crude that it led him to think that one is born alone and dies alone, and that man is only garbage once dead. He deformed the human figure to convey reality in its most excruciating moment. In his atheistic existentialism there is no room for hope. Your work, on the other hand, is open to the metaphysical question. Even if you address tragic themes such as the fear of the cold war period or the nightmare of being infected or contaminated, your attitude to the world is profoundly different. Bacon considered faith and religion pure hypocrisy. He saw faith as a ghost and religion as a way to impose social behaviors useful to politics.

**WG:** My idea is completely different. For me, faith and religion give life to a universal existence that pushes man to overcome the finite limits of life: for this reason, there is nothing false about them. Faith is fundamental to the individual, it sustains him in his existence. My religious tension is not addressed to specific religions, but expresses a metaphysical need towards the unknown. Of course, politics has always tried to exploit religion to pursue its own ends. Contrary to what Bacon himself claimed, I do not think he had no faith. Not completely, at least. I disagree with those who talk about Bacon as a man without faith.

**DP:** Bacon painted some crucifixions, but he did not consider them from the religious point of view. For him those were representations of the cruelty of the human condition.

**WG:** Put it any way you want, it's still about crucifixion.

**DP:** Not having faith does not mean not having ideals. Do not you think that these ideals can lead to utopian or visionary positions?

**WG:** I see nothing wrong with the fact that the artist can see things disconnected from reality. Often the artist imagines things detached from reality even when using realistic elements. Even Bacon does it: his work is not pure concreteness. In him the flesh is both real and imaginary, and this leads him to confront the unknown, creating that openness to religion that we were talking about earlier.

**DP:** In *Weather Report* (see Figure 4.3—same work with a different title), one of your paintings from 1989 that does not belong to a cycle, [it] shows Tiananmen Square and the entrance to the Forbidden City, with the portrait of Mao reduced to a silhouette. At the top left there are meteorological symbols and numbers indicating temperatures. 1989, the year in which you realized that painting, was marked by tragic events in China. Huang Zhuan, the critic who knows your work better than any other, has written about your installation *Temperature*[, saying] that concepts such as "climate" and "temperature" often assume a political connotation. The definition of "Cold War," though, does not make one think of meteorology. Can you tell me something about *Weather Report*? Does this painting relate with the 1989 student riots in Tiananmen Square?

**WG:** *Weather Report*, like all my works, does not refer to specific events. In my opinion, chance plays a decisive role in events, influencing how they develop. Much of what happens is accidental, but behind an effect there is always a cause. More than the events as such I am interested in what is hidden behind them: I look at the phenomenon to understand what lies behind it.

**DP:** Joseph Beuys thought that in conditions of full freedom man naturally develops his own strong spiritual life. During a debate, Michael Ende replied to him that, in order to create the conditions for freedom, there must be a strong spiritual life first. Both Beuys and Hende were followers of Rudolf Steiner, but disagreed on several points. For Ende, the will as such and free will without content are to be considered empty faculties: it is necessary to have an intuition of what one wants to achieve for the exercise of free will to make sense.

**WG:** Naturally, I appreciate Beuys' point of view. Freedom is a precious commodity, but it indicates something too broad to be defined precisely. It expresses itself differently depending on the time and place. China is a very complex country: its interminable feudal age, as well as the ancient reverential fear that the people feel for the monarch, still cast their shadow over people's way of thinking. As an artist, I think I express my creative freedom.

**DP:** To a Westerner, if a Chinese intellectual does not want to talk about politics it's because he is not allowed to do so.

**WG:** Art always has political implications. One needs to know how to read them. Some in the West will be disappointed because I do not say things that a Chinese artist is expected to say, but I do not believe that I am limiting my freedom of expression by making politics and theology interact.

**DP:** You talk about theology with the jargon of politics. Your work is a figurative political theology.

**WG:** It's a good definition.

**DP:** You have always been interested in highlighting how opposites, when coexisting, end up generating new subjects. In the *Great Criticism* cycle, for example, you have placed images of Maoist propaganda next to the best-known logos of Western commercial propaganda.

**WG:** China is basically a utopian nation. In its long historical evolution, changes in state power have had a huge impact on people. Having been born in 1957 I have experienced the ability of the state to brainwash people through the dissemination of images that propagate utopian ideas. Growing up, I realized that in Western developed countries the system stimulates people's passion for material goods through logos and products designed for this purpose. Materialism is one of the reasons for the development of the West. These two ways of psychologically conditioning people's choices share some similarities and contradictions. My task as an artist is not to raise objections: I used the artistic approach to represent the relationship between these two ways of brainwashing.

**DP:** In 2007, *Great Criticism* found a natural sequel in the *Cold War Aesthetics* series (Figure 13.3) inspired by the propaganda posters of the fifties and sixties. You have clarified yourself your intention to make everything that was exposed appear true, so as to give the viewer the impression of visiting an exhibition.

**WG:** I think of art as something real that deals with issues related to existence—that is why it affects the heart of people. I do not like refined, elegant, graceful art.. That kind of art meets the needs of the market, not of the spirit. I stopped making paintings associating the

**Figure 13.3** Wang Guangyi, *Cold War Aesthetics—People Living in Fear* (2007–8), installation with colored fiberglass and video, 215 × 60 × 30 cm/each sculpture.

images of Maoist propaganda with Western logos because, once hung on the walls, their beauty distracted from the theme that was being dealt with. This leads me to prefer the cycle *Cold War Aesthetics*, which rests on the belief that we have not really left behind all that we have assimilated during the Cold War period. Even today we experience a sense of looming danger, which my generation was also exposed to in school. The images of the posters explaining how to react to a potential nuclear explosion or the lessons on how to defend ourselves against American imperialism are not easy to forget.

Even on the other side of the world things must not have been very different. China was presented as a danger, and many people in the West still feel the effects of the Cold War. This means that our vision of the world is marked by that psychological experience.

**DP:** But today the world is not the same, many things have changed.

**WG:** Not all things. Many things seem different, but they are not.

**DP:** How do you manage to address the psychological effects of the Cold War on your people, with a didactic intent, while saying that you do not criticize or oppose anything?

**WG:** What I think is not important because what happens is not my choice. This position is linked to the spiritual dimension, to religion, to metaphysics, which tends to privilege contemplation over attempts to modify reality. The Taoist and Buddhist visions, which are very present in China, are profoundly different from those of Christianity and Marxism, which have a teleological vision of history. Taoism and Buddhism tend to consider reality by looking at the causal relationships between events on which we cannot intervene. Looking at this necessary causal relationship in Schopenhauer's terms, one naturally thinks of the link between the noluntas and nirvana. I agree with Schopenhauer when he maintains that all reality is nothing but the manifestation of a blind, irrational and infinite will, which affirms itself. Even the noblest actions, from this point of view, are an illusion hiding this blind will. We can free ourselves from this slavery only by denying the will, through an ascetic path that will lead us to deny the things that mostly express the will to live.

**DP:** As you know, this leads to chastity.

**WG:** Of course. Schopenhauer identifies the final goal of this ascetic path with chastity: in denying procreation, in fact, one denies the affirmation of the will. All this involves a form of nihilistic quietism.

**DP:** You talk about Schopenhauer as if he were an eastern thinker.

**WG:** Schopenhauer represents an element of extraneousness within the Western philosophical tradition: it should not be forgotten that his way of thinking is strictly connected to Oriental culture. But for Westerners this attitude, apart from Schopenhauer's case, exclusively falls within mysticism.

**DP:** Looking at the past could arouse a nostalgic attitude, which is certainly not beneficial for the present.

**WG:** In Buddhism, the yuan represents the conflicting and complementary relationship between the two cosmic principles yin and yang. In this relationship we can see how the future is rooted in the past and in the present. We cannot talk about hope without looking at the past.

**DP:** But from a modernist perspective, the past could also represent a burden that one should free oneself from in order to create the new.

WG: Modernism is immature because it looks at the present and the future without understanding the dialectical relationship that makes the present and the future exist precisely in their tension with the past. Taoism insists on the fact that becoming is the outcome of a relationship between opposites. Neither of the two opposites—past and future—can exist without the other.

DP: What you say brings to mind that the dialectical conception runs through all of Western thought and is particularly present in Marxism. Given that Marxism and Christianity recognize a teleological design in history—which is immanent in Marxism, transcendent in Christianity—how do you place yourself in relation to history, considering your closeness to Taoism and Buddhism?

WG: Taoism is more a cosmology than a philosophy of history. Buddhism, for its part, is predominantly a doctrine that teaches us to overcome selfishness, the desire for power, and suffering. In this context history becomes the stage of reincarnations, understood as a form of purification. There are no prizes or punishments except in earthly life, and therefore within a historical dimension.

DP: But what do you mean by politics? I have the feeling that you and I give a different meaning to this word. Western culture has its roots in ancient Greece, which considered politics to be noble. In the West, politics does not necessarily involve siding with a party, following a leader, or being part of an organized group. There is a politics that is foreign to that of parties. Your work on the aesthetics of the Cold War for us Westerners is markedly political, because it tends to raise awareness about a social condition.

WG: I agree with you, but as an artist I lean towards Augustine's view by which philosophy is the "ancilla theologiae." When Christians encountered Greek thought, they came to sometimes opposite conclusions. On the one hand Greek thought, prior to the revelation of Christ, could be rejected in full; on the other hand it could not be denied that it represented the greatest effort of natural reason to grasp the essence of the divine. All this was evident in the Platonic metaphysics of ideas and in Aristotle's God as pure act. Integrating Platonic metaphysics and Christian theology, Augustine became the Christian Plato. Thomas, on the other hand, rethought the Aristotelian categories in Christian terms.

DP: Are you referring to Augustine's *City of God*?

**WG:** For Augustine there are political institutions and then there is an invisible city, which is aimed at the realization of the spiritual good. History is the place where these two elements intersect and collide.

**DP:** God's design that drives history is inscrutable for humans. Does this view relate in some way to your cosmological vision that becoming is totally determined by cosmic cycles?

**WG:** Yes. This is why I referred to Augustine and to the City of God. As you know, we are not able to understand who works for the City of God and who works for the City of Man, precisely because we are the tools of a design that we cannot understand.

**DP:** So, to conclude?

**WG:** To conclude I would say that politics is the handmaid of theology, because it is the human attempt to realize the good within the limits of history.

**DP:** What is your view on artists who take an explicit political stance in their work?

**WG:** There are artists who have engaged or do engage with politics, and I appreciate them for the formal qualities of their work, even without sharing their positions. I admire Beuys, for example, who made his personal and artistic life coincide with social commitment. But I feel closer to Francis Bacon, who placed the human condition at the center of his work, keeping it out of political contexts. All the governments of the world have flaws, but Bacon, who was a gruff and irreverent artist, was interested in something else. Rather than politics, he attacked social hypocrisy. You are Italian, so I don't need to remind you that already in the sixteenth century Machiavelli founded modern political science by separating political action from the moral sphere. In other words, according to Machiavelli, we cannot use ethical categories when we judge the ability of a statesman to found and defend a state. This means that for Machiavelli a statesman who chooses an ally who is not transparent on the moral level—but useful for the defense of the state—cannot be judged by moral criteria, but must be appreciated for his political virtues. Bringing this discourse back to art, I would argue that if morality can be considered separate from politics, so should art. The artist has to deal with philosophy and religion because, more than politics as it is commonly understood, philosophy and religion are the spheres where the individual fully realizes her humanity.

**DP:** What is your religion?

**WG:** My mind is an indefinite enigma, but I am fascinated by the mystery of religion. The mystery of religion has a permanent influence on my art.

**DP:** We have made it clear that you do not consider yourself a political artist.

**WG:** Of course not. I prefer to call myself an artist interested in metaphysics. I'm not interested in petty politics. I consider politics a small profession that does not require any metaphysical quality.

**DP:** It is curious that you hold a markedly anti-modernist position, and at the same time you also use the language typical of the most extreme avant-gardes. The cycle dedicated to the effects of propaganda where you show shovels or newspapers in mail boxes, as well as the installations of the *Cold War Aesthetics* cycle, do not seem to me to use the language of classicism.

**WG:** The question should not be asked in terms of language. Language is not on one side or the other, but in the middle: it is the bridge that connects thought and form. Modernism has given up thinking of art and theology as a single thing, emphasizing artistic forms and languages. This resulted in a great loss. I have always been an anti-modernist, I was one already around the mid-eighties, when I painted the *Post Classical* cycle. Many have confused language with the goal, which is instead the thought to which language gives form.

**DP:** Do you consider yourself a pessimistic artist or a pessimistic philosopher?

**WG:** I prefer to consider myself a pessimistic philosopher.

**DP:** This means that you do not think your work can change society.

**WG:** Art cannot change society, but it allows us to think about the reasons why we are in the world.

**DP:** And religion? Can religion change society?

**WG:** Yes, religion can change society because it acts on the spirit.

**DP:** Are you arguing that art does not influence the spirit?

**WG:** Maybe it does, but in a small part. Being an artist, I would like art to have this ability, but I am not sure it does. It is said that art gives people pleasure, and probably this is what happens with my work, but that is not what I am interested in. I would like to change this way of seeing art. The fact remains that it is not enough for the public to look at the work of an artist for a change to take place.

**DP:** I can agree that art hardly produces concrete social changes, but you have to admit that there are works that mark our lives. Surely there is an excess of optimism in those who, like Dostoevsky, think that beauty can change the world, but it is also true that art can change the way we see the world. And if art has the ability to affect a single person's way of thinking, it has the potential to affect everyone, so it can change society.

WG: I would like art to have such an effect, but the art I've seen so far has not achieved this goal yet.

DP: The most recent Western experience would seem to show that art can have a strong impact on social change. I am not saying that art has generated social and political upheavals but, in more than one case, it has become the emblem of such upheavals. In the second half of the nineteenth century, artists such as David, Delacroix, or Courbet, for example, became the emblem of change. Think of cursed poets like Baudelaire, Rimbaud or Verlaine. These cultural celebrities have influenced social changes and the lifestyle of many people.

WG: Artists have only changed the way of being artists, they have not changed the world. The change they brought only concerns the way of making art and being artists. All artists have the dangerous tendency to widen the area of influence of art. The task of the artist is not to do politics, but to influence the formation of individuals: art and politics are two different fields. There is no perfect government anywhere in the world, but this should not prevent the artist from addressing something higher than politics, like philosophy or religion.

DP: Among the works of your *Great Criticism* cycle there is also a sculpture showing a revolutionary wielding a brush.

WG: This figure refers to the images of the Chinese Cultural Revolution. I do not use it in a revolutionary sense, but to emphasize that it has become "nothing." The figure is simple and clear, but [it] expresses the uncertain emptiness of meaning; it could imply the pain of descending from divinity.

DP: How does someone wise and knowledgeable not aspire to change society?

WG: The reason why the Eastern world has not changed with the same speed as the Western world is wisdom as it is understood in Eastern society. The wise man is such for himself, and his wisdom, moreover, leads him not to change anything, let alone society. It is his influence on ordinary people that can change society.

*This interview summarizes numerous conversations recorded in Beijing, Milan, and Venice between 2012 and 2014. © Wang Guangyi and Demetrio Paparoni 2014.*

# 14

# Dark Learning, Mysticism, and Art: A Conversation with Wang Guangyi

Yan Shanchun 严善錞

**Yan Shanchun:** How, specifically, do you view the question of knowledge and wisdom?

**Wang Guangyi:** From the perspective of reading, at least, I prefer books about wisdom or perhaps religion. This might be connected to the type of reading I did in my college days, books such as *Thomas Aquinas: Selected Political Writings*, which was connected to the mythic nature of his life. He was focused on theology and involved with the Dominicans, who challenged the Franciscans and the clerical hierarchy. Aquinas's actions made his family feel unsafe, so his brothers captured him and locked him in a castle for two years, forcing him to give up his dangerous leanings. During that time, his brothers even sent a prostitute to tempt him, but he was unmoved. He spent the rest of his days proselytizing, and wrote treatises, including his masterwork, *Summa Theologica*. He was offered positions in the Church, including archbishop and abbot, but he refused. Once, at mass, Aquinas claimed that he witnessed a miracle. He immediately stopped writing, and when someone asked him about it, he responded, "I can write no more. All that I have written seems like straw." Later, people claimed that once, when he was praying, he heard a sound from the crucifix, and they witnessed him float up into the air. I really respect his attitudes towards knowledge and life. The statement of his that left the deepest impression on me was, "Nothing is in the intellect that was not first in the senses." I have always felt that any thoughts which remain solely on the level of logic and abstraction are meaningless.

**YS:** Do you think these theological ideas have any connection with art?

**WG:** Our understanding of art is too narrow. We have always treated art as a form of knowledge and a tool; this is very dangerous. The reason our art history is so bland is that we treat it as knowledge far too much. The reason that so much art since the Renaissance lacks charm is that, in my opinion, it is too focused on facts, on anatomy, on perspective, on color theory and on composition. This knowledge has formed the structure of art, and it made art too ordinary.

**YS:** "Retina games."

**WG:** Right. That's a good term for it. I really liked that term of yours when it came out, and so did Shu Qun and the others. Art cannot get stuck on the issue of vision. That's why I've always told you that I like pre-Renaissance art, along with Chinese literati painting. Your book *The Literati and Painting* was quite good, but I still feel it was too knowledge-focused. It read almost like a textbook. It should have touched more on the essence. I think that artists like Gu Kaizhi are very interesting. An artist must have a bit of spirituality, even if it's just myth, otherwise there's no point.

**YS:** Let's get back to Aquinas. What connection does he have to your art?

**WG:** One thing that left an impression on me was his idea of the two types of revelation: the natural or normal revelation and the supernatural or special revelation that God gives man. Natural revelation is attained through observation of order in nature, which I understood at the time to be common and worldly knowledge. Such observation can lead to the truth through logical thinking. Special revelation is a revelation about the existence of God, which I understood as thoughts on questions of existence and creation, belonging to the realm of wisdom. Artists should focus on these kinds of questions. Questions such as the Trinity cannot be explained through observing the natural order. This is about revelation and it is self-evident.

I remember certain of Aquinas's passages quite clearly. He said that some of God's creations are concealed, and others are apparent for mankind to observe. He said that we can gain knowledge of His existence through the things that God has revealed, this likely being the "normal revelation," but this can only be done through a method of comparison. What interested me the most was Aquinas's importation of Aristotle's "syllogism" into Catholic doctrine. He combined reason with faith.

**YS:** Specifically speaking, what connection do these ideas have to your art?

**WG:** Looking back at it now, I think it had two influences, one being the incorporation of religious issues into art, seeing the two as a whole.

**YS:** Was this connected to your ideas at the time of the Young Northern Artists Group and "rational painting?"

**WG:** One may have led to another. At the time, we were all talking about it. Actually, I must admit that we practically treated art as a religion, which is connected to the ideas of Nietzsche. We hoped to save souls through art. We felt then that it appeared to be a trivial, listless phenomenon. It had become "retina games," focused on trifling matters. We felt that this was very harmful to Chinese art, and it was a bad aspect of literati painting. I don't think this was present in artists such as Gu Kaizhi or the paintings of the Tang and Song dynasties. I think that art should be upward-looking and healthy. Aquinas's ideas gave me this power. But I never engaged in a complete reading of his works, I don't treat them as a complete system of thought either. What interested me was the great vocabulary, one that was in keeping with the vocabulary of my artistic thinking. This is where my reading differs from yours.

**YS:** You don't think there's a discrepancy between your understanding of these words and the original spirit of the work?

**WG:** I've never thought about that. I think that's unfair towards artists, and it's unnecessary. If I came to doubt my own understanding, then I would not read such books. Such doubts can lead to a lot of problems, because I can then also doubt the accuracy of the translation. I read the works of Hegel and Nietzsche in the same way. I treated them as classics and maxims, ones that I am free to understand however I wish. What I care about is what I understand. What it once was does not matter. That is for the scholars.

**YS:** Your understanding is actually a model that already exists in your mind, and then you go to see what inspiration or supplementations their thinking can provide for your model.

**WG:** Right. I think that this is the artist's reading method, or the one with true wisdom. I believe you are saying that my model should be "prophetic." If a person lacks this prophetic model, then he is just a sheep in the flock, unable to ponder questions or create art. He can only follow the thoughts of others, or to use a modern term, he is brainwashed, brainwashed by highly trivial knowledge. I remember you quoted Lao Tzu once, something about how the more you research something, the more it loses.

**YS:** "Knowledge—the more refined your analysis, the craftier its evasions." It was Huang Zongxi.

**WG:** Right! Actually, I thought at the time that Aquinas's ideas were quite simple: one was to bring logic to theology, and the other was to bring order to the world. These ideas were very important to us in the Young Northern Artists Group. Bringing logic to bear on theology implied that there was evidence in reality for things from the other side, and that gave us a sense of direction. Meanwhile, it pushed logic beyond knowledge, giving it certain qualities of wisdom. We emphasized this in our art. That is to say, we expressed the sacred through very clear schema.

**YS:** Are you talking about your *Post-Classical* series?

**WG:** *Frozen North Pole* was along those lines, but it was conveyed more completely in the *Post-Classical* series. That is because I drew from art history. I believe in the power of knowledge and education, because as far as the masses are concerned, we still must draw from history and memory to speak. There is also a connection to the later *Great Criticism* series. The inspiration that I drew from Aquinas came from his fusion between philosophy and theology, which gave it a special power.

**YS:** That is to say, what you focused on and expressed were issues of "dark learning" (*xuan-xue*[1]), but you were not opposed to, or you required the application and use of, knowledge.

**WG:** Yes. This is the relationship between ends and means. I think that a lot of artists stop at the means, viewing them as a kind of noumenon. Aquinas's other influence for me was in terms of thinking about order. We were quite averse to a state of disorder in Chinese society at the time. Whether it was art or politics, it all seemed rather chaotic and individualist. Aquinas believed in theology and advocated the divine right of kings. He believed that a king's power derived from the Church and God, and that theological power was above secular power. In this way, a nation and its people would have a unified thinking and will, and society would have order. In a certain sense, my later placement of grids on canvas was connected to the views I had back then. The grid is a kind of visual order, one that can give order to our perceptions. This brings order to our lives, and through this order, we can verify the existence of God. This is Aquinas's "verifying God's existence through the order (or purpose) of the world." I didn't really like the liberalism or sensationalism at the Zhejiang Academy of Fine Arts, so I was always a bit vexed. For this reason, beginning around my third year of college, I was no longer an "artist" in the traditional sense. My theological impulse was much stronger than my passion for art, and this quickly led me into "contemporary art." Oh, this reminds me of another Aquinas quote that left a deep impression on me: "Theology is greater than philosophy. Philosophy is the handmaiden of theology." I turned that into: "Theology is greater than art. Art is the handmaiden of theology." Such an idea was quite in keeping theoretically with my supposedly contemporary art.

**YS:** Don't you think this conflicts with your current views on China's problems?

**WG:** Of course, my art has now basically discarded these ideas, or as Hegel would more accurately put it, sublated, which is to say that while I mostly discarded and moved forward, I retained certain internal elements. I think the most appropriate explanation would be one we were using twenty years ago, which is "logical progression."

**YS:** I remember at the time you also talked a lot about another philosopher, St. Augustine.

**WG:** Right! Augustine was perhaps a bit more important to me. I read *Confessions* many times. His thinking on creation linked up with some of my later artworks, including the *Spirit of the Material*. Augustine stressed that God created the world out of nothing, which contrasted with Plato's view that God had created the world out of matter. If God had created the world out of matter, then such material would become a limitation placed on God. Augustine believed that God was all-knowing and all-powerful, completely free. He could create the physical world completely from nothing, with no need for materials. On this point, I borrowed a bit from his ideas, and in a certain sense, I replaced God with the artist. This is connected to the later emergence of my readymade artwork *Inflammable and Explosive* (see Figure 8.1). I believed that the artist should use his own intuition to create, should create out of nothing, to discover things from within the natural state. This method was completely different from that of *Great Criticism*; it was complete "dark learning." I remember Augustine said that God created everything with one word, using his "way"—language—to create all in existence. It is the same with art. When you view something as being rich with spiritual characteristics, then that thing begins to exist.

**YS:** This is the same as the "theory of possession" we discussed previously.

**WG:** Thinking about it now, they are the same. It is also a source of ideas. Artists should have this ability, and even a bit of a gambler's spirit.

**YS:** Do you mean disciple?

**WG:** In a way, gamblers and disciples are the same, as they both act out of faith. Faith is very important. If contemporary art were to lose its faith, it would be nothing. I think it is the same with economics; money and stocks are the embodiment of everyone's faith, and if we were to believe that the world is going to end tomorrow, then stocks and money would have no meaning. It is because we have faith in tomorrow that art and money have reason to exist. Augustine's greatest influence over me has been in regards to the question of faith. Someone once raised the question about what God was doing before he created the world, and Augustine felt that such a proposition was wrong in itself. As he saw it, it was obvious that God created the world and time at the same moment, and that there was no time before creation. God does not exist within time. Though we believe that God exists and that God created the world, we shouldn't go on thinking and wondering about what God was doing before creating the world. Such doubts will strip us of our sense of security, and we will also lose the foundation for discussing art. Some suppositions are necessary. They require us to persist in our faith. If we doubt even those most basic of suppositions, then we can't talk about art or about life. Endless doubts and inferences are meaningless; they can only lead to total nihilism. Even though I am myself a nihilist, there are limits. I know there is a point at which I can no longer go on thinking and doubting. I must maintain faith in those things. I remember you once talked about a certain metaphor of Hui Shi's, about how you can divide something forever without reaching the end.

**YS:** "A foot-long rod, if divided in half each day, will last forever." It's true. As Augustine saw it, God was the creator of the world and also of time. He created time as he created the world. God transcends all change and is eternal. For God, there is no past or future, only the endless now. As for what time is, it is said that Augustine pursued this question, and eventually classified it as a function of human thought. He believed that it was inappropriate to view time as dividing between the past, present, and future. At the time, I talked with you guys about the similarities between such ideas and

Buddhist thought, but as I remember, we didn't get very far. I think your ideas were very mysterious. At times it felt like a secret society. When you discussed those terms with the others at the Young Northern Artists Group, it was like there was some tacit agreement. Some concepts that seemed quite slippery to us were, to you, so solid and interesting.

**WG:** Actually, we were just kind of feeling our way through, without really discussing or analyzing these concepts. It was enough if they just inspired our own creations.

**YS:** As for Aquinas and Augustine, we also knew some of their aesthetic ideas, such as those regarding proportions and principles.

**WG:** I was basically an anti-aestheticist. At the time, I basically just viewed their aesthetics as theories connected to the sacredness of God, wholly unrelated to the principles of visual form we talked about later, or even to the aesthetics of Kant and Hegel. My understanding of the order and proportions of form was all built on a foundation of the sacred and unknown. That is to say, I placed the grid on the canvas to provide people's vision with a form of order. Such order is merely a principle of rationality. It is aimed at the formalism that was so prevalent at the time. The aesthetics of Augustine and Aquinas did not really have that great an influence on me. Theirs was mostly a kind of harmony theory based on visual principles, along with a bit of stuff from Pythagoras; it was very physical, a concept of "beauty" as opposed to "ugliness." It was a visual concept.

**YS:** Were you influenced by the Western aesthetic theories that were popular at the time, such as those of Clive Bell or Rudolf Arnheim?

**WG:** No, not really. Even the ideas of Hegel and Kant, I basically approached from the perspective of "dark learning" rather than aesthetics. I'm starting to come around to what you said back then about the similarities between Buddhism and some of Augustine's ideas. In fact, I've been having a lot of thoughts in recent years about Eastern "dark learning" or esoteric thought. It's related to Buddhism, but it's all rooted in Augustine. In essence, I am someone who brings together nihilism and theism. One side of me is extremely nihilist, whether it comes to art or my own life. Like I said that day, I am often struck by a nameless terror, especially when I work deep into the night and I look up at the sky and feel that the world is so boundless, and therefore so unreliable. To counteract this terror, I have to create points of support for myself. Art is an important support in my life. For this reason, it is only when I infuse my art with these thoughts of emptiness that I can enjoy a sense of security for a moment. This sense of security is perhaps a god that I have created for my own soul. Thinking about it, this god I believe in, or the God that we often talk about, is not the same as the God of Christianity. It seems a bit more Zen.

**YS:** It appears so, but I think at its root, Buddhism aims to destroy such "gods." The essence of Buddhism is enlightenment. It is about seeing one's nature with clarity. It is about leaving the fairyland of vanity. It is about realizing emptiness, to break away with the grasp of ego and dharma.

**WG:** Oh, well in that case, does that make me a delusionist?

**YS:** Do you think there are any connections between you and Joseph Beuys?

**WG:** Of course. First, there was his life experience. I always pay attention to legendary fig- ures. I don't really like those scholars and artists with ordinary lives. I like legendary stuff. What I said over twenty years ago about "legends and games" expresses my thoughts on this. I feel that I must live in a legendary state, at least in terms of my art. An artist with a legendary life can certainly have much more influence over art history than an artist with an ordinary life. Perhaps Cézanne was an exception. That ascetic life at the foot of Mont Sainte-Victoire is quite legendary, though such a legend would be difficult to put into effect, but once he became a great enough artist, one who had changed art history, that tranquil life suddenly appears sacred, eliciting respect. If he were just a second- or third-rate artist, then that life would appear quite ordinary.

**YS:** You think that primarily it was Beuys's life that touched you?

**WG:** You could put it that way. His artworks and his life are part of a unified whole. We rarely see great artists with Second World War experience. Disregarding the various interpretations of Beuys's connections with the Nazis, as an artist, he certainly brought his experience of life and death in- to his art. He used special materials to express these sentiments. His injury at least gave him a firsthand experience of all this. Putting ourselves in his position, it is not strange at all that an artist with such life experience would spark a re-evaluation of artistic questions, especially in the contemporary art setting. Doubtless, artists such as us, who have experienced the Mao era and the Reform and Opening, can't just tackle problems on canvas alone. Of course, I think there are some artists who still persist with the artistic concepts of the past, and yet continue to ponder certain new artistic problems, but I can't. My life has completely changed. It has shown me that I must make new value judgements about art and everything I do.

YS: Perhaps we can talk about Beuys in a different way. Tell me about the differences between you and him.

WG: Good. That might allow us to speak more clearly. First, I think what we have in common is that we have both extended our fields of vision onto problems that are related to art but are commonly viewed as being outside of art. A very important detail about Beuys is his connection to the academy and to students. He had this godfather quality. He fully achieved this, spreading his ideas to his students and influencing a generation. I'm not like this. I don't enjoy interacting with students. He placed great importance on academia. A famous line of his is, "Wherever I am, Academy is." On this point, I am his complete opposite. There is an interesting paradox here. In art, Beuys often pursued a highly individualized experience, and his expression was also often very highly individualized, but he often liked to use "socialization," such as students or groups, to spread his spirit. My experiences are also highly individualized, but I think that the self in that personalization is a "greater self," the self in an era, and the methods or images I

choose are often ones that are very familiar to the masses.
I don't like interacting with academies, and I don't like engaging in academic associations or other such methods, even though the early Northern Artists Group was like that. In essence, I'm not suited to that kind of group life. On an even deeper level, I don't like interacting with people. This is connected to my experience of life in the North. I like meditating, rather than chatting or lecturing.

YS: Actually, in comparison, he is more like a professor or a missionary, and you are a monk. He had a social demeanor, which is in keeping with the legendary principles you mentioned. Why don't you take part in the necessary social activities?

WG: There might be another paradox here. The concepts in Beuys's works were perhaps too strong. The material qualities in his artwork were markedly behind the intellectual qualities. As a result, most of his artwork could not be materially preserved, and there were also performance works and site-specific installations. The majority of his artworks were impossible to document, but in this regard I have taken a relatively classical attitude, in that I place importance on the material aspect of artwork. I emphasize "material spirit," meaning that the spirit is presented through a certain material. This may be connected to the materialist education we received as children. I believe that there must be something tangible to be able to take on the spiritual mission, or alternatively, that the spirit or soul can only find expression through a certain physical carrier. That's my view on "spiritual possession." As a result, I don't do performance art, and I don't like so-called participation and interaction. I think all of that is too short-lived, too impermanent. All of my artworks have substantial material careers, and this implies that all of my souls have a sanctuary. I must think about my art and face it in this way to keep my conscience clear.

YS: Looking at your past understanding of art, you seem to have an elitist attitude towards it. Even though you hope to use what you call art of the "people" to discuss your own concepts, your art is essentially at the service of a minority of people removed from the masses.

WG: There is no such thing as service in art. I've never hoped to educate certain people through my art; I just wanted to raise a point, to awaken certain experiences and thoughts in them through the visual specimens I provide. Beuys believed that everyone is an artist. He of course wasn't saying that everyone could become an artist, but his goal was apparently to point out that everyone has the ability to become an artist. I think this is meaningless. As I see it, being an artist is a profession, a person with special qualities. I don't agree with his "expanded view of art." The notion that by transforming decorative things or things from life can turn them into works of art has certain pantheist and Dadaist leanings. Art is a thing for a minority of the people. I must be clear on that point. I think that Beuys's excessive expansion of art onto all objects and all behaviors is quite suspect.

YS: Do you think that his art has excessively mystical and anti-art leanings, or that his performance art was a kind of shamanistic act?

WG: I think that at least from his words and actions, such an appraisal is reasonable. I think he said something along the lines of "God and society are art." In fact, his later works were anti-aesthetic. On this point, our views converge a bit, but I am not against art history. The art history I'm talking about here is not a history of aesthetics; it is a history of visual experience. It's the same from *Great Criticism* up to now with *Under the Sky, Rivers and Mountains*. I like to use history to do my talking, to use "the people" to talk. Beuys's art was virtually never aimed at history, or at art history. He mostly directed his art towards the current individual experience, an absolute self in reality. I am different; I care about a self in society, a self in history. Truly, in a certain sense, his performance art very much resembled the acts of a shaman. He used action, while I think that "spiritual possession" is mainly a question of faith. If you believe in it, then it is there. When there is too much action, then you are treading close to shamanist territory. My ultimate questions are in art, in the artwork. This is a fundamental difference between me and him. I focus on artistic issues. Religion and God are just paths for me to solve artistic issues, to save artistic issues, or to push art up to a higher level. In fact, on this point, my thinking is in line with that of the '85 Movement period.

**YS:** Are you talking about Hegel's idea of "replacing art with philosophy?"

**WG:** Yes. This might be a clearer way to explain it. Hegel's ideas really did lead me towards my understanding of contemporary art, which is a belief that traditional art is dead, no longer able to satisfy our spiritual needs. As far as I see it, formalism has led us to spiritual degeneracy. I have always believed this. I think that the questions I ponder are about art, a new kind of art. This art is connected to traditional art history. It's just that I have extracted some spiritual things from traditional art, and slowly elevated them, enhancing their spiritual qualities. In regards to the question of art, I am a fuser of historicism and mysticism. So, my understanding of philosophy replacing art is not that ideas have completely become art, but that art and ideas have come together. The profession of art still exists. Therefore, I am not a thinker, nor am I a philosopher; I am an artist with ideas. Otherwise I would be unable to explain my current state of life and mode of behavior. It is the same with my economic life. I make my living from selling paintings, selling artworks, rather than from teaching.

**YS:** It is said that when he was at the academy, Beuys always discussed the question of God with his students. Some of the students were dissatisfied, saying that he only talked about God and society, rather than art.

**WG:** This is really something where he and I differ. In the past I always stressed my attitude that I don't like art that is too much like art, because when it's too much like art, it can easily go aesthetic. Art that pursues aesthetics or technique to excess lacks dignity and inhibits the elevation of the human spirit. I still, however, view it as art, rather than philosophy. The negative effect of Beuys is quite obvious. It led to today's art becoming accessible to everyone. Overly egalitarian art has led to the loss of dignity in art. One could also say that excessive professionalization (technicalization) and excessive amateurization will harm art, and in this sense, I am a moderate. YS So, then, how do we interpret the connections between Beuys's "everyone is an artist" and your "hands of the people?" Is it a question of identity, or of aesthetics? Beuys's assertion has a kind of Zen or Buddhist effect, as in the notion that everyone has a Buddha nature so everyone can become a Buddha, it being only a question of awareness or confusion.

**WG:** That approach works, of course, but the question I am interested in is that of "the people" rather than people. Of course, according to the past view, the term "the people" has a bit of a "flock of sheep" connotation. The term truly does have a double meaning, but I am using the term from a rather positive perspective, which is connected to the Maoist education we received. Mao said, "There is inexhaustible creativity within the masses of the people." He also said, "People, and only people, are the true momentum behind the creation of history."

**YS:** Mao Zedong's greatest impact on our generation was his elevation of the concept of "the people," writing "the people" into history. He created "the people's war" and "the people's commune." He called out, "Long live the people." There were also other terms, such as "the people's enemy Chiang Kai-shek," but all of them were "in the name of the people." If I recall correctly, I think it was something that Lenin said. Apparently, when we say things such as "the people's enemy Chiang Kai-shek," or "in the name of the people," it lacks power. For our generation, at least, this concept of the people is not the same as the concept of citizenry. Citizenry seems to be more of a legal concept, connected to such concepts as elections, constitutions and stocks, while "the people" seems to be more connected to human history. When we talk of citizens, it seems we are merely talking about questions of rights and responsibility, but when we talk about the people, we talk about questions of human spiritual civilization and the creation of physical wealth. It seems that if we are to talk about history, we must use this concept of "the people."

WG: They're both there. "The people," as I use it here, has two meanings. One is the people under some collective unconscious state. Such people have a kind of primitive imagination and creativity. They talk about all sorts of things together, and respect certain rituals. I think that this is the basis for shamanism. Otherwise, a sorcerer couldn't have so much power. That is to say, he has to draw his power, absorb qi. Without such a setting, many religions would never have been able to exist. The second meaning of "the people" refers to when one of them creates something, and it is universally received by and spread among them, becoming a very important part of their spiritual life or even everyday life. In other words, the participation of the people has bestowed this created thing with more meaning and value.

YS: Is there a difference between this participation of yours and the participation and interaction of Beuys?

WG: They are clearly different. My idea of participation is rooted in certain totemic concepts. My creation is a fixed, physical object, and everybody, through their own imagination and experience, injects it with a certain meaning, rather than changing its form and meaning. It is the addition of meaning, rather than its change. That is to say, that basic thing exists, and its direction is clear, but the participants have added things to its foundation.

YS: Do you think that interpretations of your artwork are relatively objective?

WG: It goes back to what we used to say when we debated, that "one hundred viewers will see one hundred different Hamlets." That sounds a bit cliché and meaningless, but it truly touches on some basic issues in contemporary art. I still maintain that view, which is that the final result will be one hundred Hamlets rather than one hundred Ophelias. I think that my artwork embodies this value standpoint; the images in my work come from "the people," and I think that "the people" can objectively read my work. My *Anthology* artwork indeed has certain unclear or mystical aspects, but the basic meaning is clear and graspable. For a long time, I focused my efforts on removing my own individual ideas as an artist, on removing my highly personal perceptions, striving to express a public, of-the-people concept. In reality, I can't truly know what the people are thinking, but ever since the *Great Criticism* series, I have always been rooted in this supposition. It is just a supposition, but without suppositions, the artist loses reason to exist. We are not scientists, nor are we thinkers or philosophers. We have no duty or need to disseminate objective knowledge to the public. What the artist should do is strive to imagine a world, and to imagine his artwork's meaning and its relationship to the public. As to what the true situation is? That is not my concern.

YS: So, do you view yourself as one of "the people" or as an artist who is apart from "the people?"

WG: There are two aspects of my response to this question. The artist in my mind is decidedly not the same as the people. It's like Mao's saying, that they come from the people but are above them.

YS: Mao said, "Art derives from life and is above life."

WG: It's the same meaning. My art contains the consciousness of the people, and clearly applies the language of the people, but that does not mean that I am one of the people, because I take the stance of the artist as I employ this language and consciousness, and there is an important transformation on my part. This must be clear. Beuys wasn't very clear on this question. Perhaps he wanted to destroy something, and maybe it was linked to some of his life experience, perhaps to his experience with war and the Nazis. I, however, am a builder. I don't have too much to repent for. I think that in my art, I also express a concern for politics, and this concern is rooted in my consciousness of "the people." My so-called concern for politics as art, rather than art as politics, should be discussed on this basis. Artists can choose any such themes, and they can worry about questions regarding art itself, or about education, hygiene or the environment. I happen to care about political issues, but that does not mean that I am a politician; not in the slightest. I would not engage in politics, holding rallies or forming cliques. I am just someone who thinks about political issues and uses the language familiar to me to engage in thought and expression. I know that politics as a struggle for power is a very rigorous knowledge system and behavior process. All kinds of human relationships, balances of benefits and allocations of authority are very complex, and I'm not the least bit interested in them. That is what I meant when I've said in the past that my political stance is "neutral" or "standpoint-free."

**YS:** Do you think of yourself as a "free intellectual?"

**WG:** It's almost the same as that, but not quite. It is the same in that I maintain my own independence, but different in that they maintain an intellectual stance and participate in politics, while I follow the intuition and perceptions of the artist, with no theoretical import, let alone public values. As one of the people, I think that there are many political problems in the world, and such problems, including certain massive political incidents in our own country, catalyze my artistic creation.

**YS:** Do you think that since you are not a participant, you can never know the truth behind political incidents?

**WG:** There is no truth in anything. Nobody knows the truth. I believe that even the majority of the supposed politicians who take part in these things do not know the so-called truth. We have all had the experience of seeing the so-called revelation of the truth, which turns out to be nothing more than one lie being covered by another. It is ridiculous for individuals to discuss truth in politics. One could even say that it is ridiculous to discuss truth in knowledge, including man's origins. Everyone believes that man descended from the apes, but is this the truth? I don't believe in this thing called the truth. All we have are tiny, distorted reflections of things.

**YS:** Your understanding of the truth of things quite resembles the Buddhist idea of "dependent origination" that we discussed last time. From the Buddhist perspective, the essence of things is empty, but we cannot persist in emptiness, because we will fall into the belief that life ends in death, which leads to nihilism. We cannot deny the existence of the phenomenal world. This world is illusory, comprised of various karmic relations. They are just a combination of relationships, a semblance.

**WG:** You put it quite well. We cannot grasp that truth, but if we say that there is no truth to begin with, then there is no issue of whether or not it can be grasped. If we say that the truth is, as you put it, this combination, then that says that what we can grasp is only a semblance. This suddenly calls to mind the ideas of the "false, grand, and empty" that we talked about in the past, as well as the questions of "emptiness, falseness, and the middle" that you spoke of a few days ago. I am a moderate, just as Huang Zhuan said, and just as you said, I don't persist in the empty or the false. I admit that there is a bit of suspicion of the "false, grand, and empty" in my art, but I accept such criticism with a positive attitude. This concept of the "false, grand, and empty" is very difficult to distinguish from style and form in art. All form in art history is false, borrowed from predecessors. Individual creativity is limited, history is of the people, and our artistic language and forms must all be borrowed from the people; it is just a question of how much is borrowed. Manet's *Déjeuner sur l'herbe* was borrowed from Dürer. The crux of the matter is whether or not your act of borrowing is meaningful. The question is whether or not people can perceive the production of a new meaning in a new setting. My *Great Criticism* represents an attitude of not mincing your words.

**YS:** Your understanding of Buddhism has a bit of a shamanistic feel.

**WG:** I think that as an artist, you must have your own understanding towards existing knowledge. You should not be too objective, though some objectivity is necessary. The key is that such understanding must be in keeping with the logic of your own ideas and your own art. You must make this knowledge or vocabulary into a product of wisdom, something alive, rather than dead dogma.

**YS:** Think back now to before *Mao Zedong* and *Great Criticism*, to how your concept of the people was established in earlier series such as *Post-Classical*.

**WG:** Of course, back then, I didn't have the notion of "the people." I still wanted to be a scholarly artist, meaning that I used so-called schema correction and culture correction to engage in the alteration of art history. At the time, I was mainly under the influence of Hegelian ideas, and I wanted to reconsider the issues of art history from a metaphysical perspective. Later, I shifted from a limited art history to a large art history, from the art of artists to the art of the people, and in this way, my visual experience was completely changed.

But I think there is still an internal logic to it, which is that I am still facing a historical experience, except that the scope has been expanded. I respect the word "creation," but I don't believe in the definitive significance of creation in art history. In the face of the image, our creativity is weak. This is an idea that was already clear to me twenty years ago in Wuhan discussing the theories of Gombrich. We can say today that with *Post-Classical*, I was drawing from great artists to make my statement, and after that, I drew from the people to make my statement. I'm always drawing from others to speak. What matters is that I have used the words of others to speak my own meaning. I still believe that art must be disseminated, so I choose words that all can understand, to express my meaning.

**YS:** Could you explain this people's language in a more concrete way?

**WG:** I have talked about this before. For instance, beginning with *Great Criticism*, my images have increasingly trended towards flatness, gradually chipping away at the tone in the middle. Whether it is the sketched relationships or the color relationships, everything has grown increasingly simple. Though this is connected to the primitive style of those *Great Criticism* images, with that feel of carved wood, I subsequently always consciously pursued that effect. A lot of the scenes from the *Cultural Revolution* have a sense of three-dimensional spaces. It is all basically in the Soviet art style, but done by professional artists, even the *Great Criticism* masthead pictures. But when they spoke to the people, they gave it a simplified rendering. I call this simplification "total conceptualization." Interestingly, such conceptualized images happen to have a special power. They don't make my eyes seek out those tiny changes and they let me focus on the overall atmosphere. This is the same as the people's expectations of art. The people understand it, and at the same time, they are interested in copying or disseminating such art. Such an image is clear and powerful. It has defeated the weakness of aestheticism, defeated the meaningless groans of the petite bourgeoisie. In fact, in drawing from the art of the *Cultural Revolution*, some artists have made interesting transformations. As to their value, it may take quite a while before that is known. My faith at the time was in "ceasing the aesthetic experience."

**YS:** I think that as you talk about the people, about using the people's language to speak and speaking words that the people understand, you need to explain more about your relationship to Warhol.

**WG:** In *Who Do I Like More, Warhol or Beuys*, I made the following metaphor: "One of them is the palm of my hand, the other the back." I said that Beuys was an alchemist, an artist who could make things mysterious, while Warhol turned ordinary things more ordinary, a person under the sun. My similarities and differences with Beuys are quite obvious, and the differences are probably where I'm connected to Warhol. Warhol's stuff is direct and clear; people could understand his art at a glance. He showed you what everyone saw. But this is also where the problem lies. Behind Warhol's "shallowness," I can't say that there's any depth. The very least I can say is that there is wisdom there. It's like when we're in a solemn and refined setting, and suddenly someone says something coarse—everyone is filled with surprise and strange ideas. Of course, such words have to come out of the mouth of a master, rather than a servant. The identity of the speaker is very important. I think that Warhol was one such—interesting—master.

**YS:** You feel that Warhol's art becomes meaningful when it's interpreted within a contemporary art context of intentionally seeking out the mysterious and obscure. Is this what you mean when you say that "situational logic" is more important than "formal logic?"

**WG:** You could say that. "Formal logic" can easily lead to soliloquy and endless explanation, and easily grow tiresome. "Situational logic" is marked by humanity. It is the spirit of Zen. Speaking and reading cannot be removed from the background. When a person says the same sentence against a different background, the meaning is different. This is the meaning of that term "directionality" we used to talk about in contemporary art. I have continually been extending and pushing this idea. As I see it at least, it's only when you place Warhol's stuff together with that of Beuys that you can see how much of a martyr he was. They are on the same level. Without Warhol, Beuys loses meaning, and without Beuys, Warhol becomes exceedingly ordinary. Warhol could be said to have an ordinary form of "beauty," the "beauty" of the masses. In his work you can see that he really knows how to paint. It's very well produced, very bright and full of layers. Amidst the expressionism, abstract and individualized brushstrokes and materials that flourished at the time, however, this was clearly a reactionary role. His aesthetic qualities were of the masses, but I don't think they were of the people. "The people" is a political concept, which usually seems to be tied to the concept of the proletariat, to hardship and selflessness. The concept of "the masses" seems to have certain urban connotations, of materialistic people who are focused on enjoyment and consumption. My art is a people's concept, not a masses' concept. It is on this level that the concept of "Political Pop" establishes itself (Figure 14.1). Also, one difference between Warhol and me is that the imagery in my artwork does not come from the photography industry or commercialized production; it is all created by the people and people's artists, and then I make the appropriate adjustments according to my own principles.

**YS:** Are they aesthetic principles?

**Figure 14.1** Wang Guangyi, *The Materialist* (2001), sculpture with fiberglass and millet, about 180 × 120 × 60 cm.

WG: They are aesthetic principles, but not the principles of formal aesthetics in the usual sense. My principles are relatively uniform principles, ones which fit with my own habits in viewing painting. In terms of color and form, I have made adjustments and unifications. Otherwise, I would lose my identity as an artist. This is where I differ from Beuys; I am still an artist. I am not a pure thinker, or a thinker who uses his eyes to consider problems. Comparatively speaking, I think that Warhol's stuff really is a bit shallow. His art is overly sunny, which is an American cultural tradition, where everything is so beautiful and pure, like their natural environment and their cities, without too much historical burden to worry about. We Chinese people are more conflicted. Though "the people" is a fine expression, a fresh concept that Mao Zedong created for China, the term always has an historic aspect in China, and there are things like peasant uprisings, figures such as Chen Sheng, Wu Guang and Li Zicheng, and incidents such as the Taiping Rebellion.

The people have a history; Mao Zedong found them a history. I think that Warhol and America's concept of "the masses" is a very flat thing, a here and now concept, a truly common concept. As a result, Warhol's explanation of his own artwork was also very direct, never halting or evasive. When others asked him "if it was like this or that," or even when a common audience member asked a very *naïve* question, he would usually respond, "Yes, that's what I was thinking." I remember a very famous interview with Warhol, where all he ever said was "yes" or "no." I would not be able to do that. I often say that there's something else in there, something hidden. That's because I truly feel that my artwork contains things that even I cannot be sure of, which is what we were talking about with the game of jumping back and forth between Beuys and Warhol. I'm actually quite jealous of Warhol's purity and directness, but there's something in my personality that always pulls me towards the mysterious and uncertain. It is a very painful experience, one that I must endure alone. Warhol's dissemination of meaninglessness might be connected to his choice of images. His images are not very meaningful, or perhaps are meaningless. Though the forms are clear and the schema simple, they are not the result of professionalization. Deep down, they are the products of the universal decline in spirituality.

**YS:** Could I say that overall, Beuys has had a greater influence on you?

**WG:** That is without a doubt. This is connected to national character. The Chinese and Germans are relatively solemn and have a strong sense of history. They like to meditate and have an impulse for dark learning. As I have said before, I have many contradictory aspects. In terms of thinking, in the past I really liked to use the term "antinomy." I prefer obscure, difficult language and uncertain modes of thought. It's like we say of thought, that it cannot be too clear, that it should be something invisible and intangible. Otherwise it loses its meaning.

## [B]

**YS:** We were talking about Duchamp last time. I think that another of his greatest influences on contemporary art was in the concept of play. Over these past few days I took another look at that discussion we had in 1990 about myths and games, and I think that a lot of facts today affirm our "ideals" from back then.

**WG:** I think a lot of ideas from that discussion were very important. My current state is one of a "logical progression." It feels really good when myths become reality.

**YS:** What are your thoughts on Duchamp's concept of play?

**WG:** I haven't systematically read his writings on this. My intuition is that his concept of play is very broad, possibly because of his longtime desire to destroy people's established concepts about art.

**YS:** Do you think that your art contains an element of play? Alternatively, could you talk about your art over the years in terms of play?

**WG:** No problem. First, I think that the situation in art that I face is different from that of Duchamp. He chiefly wanted to change the rules of the art game at a root level, and he really was a subversive, a revolutionary. I am not. I say that, basically, I am a builder. In the early days of the '85 Movement, I really felt that I had to destroy the monotony and blandness of art under the official system. Looking back now, that was a very short-sighted line of thinking. Later on, I quickly found what I needed, and I wasn't moved by the various movements in thought around me.

**YS:** Do you feel that your artistic issues, or what we used to call their "directedness," have always had an international background?

**WG:** That is beyond a doubt. When we were in college, we were always thinking about artistic issues in that way. Duchamp, Beuys, and Warhol were doubtless the foundation of my thinking about such issues. But that is not to say that I consider contemporary art issues from a purely Western standpoint. Just as we said last time, we have our own logic of cultural development. I would be hard pressed to say whether contemporary world art has two different logics, one logic, or many. On this matter, I will use the previous standpoint I've always held: to do things according to my own ideas and determination, and to have faith that my own thinking has universal significance.

**YS:** So what is the play element in your art?

**WG:** Talking about play can become a bit abstruse. I remember you once mentioned a book by a friend of Gombrich's entitled *The Seriousness of Play*.

**YS:** It was *Homo Ludens* (Man the Player) by Johan Huizinga.

**WG:** That book was very academic. I think it even spoke about war.

**YS:** "Play" is actually a very important concept in Western contemporary thought. Hans-Georg Gadamer also speaks along these lines, talking about the mutual participation and fusion between receivers and expressers, conscious and unconscious, about the cyclically repeating spiritual interaction in re-creation, and about "fusion" on the foundation of the teleology of self-expression. Such fusion is connected to activities of sexual awareness.

**WG:** That's too complicated; I don't really understand it. Contemporary philosophy seems a bit deliberately mystifying. Right now, I prefer more direct thinking, things that are more visual and close to life.

**YS:** When you were young, did you ever play the game "38th Parallel?"

**WG:** I'm not sure. Tell me about it.

**YS:** Thinking about it now, the name "38th Parallel" was connected to the Korean War. We learned about the concept of the "38th Parallel" from the Armistice at the time. Later, it slowly percolated into our childhood. When we were in elementary school, it was two students to a desk. In order to keep students from talking in class, the teachers would put one girl and one boy at each desk. It seemed that in each class, one strong-willed boy would end up at the same desk as one strong-willed girl, and because the desks were small, you would inevitably have one person's hand ending up on the other person's side and an argument would ensue. To solve this problem, we would draw a dividing line on the desk in pencil. We called it the "38th Parallel."

**WG:** We had this same situation.

**YS:** This 38th Parallel led to a lot of interesting stories. When one student wanted to give the other trouble, they would think of ways to use this line to cause problems. They might focus all of their attention in class on their neighbor's arm, watching to see if it crossed the line. When it did, they would get into an argument. Sometimes they would secretly redraw the line or erase it, using it as an excuse for "war." As a result, everyone focused on this 38th Parallel. Actually, in most cases, the size of the table wasn't a limit on normal study. It was this stupid "strong willed" personality that made the 38th Parallel so important. A lot of "wars" are started in much the same way. This game of the 38th Parallel became an important part of our lives at that time, helping us to understand the meaning of the existence of the collective and society. A lot of political theories of the time were included within, such as "We will not attack unless we are attacked;

if we are attacked, we must counterattack," and the idea of "choosing sides," which is that as a member of the class, you must declare your support for either A or B, and you can't just sit on the fence. There is no respect to be gained in sitting on the fence, especially for a male student. Similar to sitting on the fence, there was also a type of person known as the "uninvolved faction." This is a term from the Cultural Revolution; such people never get involved in any faction, but you must make your decision before the game begins, and stay out of the game. Once you get involved, if you maintain neutrality, then you are branded as a "fence-sitter," which is a loss of face. I think this game arose out of a surplus of energy.

WG: This story is very interesting. In a certain sense, one could say that art is a form of surplus spirit. I, however, am a dualist, and I emphasize the seriousness, even the tragedy, that lies behind such play.

YS: Huizinga and Gadamer both talk about the issue of seriousness in play. They also spoke about the relationship between seriousness and humor in play. We used that essay to talk about art. Allow me to read from it: "I think that, in the game that is contemporary art, people mostly take a humorous stance when talking about academic issues. The overly pedantic is rarely met with welcome." This also reminds me of a passage in Huizinga's doctoral dissertation on Indian drama: "It is only when seriousness and levity are combined, or even intentionally fused together as one, that certain people are able to express their deepest inner thoughts. These people's lives convey the balance of actions and thought from a period of cultural flourishing." Without a doubt, Duchamp and Warhol appeared less serious than Kandinsky and Mondrian. They appeared more humorous, more contemporary. Perhaps it is precisely because we view Duchamp as the godfather of contemporary art that when we speak of contemporary art, we treat his humor as the "situational logic" of this movement. I really appreciate that statement you once made, about how any successful contemporary artist must have a humorous side. Excessive seriousness or nitpicking can make us lose a lot of meaning and much delight. Of course, this humor must have certain academic qualities. Otherwise, it will lead to farce. Farce is a dislocation of perception, while humor is a dislocation of meaning. Farce is one party provoking another, while humor entails both parties sharing in understanding. Humor is also a kind of play, a creative game in which only highly intelligent people can partake. At the time, you said that my interpretation was very penetrating, and had the making of a maxim.

**WG:** I think that what I was saying was possibly a bit different from the others. I think that they were talking about seriousness as a part of the rules of the game, the "unanimous consent" of the participants, just like you were saying before about everyone's acceptance of the supposition of the "38th Parallel" as a boundary. I think that this seriousness is quite similar to the rule-orientation that we discussed before, such as certain "principles of technique" we used to talk about in art, like when perspective was discovered during the Renaissance, and everyone began competing in art around the rules of perspective, or when shading was discovered, and everyone competed in shading. I think that it would be better to use the term "sacredness." That's right; "sacredness" can explain the issue well. For instance, the 38th Parallel you mentioned is actually a concept about "turf and territory." When we set this line, we were aiming for a sense of security, while we were also seeking respect. Actually, we are making a supposition that will bring security to the soul, this is a sense of the sacred. This sense is not there with Duchamp. Therefore, my art is rooted in the terror of life and the grasp of this sense of the sacred. I want some supposition to affirm the truth of my own existence.

**YS:** So where do you think the seriousness, or rule-orientation, lies in your artistic play?

**WG:** If there is a rule-orientation, that would be, for me, entirely a figment of the imagination. I think that *Great Criticism* can easily illuminate the problem. I think that we could basically put it like this: *Great Criticism* is obviously my artwork, and I am that artwork's producer. In the process of its production, I am clearly in a state of play where I took the painting of another, a creation of "the people," and altered it, seeing what I as an artist could do with this "people's" creation. This has an element of play in the most ordinary sense, a bit of a challenge to boundaries, or what you could call a surplus of spirit. Meanwhile, it is without a doubt that when I complete this artwork and transmit it to society, its sense of play goes on fuller display, which is to say that when the people read their artwork that has been altered by another, they will certainly look at art and their own lives with a more positive attitude, an interaction, if you will. Of course, this is purely my own imagination. I really don't care about its real effect. It was the same with *East Wind—Golden Dragon*, even though the original was a "product" rather than a "work of art," but that's not important. What matters is that when "the people" face their creations that have been imbued with new meaning, they will certainly feel the sense of joy and participation that comes with play. We are all within our creations and without them. We are within principles but also removed from them. I will put it in more precise terms: this is a game of chess between principles and inspiration.

YS: Now I will read a passage from a previous discussion of ours about "logical progression." This is what you said: "Logical progression has two meanings for the contemporary artist: first, his works must have some form of a connection to previous art history; second, there must be some kind of connection between his earlier works (of course meaning those since maturation) and his later works. This connection can be in terms of form or motif. As for the first point, I think that aside from becoming fluent in past art history, a contemporary artist must also accurately grasp the position and significance of art in contemporary cultural movements." What is your opinion of these words now?

WG: I think that I spoke with maturity. This had a definitive influence over my later creative methods.

YS: This talk about the "sense of the sacred" behind play reminds me of what we said about "myths" at the time.

WG: These two words should be linked together.

YS: Now I will read a passage from Romain Rolland's *The Life of Michelangelo*: "Great souls are like mountain summits. The wind beats upon them, the clouds envelop them; but we breathe better and deeper there than elsewhere. The air on those heights possesses a purity which cleanses the heart of its defilements, and when the clouds part we dominate the human race ... I do not claim in general mankind can live on those summits, but that once a year they ought to ascend them on a pilgrimage. There they will renew the air of their lungs and the blood of their veins. Up there they will feel that they are nearer the Eternal. And afterwards they will descend towards the plains of life with their hearts tempered for the daily struggle."

WG: I think he's great. I think that he's not only a legend, he is also a reality. The people of that era seemed to live in an atmosphere of heroes. An age of heroes is an unforgettable era. Our lives today lack

YS: this. Go back and read Gombrich's "legend" of that German soldier. That was amazingly written.

YS: Oh, that was when Gombrich exposed Goebbels. That was a myth created by Goebbels. Goebbels used little so-called reports from the front lines to describe himself and the enemy: "When the German battleship Bluecher was sunk off the Norwegian coast in the spring of 1940, the High Command had announced, perhaps truthfully, that most of the crew and soldiers had been saved. Still, this implied that some had died, and so the Front Reporter Heinz Laubenthal told the story of the ship's last moments as he had allegedly heard it from a lieutenant-colonel: 'Suddenly the stern reared up, seven to nine meters straight into the air, and we see it clearly, there stands a man, upright and erect, his arm lifted in the German salute. I have seen statues, medieval knights of shining metal, carved figureheads of legendary fame, but I shall never forget this living symbol of a German soldier standing like this in the hour of his death … we on our island were thrilled to the marrow, a German soldier who knows how to die, a hurrah broke loose, and our fervent hearts welled over in the song 'Deutschland, Deutschland über alles.' The death of an enemy soldier was a different matter; when the reporter viewed the mangled remains of his enemy, the French conscripts, he described them thus: 'animal is too good a word for them.'"

WG: That was amazingly written. It really has the ability to inspire one's creativity and imagination. Art really needs such mythical elements.

YS: Contemporary audiences seem to have read your *Great Criticism* as a form of mockery or ridicule.

WG: That is the tragedy of this era. As I've said before, I perhaps do not belong to this era. I admit that my art contains elements of play and breaking through the rules, but such breakthroughs are constructive and creative, something upward facing. I said before that when I placed the "great criticisms" together with *Coca-Cola*, their spiritual aim was at the connections between utopia and fetishism. I think that people should approach my games from the perspective of seriousness and the sense of the sacred.

YS: In that case, do you believe that there is subjectivity in your supposed seriousness?

WG: I think that objectivity and truth are two different things. I remember in our last talk, that concept of "dependent origin" was very good. There is no such thing as something which is absolutely true, so there is no need to seek it out. This leads to nihilism, the decline of the spirit, and world-weariness. We must create a supposition, like communism or utopianism. Without a basic supposition, we cannot work and live together. On the other hand, we cannot just go off the deep end simply because these are suppositions.

**YS:** What do you think the prerequisite is for the establishment of such suppositions? Is it the number of supporters or participants?

**WG:** This is a very important indicator, but of course, I don't think that this indicator could influence my artistic decisions. I ponder this problem on a highly intellectual level. You could say that I consider a lot, from human politics, philosophy and economics to art, combining them together to engage in thought, and I try to the best of my abilities to do it on a deep level.

**YS:** When you talk about this intellectual thinking, are you talking about knowledge in the academic sense, or theoretical thinking?

**WG:** That doesn't sound quite right. I engage in intuitional thinking, or perhaps meditation. But I definitely enter the thinking of scholars into the equation. I think that such meditation touches the soul; it is very deep. Then, according to the results of my meditations, I will make a reasonable decision. Therefore, my work is not presented in some extreme form. I am quite a believer in the "middle path."

**YS:** This reminds me of a saying: "Pursue great breadth and also minuteness in order to reach the heights of wisdom and the actualization of the Mean."

**WG:** Who said that?

**YS:** This is from *The Doctrine of the Mean*. The original text is: "Follow the path of inquiry in a virtuous manner, pursuing great breadth and also minuteness in order to reach the heights of wisdom and the actualization of the Mean, reviewing the old and learning the new."

**WG:** That is very well said, especially the part about "reviewing the old and learning the new." This is completely in line with my past trajectory of schema correction, right up to *Great Criticism*. This is a kind of historicist and humanist attitude.

**YS:** I think what you're saying about this kind of supposition is actually a mystical thing. This is not the same as those suppositional play themes in common art history, such as those competitions in the West over perspective, lighting or the principles of color, or principles in Chinese painting regarding brushstrokes or other flourishes.

**WG:** Of course. My suppositions are, for the most part, not technical but schematic or spiritual. This is in keeping with the "mystery" I posited during the '85 period, except that its implications gradually expanded.

**YS:** I will read another statement of yours from the past. Let's see how you feel about it now. You said, "This 'mysterious thing' is very difficult to express in my own artwork. I think that it can only serve as an impetus to elicit our interest in the art industry. Once we enter into the picture, the issues we face are entirely about 'technical operation.' The artist can have God in his heart, but when he is searching for God, he has to attend to the trivial technical details with a high level of rationality and care. I believe, however, that as a contemporary artist, there is a necessity to take the difficult path of expressing 'something mysterious,' and it is precisely because of this, that I have views regarding certain domestic critics who infinitely exaggerate the role of these 'mysterious things' in art. The method of relying excessively on one's own imagination to explain the mysteriousness of an artwork will lead to a loss in its academic value, and for those artists who are still in their development phase, this will be even more harmful." You then went on to give an example from Gombrich talking about certain academics who engage in deliberate mystification.

**WG:** Looking back now, perhaps there is a need to add to this. I think that the presence of "something mysterious" is necessary in art. When art loses its sense of mystery, it becomes a mere craft, and so in this sense, I have always been a defender of traditional artistic values. As for the mention of certain critics' infinite exaggeration of "mysterious things," I meant that they completely misunderstand the artist's original intent, and, completely removed from the context of art history, they engage in an interpretation that is wholly based on their own imagination.

**YS:** Do you think that there are any similarities between this "something mysterious" and the "sense of the sacred" in your art that you now talk about?

**WG:** There is a definite connection, but mysterious things are not necessarily sacred, while sacred things are certainly mysterious.

**YS:** Your sense of the sacred is more of an intuition about life.

**WG:** You could say that. Much of it is a fear of death and the unknown. As a result, I must posit something for me to rely on. You could call it a myth of my own making. In this way, I connect play, myths and art all together. Right now, I think that a lot of problems I'm pondering seem to be converging towards a single understanding.

## [C]

YS: Today let's talk about some specific issues of art history, combined with your own artistic issues. Which classical artists had the most important influence for you?

WG: Of course, in general, such masters of Western art history as Michelangelo, Leonardo da Vinci, and Rembrandt had a profound impact on me, and during my *Post-Classical* period I engaged in some "corrections" of their "schema," which is rooted in our basic art history background. The artists I think I would particularly like to talk about are Bernini and Chardin.

YS: The seventeenth-century Italian sculptor Gian Lorenzo Bernini and eighteenth-century French painter Jean-Baptiste-Siméon Chardin?

WG: I think these two artists are particularly important, especially to me. I think I can describe their artistic demeanors: Bernini is "splendid craziness" and Chardin is "sacred plainness."

YS: Today's art historians have a rather high opinion of Chardin, often linking him together with Cézanne and Morandi.

WG: I think that is normal formal and stylistic research, a kind of research into history and context. I discovered Chardin through an intuitive method. I remember I mentioned him in a discussion back in March or April. I was in college, and I started imitating his techniques in a life-studies class, and I decided I might as well just move his still-lifes into my pictures.

YS: What kind of force attracted you? At the time, Chardin was almost completely out of our field of vision, and few people talked about him in China. In terms of still-lifes, aside from Cézanne and Van Gogh, we might talk about some seventeenth-century Dutch still-life painters, or maybe even about certain objects in Vermeer's paintings.

WG: I found that in Chardin's paintings certain things related to Kant's concept of "things-in-themselves." I was reading Kant at the time, and I also felt that those qualities in Chardin's paintings were related to Aristotle's "material cause." I felt that he seemed to be explaining some sort of material force, and that this force also possessed a sort of world-creating spirituality. I was also quite enamoured of ancient

Greek philosophy at the time. I really liked some of Plato's ideas, especially his theory of the cave. His allegory was quite vivid; he was talking about a question of education or knowledge. I think he said that some captives were locked in a chamber like a cave. Some of the captives had grown up inside, but their necks and legs were bound, and they could only see the back wall of the cave. A torch burned behind them. There was a paper screen between them and the torch. Behind the screen, were people facing the light of the fire. They held all kinds of puppets in their hands, and would raise them over the screen, making them do strange movements. The torch cast the shadows of these puppets onto the wall as images, and the captives believed that the images were real. Then, one of the captives was released from his bonds. He stood up and saw everything around him. He thought that what he was seeing was not real, and that the shadows he had seen before were the truth. If someone were to then take him out of the cave and into the sunlight, he would be dazed by the sun's rays, seeing nothing. He would hate that person, hate him for making him unable to see the truth. This story is quite vivid and has always been implanted in my memory. I often use this allegory to think about the questions of human knowledge and truth. I'm always wondering, is there some kind of knowledge that can bring people out of the cave and show them the true world? If we all live in the cave, then maybe we should just believe in our current perceptions and not seek any trouble. This allegory also eventually led me to distrust knowledge to a certain extent, and to grow confident in my own intuition. Another way in which Plato influenced me was through his theory of insanity, basically the idea that artists are assisted by divine inspiration.

**YS:** Oh, that was in the *Ion* dialogue. Let me find it and read it: "For all the good epic poets utter all those fine poems not from art, but as inspired and possessed, and the good lyric poets likewise ... For a poet is a light and winged and sacred thing, and is unable ever to indite until he has been inspired and put out of his senses, and his mind is no longer in him: every man, whilst he retains possession of that, is powerless to indite a verse or chant an oracle. Seeing then that it is not by art that they compose and utter so many fine things about the deeds of men—as you do about Homer—but by a divine dispensation, each is able only to compose that to which the Muse has stirred him."

**WG:** I think that his theory of insanity is very interesting, and vivid as well. I think he used a magnet as a metaphor, meaning that such insanity spreads like a disease. It is very vivid. People like Homer have a talent for writing poetry, not because of a certain skill or technique, but because there is some divine power driving them, and this miraculous power is like a magnet—not only does it attract this poet, turning this poet into a magnetic ring, it also can attract others, one by one, until a massive magnetic chain is formed. This is basically connected to my later ideas about "possession" and "the people," which we could call "the people being possessed." This is also basically the source of my ideas on "possession of the soul." You could put it this way: Plato's allegory of the cave led me to doubt all knowledge, while the "theory of inspiration" or "theory of insanity" led to my faith in "wisdom" and "the spiritual." I think that the illustration from the Gospel of Matthew in Gombrich's *The Story of Art* is wonderful; it feels like a sort of spiritual possession, while the form is also very good, the brushwork imbued with a nervous rhythm. It is in no way inferior to the effects in Van Gogh's later work. Someone should carefully research these medieval hand-copied illustrations. I think that they are definitely linked to expressionism.

**YS:** You don't think this might be your own projection?

**WG:** Perhaps, but tell me, what can an artist do aside from projecting? Does truly objective knowledge exist? Does definite meaning exist? Do you believe those narratives of art history? I think that "endow" might be a more apt term than "projection." Yes, "endow" is a good word, and it is very close to my past religious emotions. For instance, "God endowed something" or "the people endowed something."

As an artist I would say that I endowed this artwork or object with something, or even that I endowed Plato's theories with something. This is good; it is more accurate than projection. Projection seems to be a psychological term. This calls to mind the term "brainwashing" that we were discussing before. I think that "endowing" and "brainwashing" are perhaps paired concepts, one positive and one negative. When I endow an artwork with meaning, and it is affirmed by people, which is to say that they accept this meaning, we often say that they have been "brainwashed," like people today with Apple iPhones. Steve Jobs was an endower. From this perspective, perhaps I play such a role in art.

YS: Actually, this "endowment" and "brainwashing" are somewhat connected to the play that we were talking about. When people participate in the game, whether it is the game of "utopianism" or the game of "fetishism," we often become the "endowed." Confucian offerings are a game of high-level spiritual activity. The concept of "offering to the spirits as if the spirits are present" is both a goal of the game and a rule by which it is played. Actually, Confucius here defined a final boundary for these "spirits." The "spirits" exist within this game in which we participate together, and there is no need to pursue the question any further. Through this ritual or game, we all affirm this existence in our hearts, meaning that through the collective will, we have confirmed their existence. As a result, our souls have respect for the void, and we gain a sense of security, because "they" also affirm the existence of these spirits. In this way, there is a benefit to our lives and to the social order.

WG: When I first looked at Chardin's paintings, I truly felt the existence of a kind of "spirit," though of course this game was one I played with myself. It was a game of self-entertainment, like solitaire. I really got into the game. Chardin's still-lifes give people a great sense of sacredness. The things in his paintings are somewhat removed from the real objects and, in comparison to the Dutch still-life painting that preceded him, they don't have as much of that quality of realism, but I think his art has its own special texture.

YS: He was a painter who placed great emphasis on the structure and brushwork of the picture. In this regard he inspired Cézanne and Morandi.

WG: I think that a certain amount of will has been infused into this rendering of his, though the intent markedly differs from Cézanne and Morandi. Cézanne and Morandi were formal to excess. Chardin's formal will lies in his grasp of the subject. He is unwilling to entirely depart from the subject. We could say that he is immersed in it, but also outside of it. The sense he gives people is of a natural state, but it also has spirituality. It is a kind of "ordinary sacred object." Yes, I think that this is a good description for it, an "ordinary sacred object." This concept of the sacred object is connected to Kant's "thing-in-itself."

YS: I'd really like to hear how you endow Chardin's potatoes and earthen jars with Kant's concept of the "thing-in-itself."

**WG:** As I see it, Kant's "thing-in-itself" is a concept that is at once extremely ordinary and also extremely sacred. He established a "thing-in-itself," something that our rational minds can never recognize, but he is also constantly stimulating our perceptions; we have perceived its existence, but we do not know the precise reason. Behind it, however, there is certainly a revealer that supports it.

**YS:** According to the explanation that is currently prevalent in academia, Kant had three goals in establishing the "thing-in-itself": the first was to ensure that the object, constructed of the conscious impressions produced by its stimulation of our senses, was substantive, meaning that knowledge has objectivity; the second was to establish a boundary for our cognition, limiting knowledge to the realm of our perceived world, meaning that knowledge is limited to the phenomenal world; and the third was to leave room for the free will, undying spirit and existence of God that, though unknowable, should be believed in. That is to say, we must suspend our knowledge to leave room for faith.

**WG:** That is well said, but it is a rather pedantic explanation. The information I draw from his concept of the "thing-in-itself" is this: behind the object we see, there exists a mysterious force, which leads it to appear before us in a special way, and this force is not something that we can understand through knowledge. At the time, I saw such a force in Chardin's still-lifes. I can't say more than that; I am unable to use the language of common knowledge to describe it step by step.

**YS:** When we spoke about Kant's aesthetic issues back then, we often spoke of his idea of "disinterest," talking about "purposiveness without purpose" together with "formal beauty."

**WG:** I'm actually not interested in "beauty" and "aesthetics." What I'm interested in is a purely perceptive thing, and things that are connected to this perception and the spiritual.

**YS:** Then how do you think that in Chardin's still-lifes there exists something that transcends normal "beauty?"

**WG:** Perhaps his pictures, at first look, are not pretty, nor are they all that real, especially when placed side by side with those Dutch still-lifes. For instance, he was always perplexed by that rabbit he was painting. He was always wondering whether or not to paint its fur in a real way. This was perhaps the motivation for him to paint still-lifes, but many artists from centuries past in art history, such as Dürer, long ago had the ability to paint that fur realistically. So Chardin must have had his own reasons for not painting like that. His paintings appear naïve, even a bit warped, but that warping was not in a cartoon manner, because such warping is linked to humor. I call this warping of Chardin's the physical warping that takes place when the human spirit develops towards sacredness. This is actually common sense taken from our lives. For instance, when we are particularly happy or particularly angry, we discover that the external world takes on this altered sense of motion, and we will also feel that our bodies are swelling or contracting. This is quite apparent in Michelangelo's sketches. The people in his sketches have highly developed muscles with small heads, like they are made of clumps of flesh, but overall, Michelangelo's figures have exaggerated elements, and this is definitely linked to his wish to express the concept of the powers God "endowed" man with. The propaganda paintings of the Cultural Revolution are like that as well. My *Great Criticism* contains that idea, that of physical warping caused by the increased sacredness of the human spirit.

YS: I think that Chardin's art has a certain dramatic effect. There is a bit of a stage effect in the relationship between the light and the still objects, which seems to have a connection to Caravaggio. Chardin's figures also have another tendency; his depictions were all of extremely ordinary kitchen workers and washerwomen. His figures seem to be slightly imprecise, and this seems to have influenced Jean-Françoise Millet.

WG: This also appears to have a connection to Van Gogh's *Potato Eaters*. Nowadays I feel that this is Van Gogh's greatest work, while *Sunflowers* and *Self Portrait* are still quite stylistic. It depicts the kind of hardships man faces under those religious conditions. The painting basically affirms a sentence from the Bible, in which God says that man must toil to survive. Some of Chardin's paintings of the human form are very interesting. For instance, that open drawer in *House of Cards* is so enticing to the imagination. He makes you think that there must be something mysterious in that drawer. The term "house of cards" symbolizes the futility of mankind's efforts, but perhaps in that drawer hides the very God who makes all of mankind's efforts futile. Also, this miraculous force happens to occur within our everyday lives, occurring in the games of our subconscious.

YS: You really have quite an ability to "endow." What can you endow Bernini with?

WG: As a successful, lauded palace artist, I think that Bernini was a very confident man, and this confidence reflected his highly developed expressive abilities in sculpture. I would say that he is an artist with the ability to change physical properties. His *Ecstasy of St Teresa* is his boundless imagining of the sense of joy at bathing in the rays of God. He has bestowed Teresa's expression with the highest level of happiness that mankind can attain on this mortal coil. This virtually collapsed joy moves every viewer. He masterfully expressed Teresa's combined feelings of both suffering and joy in her infinite love of God. In the past I called this experience the "peak experience" and the "spread of the spirit."

YS: Is this a bit like Li Shutong's "mixture of tragedy and joy?"

WG: That feels a bit too academic, and has a sense of aloofness. Bernini's feels as if it is of this mortal world, and it even has associations with the ecstasy of sex. In this regard, Bernini's greatness is the same as Chardin's, in that he has conveyed the spirit of the next world in reality, the only difference being that Bernini's is a splendid expression while Chardin's is ordinary. The splendor of Bernini's expression is in his deft sculpting of the ripples in the clothing and clouds, removing all sense of the stone's heaviness. His skill was certainly instrumental here. The light refracted by the metal strips Bernini inlaid in the stone serve to add to the dramatic effect. Actually, I think that this dramatic effect is somewhat similar to Chardin's. Chardin's is a drama for commoners, while Bernini's is a drama for the aristocracy.

YS: This dramatic feel seems like it may be connected to our visual artistic experience of the Cultural Revolution. The model operas are a typical case, as is Mao's halo.

WG: That's for sure. Actually, the forms and layouts of the figures in the *Great Criticism* posters are connected to the stage arts of the time, as well as the loyalty dances. Speaking of the Cultural Revolution, I just thought of the "mango affair." I think this can illuminate my theories on "endowment." It is said that an African friend gave a mango to President Mao, and Mao gave it to a worker's propaganda team, the Mao Zedong-thought propaganda team. The workers felt that since Mao had given it to them, they shouldn't eat it, and so they placed it on display for all to see as a show of Mao's love and care for the working class. This mango quickly became a sacred object, and many replicas appeared. They even encased it in glass as a demonstration of its sacredness. News reports across the country said that people surrounded the mango, welling up with tears as they cried, "Long live [President Mao]." In reality, no one was clear about the source of this mango or the story behind it, but in this situation, the mango became the best carrier for the feelings of devotion towards President Mao that the people had endowed themselves with, and the golden color and ovular shape were quite appropriate. This is "the people's" power of endowment; self-endowment, self-frenzy.

**YS:** This seems a bit like Plato's theory of the "magnetic stone." It's quite dramatic.

**WG:** I think that "the people" are often in this state where in most situations they are endowed, but sometimes they have the impulse to endow. Once this impulse is catalyzed, the entire face of society is fundamentally changed. Therefore, I say that the people are also often in a state of purposelessness or even lacking will. Actually, leaders and artists are the same; many great historical events and artworks were not planned in advance, and they are not the result of reason or self-determination. Hitler, a figure who appears to have had a powerful will, often also needed the support of power beyond his own. He sent Himmler to look for the Holy Grail, and when it wasn't found, he lost faith in victory. I believe that to a great extent, art is the result of a form of collective blind action. We cannot give art a highly rational and intellectual definition. In my opinion, art is a product of faith. I've been rereading Plotinus over the past few days, and I think that his ideas fit very well with my ideas today. When talking about the highest essence, he emphasizes that man must have an ability to see. Let me read the original. It is magnificent: "But it is requisite to perceive objects of this kind by that eye by which the soul beholds such real beauties. Besides it is necessary that whoever perceives this species of beauty, should be seized with much greater delight, and more vehement admiration, than any corporeal beauty can excite; as now embracing beauty real and substantial. Such affections, I say, ought to be excited about true beauty, as admiration and sweet astonishment; desire also and love and a pleasant trepidation. For all souls, as I may say, are affected in this manner about invisible objects, but those the most who have the strongest propensity to their love." A later passage is also very interesting. He says, "Everyone must become divine, and of godlike beauty, before he can gaze upon the beautiful itself." He then follows with a wonderful passage: "If you become thus purified residing in yourself, and having nothing any longer to impede this unity of mind, and no farther mixture to be found within, but perceiving your whole self to be a true light, and light alone; a light which though immense is not measured by any magnitude, nor limited by any circumscribing figure, but is everywhere immeasurable, as being greater than every measure, and more excellent than every quantity; if, perceiving yourself thus improved, and trusting solely to yourself, as no longer requiring a guide, fix now steadfastly your mental view, for with the intellectual eye alone can such immense beauty be perceived."

**YS:** That is Zhu Guangqian's translation, isn't it? He often mixes in terminology from the sutras and the Dao De Jing, which makes it appear all the more mysterious.

**WG:** Oh, yes. What I am interested in is his concept of "vision." I think it's actually the same as my concept of "endowment." That is to say, only when you make yourself sacred can we endow objects with sacredness. This is the "mango effect." Bernini's greatness was his provision of the most perfect tangible view of the people's love-like passion for God. Objectively speaking, however, aside from the *Ecstasy of St Teresa*, Bernini's other works aren't all that great. In this regard, he is not as great as Chardin. Chardin was like a peasant, facing the picture with a form of mundane sincerity. It is said that he painted very slowly. Bernini, on the other hand, could be accused of flaunting his skills. In the *Ecstasy of St Teresa*, his skills were applied perfectly, as if his form was bathed in a spiritual halo. To use Hegel's words, the spirit flows out of the form. This brings me to something interesting. When I was reading St. Augustine's *Confessions*, I was struck by some of his unique vocabulary. For instance, "Awake, ye who sleep, and arise from the dead, and Christ shall give you light." This was taken from the Gospel of St. Matthew. I love this idea of illumination. I hear that someone wrote a book entitled *Memory and Illumination* about the theology of St. Augustine.

*Originally published in Huang Zhuan,* Thing-in-Itself: Utopia, Pop and Personal Theology, *Guangzhou, Lingnan Art Publishing House, 2012, first edition pp. 138–93.*

## Note

1 "Neo-Daoism" (or "Neo-Taoism" in the "Wade-Giles" system of romanization) names the focal development in early "medieval" Chinese philosophy, from the third to the sixth centuries CE. In Chinese sources, this development is called 玄学 *xuanxue*, literally the "learning" or study (*xue*) of the "dark" or mysterious and profound (*xuan*). See Chan, 2017.

## Reference

Chan, A. (2017). "Neo-Daoism," *The Stanford Encyclopedia of Philosophy* (Spring Ed.), Edward N. Zalta (ed.), <https://plato.stanford.edu/archives/spr2017/entries/neo-daoism/>.

# Index

Abramović, Marina 111, 121, 125, 206
Adorno, Theodor Ludwig Wiesengrund
   113–14, 119, 123, 129, 133–4
Adrià, Ferran 205
Aeschylus 233
Agamben, Giorgio 112, 131
Ai Weiwei 83, 121, 123, 132
Anders, Günther 114
Andina, Tiziana (安提强) 128
Aristotle, 26, 43, 173, 174, 178, 238, 244, 271
Arman 206
Arnheim, Rudolf 249
Attali, Jacques 115
Augustine 238–9, 247–9, 279

Bacon, Francis 232–4, 239
Bacsó, Béla 128, 139
Bada Shanren 227–8
Bardini, Thierry 113
Bataille, Georges 232
Baudelaire, Charles Pierre 241
Baudrillard, Jean 111–13, 115–19, 123, 125, 134–5
Beecro, Vanessa 206
Bell, Clive 249
Benjamin, Walter 56, 112
Berenson, Bernard 165–6
Bernini, Gian Lorenzo 271, 276–7, 279
Beuys, Joseph 41, 65, 111, 125, 127, 129–32, 156–7, 164, 192, 206–7, 234, 239, 250–6, 259–63
Beyoncé 123
Bittner Wiseman, Mary (明玛丽) 89
Bloom, Allan 128
Böhme, Gernot 217
Bostrom, Nick 38
Bottinelli, Silvia 206
boundaries 17–29, 49, 103, 217, 230, 266, 274–5
Bourdieu, Pierre 125
Brancusi, Constantin 55

Breitz, Candice 150
Brilliant, Richard 116
Brock, Bazon 111, 125–6, 139
Buddhism 9, 140, 231, 237–8, 249–50, 254, 257–8

Cannarella, Maria 201
Carême, Marie Antoine 205
Carroll, Noël 148–52, 158
Castiglioni, Giuseppe 2
Caygill, Howard 112, 120
Certeau, Michel de 115, 130–1
Cézanne, Paul 250, 271, 274
Chang, Christina 115
Chardin, Jean-Baptiste-Siméon 271, 274–9
Christo 111, 121
Clark, Andy 75
Cohen, Leonard 119, 121, 126
Cold war 196, 213, 215, 233–8
Collingwood, 175
Confucius 9, 226, 274
Courbet, Jean Désiré Gustave 241
Cultural Revolution 7, 9–10, 31, 72–9, 81–2, 84, 89–96, 98–103, 105–6, 120–1, 185, 192, 212, 241, 259, 265, 276–7

D'Ayala Valva, Margherita 206
Danto, Arthur Coleman 21, 41, 111–12, 117, 119, 121, 123, 127, 128, 130, 132–4, 227
Darwin, Charles 34
David, Jacques-Louis 54–56, 182, 241
Debord, Guy 116
Delacroix, David 241
Delacroix, Eugène 177
Deleuze, Gilles 113–14
Deng Xiaoping 78
Derrida, Jacques 95, 114, 179, 195
Dick, Philip K 113
Dickie, George 152
Donovan 122
Dostoevsky, Fyodor Mikhailovich 241

Dubois, Urbain François 205
Duchamp, Henri-Robert-Marcel 4, 111–12, 121, 123, 130–2, 136, 161, 183, 206, 262, 263, 265–6
Dürer, Albrecht 275

Eliasson, Olafur 206
Ende, Michael 155–156, 234
Engels, Friedrich 37, 44, 60, 201, 225
Escoffier, Georges Auguste 206
Eydt, Alfred 34

Fang Lihua 196
Fang Lijun 88
Ferraris, Maurizio 75
Feuerbach, Ludwig 215
Fillìa 206
Foster, Hal 117–18
Foucault, Michel 100
Franco, James 121
Fried, Michael 114

Gao Minglu 8, 10–11, 90
Gao Xingjian 75
Gillick, Liam 112
Giotto 160
Gombrich, Ernst Hans Josef 8–9, 11, 51, 92–4, 192, 230, 258, 263, 268, 270, 273
Gore, Leslie 115
Greenberg, Clement 52
Gu Kaizhi 244–5
Guevara, Ernesto 56, 96
Gunkel, David J. 113–15
Günther, Hans Friedrich Karl 34–5

Hamilton, Richard 98–9, 115–16
Hegel, Georg Wilhelm Friedrich 4, 8, 11, 21–2, 27–8, 41, 129, 135, 150, 154, 195, 245, 247, 249, 253, 258, 279
Heidegger, Martin 17–18, 126, 128–9, 140–1, 232
Himmler, Heinrich Luitpold 278
Hitler, Adolf 34, 278
Holbein, Hans 51, 135, 150
Homer, 128, 272–3
Honnef, Klaus 125
Horkheimer, Max 133
Huang Rui 7

Huang Zhuan 8, 154–6, 158, 200, 209, 234, 257
Huang Zongxi 246
Hui Shi 248

Indiana, Robert 102

Jagodzinski, Jan 131
Jean Claude 111, 121, 138
Jesus Christ 37, 44, 61–3, 65, 133, 135, 164, 172–3, 177, 179, 182, 186–7, 191, 201–2, 226, 229, 238, 279
Ji Li Jiang 76
Jiang Jieshi (Chiang Kai-Shek) 72
Jiang Yi 93
Jiang Zhaoke 7
Jobs, Stive 273
Jones, Quincy 115

Kant, Immanuel 11, 23–8, 35, 37, 48, 123, 125, 192, 200, 217, 227, 229, 249, 271, 274–5
Kaprow, Allan 206
kd lang 123
Koestenbaum, Wayne 117
Koons, Jeff 134
Kosuth, Joseph 41
Kuhn, Thomas 8, 9

Lamark, Jean-Baptiste Pierre Antoine de Monet, chevalier de 34
Laozi (Lao Tse, Dao De Jing) 9, 184, 187, 245, 279
Lenain, Thierry 116
Lenin 37, 44, 60, 201, 225–6, 254
Leonardo da Vinci 37, 44, 61, 164, 201, 216, 271
Lessing, Gotthold Ephraim 103
Levay, William J. 114
Li Shutong 277
Li Xianting 8, 79
Lichtenstein, Roy 102
Liu Bocheng 79
Liu Shaoqi 78
Liu Yan 10
Lombroso, Cesare 35
Longyu 71
Lu Peng 11
Lyotard, Jean-François 2

Ma Desheng 7
Ma Jian 84
Machiavelli, Niccolò 239
Mantegna, Andrea 37, 61–3, 135, 160, 165, 201, 226
Mao Zedong 7, 10, 17, 19, 21–2, 25, 47, 48, 56–7, 59, 62, 72, 77–8, 81, 83, 91–2, 95–6, 119–21, 131–2, 182–4, 212, 223, 254, 258, 261–2, 277
Marinetti, Filippo Tommaso 206
Martin, Emily 128
Marx, Karl 37, 44, 60, 126, 134–5, 195, 199, 201, 223, 225, 226
Matisse, Henri 160, 178–9
May Fourth Movement 7
McLuhan, Marshall 116
Michelangelo Buonarroti 17, 19–21, 25, 172, 176–7, 179, 182, 229–31, 267, 271, 276
Moleschott, Jacob 215
Monroe, Marilyn 47, 56, 119, 121, 132, 137
Morandi, Giorgio 271, 274
Morawski, Stefan 103–104
Munch, Edvard 176
Murakami, Takashi 160

Nancy, Jean-Luc 112
Navas, Eduardo 113
Newman, Micheal 112
Nietzsche, Friedrich 2–4, 8–9, 11–14, 42–3, 112–13, 119, 125–6, 128–9, 133–5, 154, 245
Northern Art Group 8–11, 155, 245–6, 249, 251

Okakura, Kakuzō 111, 128–30, 134
Orozco, Gabriel 150
Osborne, Peter 112

Paladino, Mimmo 80
Panofsky, Erwin 164–5
Paparoni, Demetrio (德沐) 80, 88–9, 160, 164, 200
Pasolini, Pier Paolo 63
Pawlenski, Pjotr Andrejewitsch 125
Peterson, Jordan 114
Picasso, Pablo 4, 43, 55, 160, 171–2
Pirandello, Luigi 22
Plato 7, 23, 28, 49, 113, 128, 173–4, 178, 280, 225, 238, 247, 272–3, 278

Pop Art 46–7, 79, 81, 87, 89–90, 93, 95–6, 98–100, 102–3, 111, 99–146, 155–6, 212, 228, 260
Pope Innocent X, 64–5, 164
Pope John XXIII 37, 44
postmodernism 1–3, 5, 100, 103, 127
Pound, Ezra 128
Presley, Elvis 56
Psy 123
Pythagoras 249

Qing Qianlong 6

Rabinow, Paul 112
Radford, Colin 174
Rauschenberg, Robert 114, 121
Rawls, John 38
Ren Jian 8, 10
Richter, Gerhard 160
Rickman, Alan 121
Rimbaud, Jean Nicolas Arthur 241
Robinson, Jenefer 175
Roth, Dieter 206

Sawall, Marina 126
Shi Lu 78
Shi Xinning 132
Shitao 228
Shroud 20–1, 23, 26, 37, 48, 61–5, 164
Shu Qun 8–10, 244
Smith, Karen 132
Smith, Terry 112
Spoerri, Daniel 206
Stalin 37, 44, 60, 201, 225–6
Stars Group 7–8
Sun Yat-sen 71–72

Tan, Fiona 150
Thomas Aquinas, 243–247, 249
Tiravanija, Rirkrit 150
Tiravanjia, Rirkit 206
Tsai Ming-liang 150

Ulay 111, 121, 125

van Gogh, Vincent 176, 271, 273, 276
Velázquez, 55, 64
Verlaine, 241
Vermeer, Johannes 271

Virgin Mary 61, 65, 172–173, 177, 179, 230
Virilio, Paul 111–112, 123

Wain, Louis 176
Wang Guangyi (王广义) 88
Wang Xiaojian 8
Warhol, Andy 45, 47, 56, 111–112, 116–117, 123–124, 160, 184, 192, 207
Waterfield, Robin 128
Wilke, Stefan 126
Wollheim, Richard 51–52

Xu Beihong 6
Xuantong (Pu Yi) 71

Yan Shanchun (严善錞) 11, 196, 243
Yu Hua 76
Yuan Shikai 71–2
Yue Minjun 88

Zhang Xiaogang 88
Zhou Yan 8
Zhu Guangqian 279

www.ingramcontent.com/pod-product-compliance
Lightning Source LLC
Chambersburg PA
CBHW070019010526
44117CB00011B/1641